Designing E-Government

Law and Electronic Commerce

Volume 12

The titles published in this series are listed at the end of this volume.

Table of Contents

Chapter 1

Electronic Government. Variations on a Concept

Corien Prins

In Spring 2000, a report of the virtual think-tank debate entitled *Boosting the Net Economy 2000* was put online.[1] The debate focussed on four themes, one of them being e-government. A particularly interesting topic raised on theme was the consequences and opportunities which could result from the global character of online communications for local communities and governments. The report states on this point: "There is no natural law that says a citizen must make use of his/her public services from his/her own government. Services may increasingly be delivered by private sector bodies and eventually by the government of another state, using the Internet." Although the report acknowledges that we are a long way from such a possibility, it also underscores that "governments should be aware of the growing number of alternatives available to their citizens for online services and make sure they are well-placed to compete". In an online world where borders seem to be no longer relevant and people have free access to global information, citizens become aware of the differences between what one government delivers and what another government may offer.

Whether the radical scenario of the virtual think-tank will one day indeed become reality remains to be seen. It is, however, inevitable that our online society will affect our government services, the terms and conditions under which political actors and civil servants operate, and more in general the manner in which public bodies function. According to Britains e-envoy, Mr. Allan, "Government is going to have to behave more like the innovatory businesses on the Internet in recognising the role of individual initiative."[2] Whether the implementation of the various agendas presently created for electronic governments results in radical institutional and inter-organisational changes, new forms of governance, more efficient and flexible public sector mechanisms, more empowered citizens influencing policy priorities, totally new policy-making processes, or (commercially oriented) governments that sell the public information held in their vast amount of databases largely depends on the strategies proposed in these agendas and thus the roads that public sector bodies will follow to move towards a digitisation of their services and operations. At the moment however, it is still difficult to fully grasp the meaning, opportunities and limits of the concept 'electronic government'.

---

1   The debate was designed, managed and hosted by the new media and electronic publishing company Headstar (www.headstar.com) and held between April 3 and April 7 2000. The report is available at: http://www.netecon2000.com/report.html.
2   Statement in: C. Grande, 'E-envoy vows to raise Internet use by ministries', *Financial Times*, 10 December 1999.

1

J. E. J. Prins (ed.), Designing E-Government, 1–5.
© 2001 *Kluwer Law International. Printed in the Netherlands.*

This does not mean that no important steps have been set on the road to a digitised government. To date, governments have widely recognised the potential of new information- and communication technologies (ICT) to bring about fundamental renewal, not only in their functioning but also in their presence towards other organisations, societal groups or individuals. Both in their relationship with the citizen (for instance: democratic processes, public service delivery, or policy implementation), inter-organisational arrangements (for instance: policy co-ordination, policy implementation, or public service delivery), and in intra-organisational activities (for instance: policy development, operational activities, or knowledge management), ICT promises enormous opportunities to increase efficiency and effectiveness in all kinds of policy sectors.

In 1993, the US government was the first to launch an initiative[3]. Subsequently agendas were issued in among others the United Kingdom (the Green Paper entitled '*government.direct*')[4], Australia (entitled '*Clients First*')[5], Canada[6] and The Netherlands[7]. International organisations such as the G8[8] and the European Commission also addressed the issue. The Commission launched the *eEurope*-initiative, which focuses among other things on government online. It is the Commission's intention to ensure that citizens have easy access to government information, services and decision-making procedures online.[9] The initiative was adopted by the European Council at its Lisbon summit in March 2000. Some countries set a step further than a mere agenda. Finland has even implemented specific legislation on the issue. On 1 January, 2000 the Act on Electronic Services in the Administration entered into force.[10] The prime objective of the Act is to improve the smoothness and rapidity of electronic services in public administration, as well as the data security.

In the meantime, the US government has already greatly expanded citizen access to online government information and services and proposed initiatives that build on the 1993 Administration's efforts, led by Vice President Gore. On 24 June 2000, the US government unveiled a series of new initiatives to give the American people - what President Clinton in his first-ever Saturday webcast addressed to the Nation claimed to be - "the "Information Age" government they deserve". Clinton stated that the new

---

3   National Performance Review, Washington 1993. See also: Office of the Vice President, *Reengineering Government Through IT*, Accompanying Report to the National Performance Review, Government Printing Office, Washington DC, 1993 (http://www.npr.gov/library/reports/it.html).

4   Office of Public Service, *Government.direct. A Green Paper on the Electronic Delivery of Government Services*, Cm 3438, HMSO, London, November 1996. Available at: http://www.citu.gov.uk/greenpaper.htm. See for a discussion: Ch. Bellamy, J.A. Taylor, '*Understanding government.direct, Information Infrastructure and Policy* 6 (1997/1998), p. 3.

5   *Clients First. The Challenge for Government Information Technology*, 1 March 1995. Available at: http://www.dofa.gov.au/pubs/itrg/itrg-tc.html).

6   *Blueprint for Renewing Government Services Using Information Technology*. Available at: http://www.ifla.org/documents/infopol/canada/tb-bp.txt

7   *Actieprogramma Elektronische Overheid*, TK 1998/1999, TK 26387. Available at: http://www.minbzk.nl/e-overheid.

8   See: http://www.open.gov.uk/govonline

9   Available at: http://europe.eu.int/comm/information_society/eeurope/

10 http://www.om.fi/2838.htm

initiatives will "cut red tape, make government more responsive to the needs of citizens, and expand opportunities for participation in our democracy."[11] By the end of 2000:

- Citizens must be able to search all online resources offered by the federal government from a single web site called 'firstgov.gov';
- Citizens, small businesses and community groups must have one-stop access to roughly $500 billion in grants and procurement opportunities.

In the UK, also, follow-up recommendations and targets have been published: by March 2001, 90 percent of routine government procurement is to be done electronically with all public services capable of being delivered electronically by 2008.

Shaping new forms of governance in an information age requires knowledge of the dynamics of the electronic processes and structures in the public sector as well as an adequate insight in the capabilities associated with information- and communication technologies. It also asks for close attention to (new) practical and ethical obstacles and dilemmas touching upon security, fraud, liability, intellectual property, free access, national security, equality and – perhaps most important of all - privacy. In the end, the success or failure of establishing a (fully) digitised government highly depends on an adequate understanding of all dimensions of the endeavour. Only when the dimensions and implications are fully grasped, we are able to answer questions such as if there is a need for specific measures (law making, subsidies, and education) to stimulate certain directions of change. For does not the scope and effect of such measures depend on whether a single design for electronic government is derived from the developments, or that diverging developments towards electronic government, governments, or even governance, are to be perceived?

This book aims to support further understanding of and knowledge on the dynamics of electronic government and hence, the future of this endeavour. The aim of this book is to draw lessons (cross-national, between policy sectors and across administrations) from the design of electronic government and from evaluations of electronic government in practice. Prime impetus for the book was an international conference held in Tilburg, The Netherlands, in May 2000 on electronic government. The book contains both papers presented at this conference as well as chapters specifically written for the occasion of this book.

The book explores both visions on electronic government and gives examples of an already active electronic government. Its prime goal is to focus at directions of developments on the crossroads of technological innovation and organisational change in governments, together with evolving barriers and opportunities for further change. Thus it aims on providing lessons for learning from both designing future electronic government and outcomes of electronic government in practice, across countries, policy sectors, and technological innovations.

Given the aim of this book and the limitations of this traditional - paper-based - medium, not all of the issues which have been risen in relation to electronic government

---

11 See: http://www.whitehouse.gov/WH/New/html/e-government.html

can addressed. Several topics, some of them even high on the policy agenda (such as access to government information[12]), have therefore not been approached here.

The book starts with three chapters that deal with the different clusters of electronic government activities: e-governance, on-line democracy and electronic service delivery. In Chapter 2, Perri 6 focuses on the first cluster: the use of ICT to support policymaking. After discussing the rise of e-governance and tools used, he focuses on the different theories that have been developed on the impact to e-governance systems across government. John Taylor and Eleanor Burt look in Chapter 3 at the second cluster: on-line democracy. They argue that ICT is infusing all democratic impulses within the polity, whether those impulses are towards direct, representative, or pluralist forms of democracy. ICT offers important opportunities to re-shape and revitalise democracy in all its forms. Charles Raab subsequently discusses, in Chapter 4, the third cluster: electronic service delivery. He thereby focuses on proactive service provision. After these three contributions on the individual clusters of electronic government, Klaus Lenk and Roland Traunmüller deal with the overall concept of electronic government. In Chapter 5, they advocate a broadening of this concept, thereby discussing four perspectives on a digitised government: the citizen's perspective, the process perspective, the (tele)co-operation perspective and the knowledge perspective.

The Chapters 6 through 9 describe electronic government developments in several countries around the world. From these chapters is becomes clear how e-government strategies are designed in individual countries and how the governmental organisations of these countries implement the concept of electronic government. Miriam Lips explores in Chapter 6 the policy agenda's in countries that played a key role in initiating the concept of a digitised government. She discusses developments and experiences in the US, Singapore and Australia. By comparing the e-government developments in these countries, she explores a possible tendency towards a single model of e-government. Koen Zweers and Kees Planqué subsequently discuss in Chapter 7 the initiatives in the United States, both at a federal and a state level. They analyse various state web sites and consider the trend from an organization-based approach toward a client-oriented e-government approach. Frans de Bruïne, in Chapter 8, looks at e-government developments from the perspective of the European Union. He describes the ambitious *e*-Europe initiative, explores the strengths and weaknesses of Europe when it comes to introducing electronic government and stresses what is at stake in Europe. In Chapter 9 Roger van Boxtel explains the developments in The Netherlands. He touches upon several policy documents and projects he initiated as the Minister responsible for e-government developments. Finally, Silvio Salza and Massimo Mecella discuss the steps taken by the Italian government in Chapter 10. It becomes clear from their discussion that various legal and organisational questions emerge in the process of introducing e-government activities and that an adequate implementation of a digitised government requires legislative action on a large number of relevant issues.

Having gained both an understanding of the concept of e-government as well as an insight in the initiatives of major countries around the world, the book subsequently focuses on several of more specific developments and challenges surrounding e-

---

12 New electronic media such as the Internet provide such new and far-reaching information processing functions that they cry for application to government information. It is recognised in various policy documents that the availability of these media asks for a re-interpretation of the governments' duty to provide access to government information.

government. Wim van der Donk and Bram Foederer focus in Chapter 11 on social movements and the influence of ICT on their way of functioning. They aim at generating conceptual tools that may help designing a more systematic comparative research into the hypothesis that ICT's are changing social movements. Matt Poelmans further explores the client-oriented (in his words 'citizen centred') approach, by describing, in Chapter 12, the Dutch initiative 'Public Counter 2000'. Customer orientation, meaning focussing on citizen's needs and establishing citizen's demand patterns are concepts at the very heart of this initiative.

The book ends with two chapters on challenges the concept of e-government faces. First, Herbert Kubicek and Martin Hagen discuss, in Chapter 13, the inevitable interaction between e-government and e-commerce and the implications of this interaction. They argue that e-government and e-commerce need to be integrated to an overall concept of electronic services, because that is what customers and citizens will in the end claim. Using the ongoing Bremen Online Services project in Germany as an illustration, they claim that an integration is the only way to achieve economically sustainable solutions. In the final Chapter 14, another key challenge to e-government is explored: the implications of the use of mobile telephone. Christopher Theunissen describes the present use of this new technology together with possible scenarios relating to its future potential use for electronic government purposes. He thereby specifically addresses the benefits it may have for developing/partially developing states such as South Africa.

In conclusion, having read all of the chapters of this book, it becomes clear that we are standing on the crossroads of E-government development. In the coming years many choices will have to be made regarding the direction E-government ambitions will, can and must evolve. This will at least require an optimal interaction between the goals and ambitions stipulated in the various action plans and day-to-day practice of those who have to implement these. What also becomes clear is that various similarities exist between E-government developments around the world. However, various factors restrict the evolution of a uniform E-government model. These are, among others cultural differences, diverse approaches to public policy as well as technological developments. The E-government of the future thus depends on the choices which are going to be made in the coming years. This book is thus intended to provide the reader with some of the necessary tools to find the possible variations on the E-government concept.

Finally, some acknowledgements are in order. I first would like to thank all of those who contributed to this book. Their willingness to make creative and stimulating contributions is highly appreciated. I further own thanks to all of those who organised the May 2000 conference: Miriam Lips, Monica den Boer, Luuk Matthijssen, Marcel Boogers and Marijke Nobel. This book greatly benefited from this occasion. Likewise, it benefited from the views presented by those who participated in this conference, either by delivering a paper or by contributing in the workshops. Finally, I am indebted to Vivian Carter, who took care of organising the contacts with the authors and edited some of the contributions to this book. She was crucial in helping to make this book what it is.

Chapter 2

E-governance. Do Digital Aids Make a Difference in Policy Making?

Perri 6[1]

1 Introduction

Across the world, politicians make much of their strategies for modernising government, using new technologies (Heeks, 1999). Under that rubric are three different clusters of activities:

- electronic service delivery: Most of the effort, money and political attention available for electronic government is devoted to the provision of services on-line to citizens and businesses through the phone, the personal computer or the digital television (6 et al, 2000).
- electronic democracy: New legislatures, such as those in Scotland and Wales, are using electronic voting systems in their chambers, and there is some interest in on-line consultations with citizens (6, 2000b).
- e-governance: Less attention has been devoted to digital support for policy making; decision making; group work between ministers and their juniors, senior civil servants working on policy formulation, development and management, and with policy advisors who are contracted to provide confidential policy support.

This third cluster is the present focus. It has been too little studied (Kraemer and Dedrick, 1997), and yet may well be of fundamental importance to the nature of democratic life.

1 Acknowledgments: I am grateful to Cisco Systems Ltd and to Nick Penston in particular, for financial support for the programme of research on which this paper is based. I am grateful for their comments on earlier draft of a longer paper from which the present one is taken, to Christine Bellamy, Paul Frissen, Brian Hogwood, Helen Margetts, Lawrence Pratchett, Fred Thompson and Steve Woolgar. None of them should be assumed to agree with my arguments, still less be held responsible for my errors. A slightly different version of this paper was given at the Political Studies Association 50th annual conference at the London School of Economics, 10-13.4.00 and a shorter version will appear in 2001 in the PSA Yearbook 2000, MacMillan, Basingstoke

J. E. J. Prins (ed.), Designing E-Government, 7–27.
© 2001 *Kluwer Law International. Printed in the Netherlands.*

One way to classify e-governance systems is roughly according to the main tool for which they are used; of course, there are overlaps because some tools are put to more than one use. There are tools for:

1. generating understandings simple data systems enabling dictionaries of key terms in the dialects of different policy-makers from different professional or organisational cultural backgrounds who are collaborating to understand one another's vocabulary;

   idea generation tools; graphical problem structuring tools (modelling in software procedures such as soft system methodology, robustness analysis, strategic options development and analysis: Rosenhead, 1989); mental mapping and mental representation tools that enable users to develop graphical representations of their own or others basic conceptual approach to problems; argumentation support tools to help multiple groups of decision makers working simultaneously to generate options, identify pros and cons, track multiple flows of argument and debate (Conklin, 1999; Buckingham Shum, 1998; Dennis et al, 1997); electronic whiteboards for graphical representation of connections between ideas (Massetti, 1998); and scenario building tools;

2. collecting data or observations search agents; digital agents based on neural nets for context sensitive searching or editing or précis or transactions (6, 1999a); sensors; and communication recording and storage systems;

3. organising and analysing data on events, conditions, problems, processes that have been observed spreadsheets and budget systems, one of the earliest areas of large-scale e-governance (e.g. the French 1980s SIAD Mairie system: Klein, Roux and Villedieu, 1991); organisational memory tools (Buckingham Shum, 1998); document profiling systems in shared work spaces that enable users on saving documents to provide hypermedia linkages to related documents, to identify key relationships with key organisation documents; some electronic document management systems use bar codes on paper documents to enable their linkage with electronic versions (Prinz and Syri, 1997); hypermedia geographic information systems (GIS); training simulation systems for decision makers, for example for crisis management; and formal models;

4. supporting communication and transaction e-mail, electronic conferencing; video-conferencing systems (Mosier and Tammaro, 1994); meeting management tools (Niederman et al, 1996); tools to model and manage conflict, come to consensus or operate a decision procedure such as weighted voting or arbitration (Watson et al, 1994); argumentation support systems; and electronic document interchange;

5. modelling decisions and advising on possible consequences spreadsheets; expert systems e.g. to test consistency and precision in draft legislation in e.g. social security (Portman, 1988, 77-9) or immigration (Frøkjaer, 1989); neural nets (Whitby, 1996; Berry et al, 1998); modelling systems for problems such as criminal activity, integrated with resource allocation tools (Borins, 1998, 132-133); and there are

6. environments that provide integration and storage for the other categories intranets and the world wide web are the most important example; however, in many cases only the simplest functionality of intranets is actually used (NAO, 1999).

Categories 1, 3, 4 and 5 include the tools often called (group) decision support systems (GDSS) (Finlay and Forghani, 1998; Jones, 1994; Karagiannis et al, 1994).

This category is not wholly distinct from that of "knowledge management" (KM) tools, but the general difference is that KM tools are supposed to manage stocks of knowledge, while GDSS tools manage flows.

2   The Rise of E-Governance

The early decades of computing, however, e-governance was the area in which most progress was made. The development and relatively cheap availability of spreadsheet software had an enormous impact on the process by which budgeting was done in government, initially on mainframe systems in central government in the 1970s, and then in the 1980s, on PC based systems at every level including the smallest local authorities. France was well ahead of the UK when by the mid-1980s many local authorities were using the SIAD Mairie – systems which provided at least finance directors   rather few elected politicians used it themselves in those years – with an integrated financial management, project planning and transaction data interrogation system with an underlying expert system engine for modelling alternative budget scenarios which allowed a variety of scenarios to be tested on a wide variety of data and projections, including non-financial data where relationships could be identified or modelled (Klein, Roux and Villedieu, 1991) At least, these tools should have enabled policy makers to ask the kinds of questions that would make it possible for them, if they had the political courage, to explore, propose, and justify larger than normal scale changes. Of course, there were many other factors at work in those years that also put pressure on governments to raise incomes, invest capital, and spend differently. Spreadsheet technology can have provided no more than a means by which those pressures could be responded to, and by which policy makers could gain a better understanding than traditional paper methods offered, of the options that were believed to be available and their implications. Policy makers were able using such tools in very short spaces of time to compare costs and expenditures, assets and liabilities in a variety of different ways, and to run projections based on different assumptions. It seems reasonable to hypothesise that, insofar as any one development can shake the long-standing and institutionalised tendency of governmental bodies to make budget changes incrementally, this development should have equipped politicians willing to do so to make decisions of a more radical kind: van de Donk, 1998 offers some evidence of non-incremental decision-making. However, the thesis requires more testing: to date, rather little work of a cross-national nature has been done to evaluate the success, even in their own terms, of the reforms to the budget process adopted across the developed world in the 1980s and 1990s (Caiden, 1998) However, the quantitative methods developed by True et al 1990, lend themselves well to this question.

But the spreadsheet was by no means the whole story. Techniques of modelling and simulation brought new analytical capabilities to economic policy makers in the post-war years. Indeed, after the military applications, probably the next major category of central government use of computing power in the age of the punched card and the mainframe was the running of assumptions on economic models. Today, the British Treasury's model of the British economy is available on the World Wide Web and analysts can run their own favoured assumptions on it and see what consequences it would project.

From the 1960s onward, analysis has been conducted electronically of data captured from transaction processing systems in, for example, social security, immigration and other fields, in order to alert policy makers to trends, exceptions, anomalies, patterns, which can at least stimulate further questions if not always rigorously test hypotheses. Spreadsheets and statistical packages have been used to construct scenarios and projections from these kinds of administrative and performance data, to support decision making. Early commentators had high hopes that the widespread use by salaried professional policy analysts of such systems would herald an era of more sophisticated, better informed, more rational policy making (Stevens and McGowan, 1985, 177-183)

By the early 1980s, modelling and simulation was being attempted in the field of environmental policy making, as evolutionary change models came to be tractably modelled in the "artificial life" tradition (Ward, 1999), at the same time as environmental policy makers began to demand systems by which environmental impact assessments of proposed initiatives could be undertaken.

Expert systems were first used in such policy making contexts as social security benefits in the 1970s in the USA and then employed on a much larger scale in the UK in the second half of the 1980s, in order to test the consistency of current regulations, identify anomalies and vague areas, and to explore the implications for proposals to change entitlements and help policy analysts prep are instructions to legal draughtspeople (Portman, 1988, 77-9). Today these systems are used by every front-line benefit officer to calculate entitlements on individual cases, and by every Citizen s Advice Bureau worker to provide entitlement advice, but their first uses were policy analytical in nature rather than in service provision. Expert systems to model British immigration and nationality law in the language Prolog were developed in the 1980s by Professor Robert Kowalski of Imperial College London, but were not extensively used inside the Home Office (discussed in Frøkjaer, 1989).

Models based on neural nets only came into use in government at the end of 1980s initially on a modest scale, and then principally in assisting professionals in such fields as public health epidemiology, civil engineering and some technical aspects of financial management, to analyse and diagnose complex systems.

Moving for a moment to a level that is at least in analytical theory below if not always in practice separable from that of policy and strategic decision making, by the 1980s, management and case decision making in government was beginning to be able to draw upon more sophisticated tools. For example, by the end of the 1980s, central police agencies were being equipped with quite sophisticated modelling systems for criminal profiling and analysis of data in order to support detective work on particular investigations. Electronic document interchange (EDI) systems were introduced to handle legal, financial and procurement systems, and some systems were designed to support extensive integrated analysis and oversight of flows. Some departments have experimented with shared work space systems and accounted document flow systems to track the movement of copies of documents between individuals, identify editing changes made, alert owners to documents that have not been edited or passed on, etc. For example, there are studies that suggest successful experimental use of such systems in some German federal ministries (Prinz and Syri, 1997)

Geographic information systems (GIS) have been developed since the mid-1980s to bring together, ideally from a small number of visual cartographic images, hypermedia databases of information relating to territories and localities. Data packaged in such systems include census, epidemiological, economic profile, land use and environmental information. These have been used by policy makers for various purposes, but the first and perhaps still the most extensive use is in local land use planning. More sophisticated systems are integrated with modelling tools that allow causal relationships to be explored, and there are some innovative examples of their use in decision making at the policy level in the USA (Borins, 1998, 132-133 reports the police department in the Florida city of St. Petersburg using GIS to explore and test explanations of patterns of crime and to model the potential impacts of alternative resource deployment strategies in policing).

In support of communications between policy makers, electronic mail systems were introduced in many departments and authorities in the early 1980s, using a variety of mutually incompatible systems and standards. Only by the beginning of the 1990s were most pre-Internet standards abandoned. Secure but simple e-mail listserv systems began to proliferate to support idea sharing among policy makers. Video-conferencing systems were in modest levels of use in some departments by the end of the 1980s.

Intranets came into general government use during the first few years of the 1990s and while take up was high in some fields of government, actual use was of a limited subset of the features of such systems. In many departments and authorities, intranets were often used as little more than over-engineered internal e-mail systems (Comptroller and Audit General, 1999). Off-the-peg groupware such as Lotus Notes is used in some parts of government, but often only for very simple shared data requirements such as external contact management.

The development of the World Wide Web in the 1980s as a government resource enabled policy analysts and those policy makers with the time and inclination to search with varying degrees of difficulty for public information of varying quality with which to help build arguments. By the end of the 1990s, in at least some fields, international agencies offered some accredited and high quality and restricted access materials to policy makers over the web. Some of these bodies have experimented with on-line electronic conferences run over restricted access web sites.

Political parties have invested extensively in decision support systems geared exclusively to political communication, such as the Labour Party's "Excalibur" system. More recently, such systems have been developed within government. The Cabinet has announced that ministers will have access to a new system that will provide best arguments for and salient facts and statistics illustrating all current policies, programmes and performance.

Figure 1 offers a stylised chronology of the early stages of adoption that is, later that original invention or first experiments but prior to widespread use into British government of e-governance tools by category.

For simplicity, I shall refer to those tools that have reached early stages of adoption - if they have done so at all - only in the late 1990s and 2000s as second wave tools . The distinction from the first wave tools that reached early stages of adoption 1980s and before is basically a chronological one.

Figure 1: A stylised chronology of early adoption of e-governance tools

	1970s and before	1980s	1990s	2000s
understanding generation			problem structuring tools	
data collection				digital agents
data organisation and analysis	analysis of transaction data, economic modelling in treasuries	spreadsheets	. hypermedia geographic information systems, land use development simulation	
communication support		video-conferencing	e-mail, electronic conferencing, bar code document and decision flow tracking	meeting support, argumentation support
decision modelling and advice		expert systems, initially in case decision, then in consistency testing for law	neural nets experimented with in case decisions	neural nets
integrated environments			intranets, World Wide Web, groupware	

It seems to be the case that Britain is somewhat behind other developed countries in the use of many of the more advanced e-governance systems. Policy makers in Australian state governments, such as Victoria, for example, tend to make much more use of at least the more straightforward groupware such as Lotus Notes and to use intranet systems for more than just internal electronic mail, but also for electronic calendars, document interchange, document work flow management and project management (see <htttp://www.mmv.vic.gov.au/>). In New South Wales, for example, sophisticated computer assisted performance management systems have been the basis on which systems for policy decision support have been developed (Hasan and Hasan, 1997). Yet even in Australia, it is not clear that these systems are being fully exploited.

The reasons for the slow adoption of more advanced include: design weaknesses due to assumptions by designers of excessive rationalism in policy making (Bannon, 1997; Kling, 1997) and overly optimistic design assumptions about the willingness of politicians to share information with each other; institutional forces (Bellamy and Taylor, 1998) such as technological frames (Bijker, 1995), policy network structures (Pratchett, 1999), perceived costs of setting up and limited gains from use (Bugler and Bretschneider, 1993; Kraemer and Dedrick, 1997); and difficulties in persuading publics to approve of additional expenditure on decision support when service provision spending is constrained (Pratchett, 1999; Ranerup, 1999). However, the global trend toward more joined-up government (6, 1997, 6 et al 1999; 6 et al, 2001 forthcoming), more syndicated cross-national co-ordination in governance (6, 2000a), generational change among policy makers and design improvements may well increase the demand for and use of e-governance tools.

3   Theories of E-Governance

What might be the consequences of significantly increased take-up of more sophisticated and recently developed e-governance systems across government? Will these tools sustain better governance, by the standards and interests of any of the principal interests that shape policy processes? Is it meaningful even to ask whether they could better support anything recognisable as the public interest? Broadly, there are four rival types of theory on offer. Each can be read as one possible future scenario for understanding the potential impact of e-governance.

3.1   Rationalisation

First, there are those who argue uncompromisingly that the use of these technologies represents a major once-for-all improvement in the capabilities of governance and in at least the possibility of rationality in decision-making (Stevens and McGowan 1985, 177-183; more recently, Tapscott 1997). The only price is the cost of investment and some running costs. Indeed, on this view, these systems will steadily reduce the costs of acquiring, ordering, coding, organising, selecting, managing and using information. Therefore, the systems will more than repay their initial costs over their life (argued by, for example, Reschenthaler and Thompson, 1996). This optimistic view is based on classical cybernetic theory (Wiener, 1948): it holds that that (using Overman and Loraine's 1994 summary), information decreases uncertainty, slows entropy, increases control (decreases variance) by feedback and deviation correction, and in general that more information enables more control (or at least up to a point that we have not yet reached, if the relationship between information and control is conceived as curvilinear).

It is relatively straightforward to obtain evidence for the control theory if one limits oneself to asking no-longer-new, now familiarised decision-making users about their satisfaction with a particular technology, as studies of e-governance in Norwegian (Ytterstad and Watson, 1996) and Australian local government find (Hasan and Hasan, 1997). However, people tend to engage in rationalisation and cognitive dissonance reduction, and so they tend to report that the technology provides them with valuable information and with greater control. Van de Donk (1998) presents some qualitative evidence for reduced incrementalism in budget-setting arising from the introduction of spreadsheets and more advanced financial planning tools, but the thesis still lacks the comparative quantitative support it would need. Such subjective evidence needs to be treated with great caution, for all the reasons now well-established in the studies on limited rationality in the policy process.

3.2   The Price of Reason

A second group of theories accepts at least the possibility of greater control, quality and rationality in decision-making, but insists that this comes at a price. These theories argue that safeguards are needed, lest that price be too great in terms of:
*   citizens individual liberty and privacy;
*   citizens collective (democratic) influence over governmental decisions (Raab 1997);
*   politicians control over decision-making agenda in favour of civil servants or officers "infocracy" (Zuurmond 1998) or an oligopoly of private contractors (Margetts and Dunleavy 1995); and/or
*   civil servants capability to exercise constraint upon populism of politicians;
*   or alternatively, bureaucratisation, as decisions that can be made using algorithms are pushed down the hierarchy from politicians to salaried officials, because they cease to be regarded as policy matters at all (Bugler and Bretschneider, 1997);
*   more personal benefits for policy makers (Nedovic-Budic and Godschalk, 1996; Berry, Berry and Foster, 1998);
*   erosion of meaningful relationships among decision makers (Wilson, 1999);
*   even in the short term, loss of quality in decision making because the focus on quantitatively measurable dimensions leads to neglect of less easily measured aspects of public programmes (Power, 1997);
*   loss of commitment to decisions made on the advice of computer based neural net models and expert systems, due to the reduced user control and understanding of the model, and the larger numbers of options generated (Landsbergen et al, 1997); or
*   in the long term, humane values - Weber's iron cage of rationality (Weber, 1958, 1976; Winner, 1977; van de Donk, 1998).

The most extreme version of this view is perhaps that of the governmentality theorists who argue that government technologies and rationalities, including e-governance tools, have become steadily more invasive through their extension of knowledge and information about populations, and their exercise has supported socialisation steadily to shape citizens into more docile subjects of authority (Burchell, Gordon and Miller, 1991; Barry, Osborne and Rose, 1996; Dean, 1999; Rose, 1999).

None of these claims is wholly compelling, and often depends on highly selective use of anecdote. The bureaucratisation thesis, for example is vulnerable to the powerful counter-example of monetary policy: the automatic correction mechanisms popular in the 1980s have been largely abandoned and the importance of judgment recognised.

Again, evidence for loss of meaning and of commitment is rather anecdotal, or confined to experiments, and does not necessarily support generalisation. Sometimes, norms, customs, rules, roles, practices that have worked well in face-to-face or telephone settings will be carried over successfully to the groupware context. This was the finding of a study of a network of British general practitioners in the National Health Service who began to exchange information about a range of practice management, prescribing, purchasing and health policy issues in which they were involved (Fox and Roberts, 1999). This finding seems to be explained by the particular institutional setting within which the on-line network was embedded. But it cannot be assumed in advance that this transfer will occur automatically. One study attempted to test for such changes by predicting what roles a group of people in an experiment would play in such a setting, based on how they behaved in face-to-face groupwork, and what roles they would want to delegate to the software, and then compared these predictions with roles observed. The main finding was that people played fewer roles than expected, and that at least some but, to the surprise of the experiment designers, relatively few participants described the software as playing the roles of recording the group memory and monitoring procedure, and a few saw the software as group facilitator and motivator (Zigurs and Kozar, 1994). It may be that, unlike the medical case, the institutional setting within which the experiment was embedded was simply too thin to provide existing norms that could be carried over. It is very difficult to avoid Hawthorne effects in designing experiments of this kind, and even in designing studies in working organisations, and so it is hard to know what weight to put on such results.

So far, the move to reduce arbitrary administrative discretion by street level bureaucrats in public service decision making about individual entitlements such as cash benefits (stressed in the recent e-governance literature by Snellen 1998), has not been the thin end of the wedge for the substitution of automated decision-making in policy judgment, or the final coming of Weber's (1958, 1976) 'iron cage' of bureaucratic rationality. Despite the burgeoning investment by governments in the technologies listed above, there is little evidence of policy makers in finance ministries or land use planning departments following wholesale and mechanically the recommendations that are cranked out casually for them by junior staff from often still crude software models.

3.3   Noise, Fragmentation and the Erosion of Reason

The third view is the most pessimistic. The claim is that e-governance will actually erode rationality generally. It points to the pathologies of excessive demand for policy analysis thus delaying action – paralysis by analysis – the bloating out of the policy advice industries among think tanks and consultancy firms, the problems of sheer information overload, the allegedly lesser ability of the public sector to manage information well than of private citizens or businesses, and the obsession with the already measured that distracts policy makers attention away from tacit, implicit, qualitative, unstructured factors and toward formal, explicit, quantitatively measured, structured factors and information. Finally, and perhaps most crucially, this theory fears that, due to mechanical rule following as suggested by overly simple data interpretations, overly simple modeling, and by overly simple expert system flows from analysis to recommendation, the cultivation and the exercise of judgment in decision making will be crowded out. This view wholly rejects the cybernetic faith that information is control, and prefers the trope of information as noise.

Again, if one asks a different set of questions about coping with workload from those asked by many studies that find satisfaction with growing control, then by the power of suggestion by the phrasing of a question (for example, using leading phrases that hint as information overload), one typically gets data that can be used to support the noise theory of information.

3.4   Technology as Totem, Fetish Arena and Foil in Ritualised Social Conflict

The theories in the fourth and final cluster argue that there will be no very fundamental and independent impact of technology itself on technical or political rationality of decision-making. Rather, both continuities and changes in governance are driven socially and politically, and technologies are means, occasions and totems for conflict over preservation ("conservative" social and political shaping) or change ("radical" social and political shaping) of styles of governance are changed or preserved (Mackenzie and Wacjman, 1985; Bijker, 1995, Bijker and Law, 1994). Indeed, e-governance technologies are not "neutral". Rather, design responds to social pressures in order to make social organisation embodied and implicit in the technologies (Akrich, 1994).

Some of the earliest studies of e-governance in US political science, in the era of the mainframe and the mini-computer, found that technologies were essentially used for purposes and in rituals of coming to political judgment that were long-established: Danziger and Kling (1982) and Kraemer and Dutton (1982) describe this as rein-forcement politics, which corresponds to conservative shaping. It could be argued that the Dutch research on e-governance which shows the promotion of horizontal co-ordination styles of policy-making and public management (Frissen, 1999), and modest experimentation in public consultation, shows more conservative than radical social and political shaping at work. While the rigidities of the traditional pillars may be almost dismantled by now, the Dutch tradition is perpetuated, of relying upon relatively autonomous networks of organisations in both implementation and rule-making, which are not dominated by politicians. By contrast, the British case shows conservative social shaping of the opposite kind: technologies of e-governance are selected and used to perpetuate the British commitment to the dominance of the political executive, and secondly to continue the role of elected politicians as story-tellers and leaders in public. Therefore, we find British politicians committed to seeing the development of digital television and to chat rooms mass media for which politicians already possess the requisite communication skills and to more leadership-centred technologies of e-governance for decision-making. However, the prospect that most citizens might access digital services using mobile phones, which provide far fewer opportunities for the kinds of political communication that politicians need to engage in, rather than digital television, is one that politicians find disconcerting. All this reflects the prior political culture, at least at national level, that characterises the Westminster system.

Crucial to the shaping of technology in the exercise of governance on this view, are the rituals that policy makers perform that legitimate their decisions (Kertzer, 1988; Edelman, 1988; 6, 2000c). New intellectual technologies can provide an array of ritual resources for demonstrating to wider publics the grounding and authority of their decision-making practices, but in fact, the underlying style or rationale of decision-making remains fundamentally politically driven. Information, on this view, is neither control nor noise. Rather, it is a totem not in any derogatory sense, but rather in the vitally important political sense that all societies depend for their cohesion on symbols and rituals of their collective decision-making and the judgment of their policy makers, and the real, indeed vast, importance of information is to be found here.

Historical and ethnographic work on long run usage by policy makers of information technologies tends to provide more support for the totem theory (e.g. Nidumolu et al, 1996), as does some survey work with a less conventional design (e.g. Overman and Loraine, 1994). Ethnographic research on the use of e-mail provides further good evidence that all projects for social shaping provoke counter projects. Romm (1999) shows that even a supposedly simple and low bandwidth technology like e-mail does not greatly constrain its users; Lee (1994) shows that bandwidth in use is as much as function of interpretation, implicit and tacit knowledge as of technical characteristics of the medium. For it is used by rival groups, subaltern and superior, and horizontally opposed factions, to their own ends: Romm shows that each exploits certain features of the technology multiple addressing, recordability, processing and routing to pursue their own goals. In this sense, e-mail merely reminds us of the longstanding finding in organisation studies that the flows of power, information and knowledge in organisations almost never follow the official organisation chart (Scott, 1992). E-mail does not deepen or exacerbate these informal networks of power and information, but merely provides them with new means to pursue their particular goals. This suggests that the hypothesis that because of e-mail, certain groups of policy makers will gain power at the expense of others, because they are gaining control (rationalisation, perhaps at a price) perhaps local chairs at the expense of leaders, or ministers at the expense of premiers, or civil servants at the expense of politicians generally should be rejected. The technology is almost certainly not responsible. Rather, people use technologies as occasions, foils, symbols, tools, ritual objects, to develop and institutionalise the forms of solidarity they are committed to.

If there are changes in norms, customs, practices associated with moving to computer supported decision making among policy makers, that may at first sight provide evidence for the rationalisation at a price theory, we should be alive to the possibility that what is really taking place is radical social shaping. That is to say, the introduction of new technologies into groups of decision makers is also being used as the occasion and the opportunity for making other changes that superior decision makers want to make. Indeed, the conventional management literature argues that this is exactly what good manager should do with technology, in order to avoid wasting investment on automating bad old ways of doing things (e.g. Hammer and Champy, 1995). There is an extensive body of work that shows that where superior decision makers use the opportunity to introduce more control, surveillance and accountability upon the work of lower decision makers, the technology will be experienced as introducing rationalisation at the price of discretion, autonomy and freedom of action (Overman and Loraine, 1994; Hayes and Walsham, 2000; Shapiro et al, 1991). Academic researchers, being peculiarly sensitive to threats to their own intellectual freedom, can often tend to be more sympathetic to claims to autonomy in decision making by other groups than, for example, national politicians or national civil servants are, and this can lead them to represent social shaping of certain kinds whether conservative or radical relative to institutional starting points chosen for the period of a study as rationalisation at a price. However, many of the findings support the view that projects for radical social shaping of decision systems typically provoke counter-shaping projects of a more conservative or differently radical nature (and vice versa), because users are ingenious in using such systems for their own private benefits, subverting the intentions of superior decision makers who may be seen likewise as shaping the technology as much for their private ends as for organisational goals (Shapiro et al, 1991).

Much of the evidence for the noise theory comes not so much from studies of use of computers by policy makers, as from studies of accountability in public management. Successive studies of the actual use made of performance indicators which are, of course, now typically collected, coded, submitted, analysed, collated, and now published electronically have found that much of the information is not read, not used at all, or provides more complex pictures than those who hold public services to account really want or think that they need (Carter, Klein and Day, 1993; Grønbjerg, 1993; Heinrich, 1999).

But again, this reading of these findings is not uncontested. Many recent commentators looking at audit and accountability mechanisms in the public sector see these as evidence for the totem theory namely, that rituals of accountability are being performed, symbols displayed, without necessarily achieving the substance of control (Hogwood, Judge and McVicar, 1998; Power, 1997). One important substantive effect, these theories would suggest, of the development of e-governance tools principally to handle quantitative information has been a reallocation of that scarcest of resources in government, namely policy makers attention (March and Olsen, 1976), to those problems that lend themselves to highly formal treatment. Had there been, for example, greater development and use in government of charting, creativity and soft systems methodology tools (Checkland and Scholes, 1990; Checkland, 1989; Ballantine and Cunningham, 1999), which have developed some of the ideas of the late great Sir Geoffrey Vickers (Checkland, 1994; Vickers, 1995) attention to problems might be allocated differently, but that selection of technologies would only have taken place had the institutional pressures upon policy makers been rather different.

Precisely because the noise and totem theories differ in their basic conception of information from the qualified cybernetic consensus of the first two, it is possible for them to come to opposite conclusions about the impacts of new intellectual technologies on leadership and collective action from their conclusions about the impacts on decision making. For the very characteristics of being either noise and totem that can undermine the quality of decision-making may in fact increase the capabilities of politicians to engage in leadership and collective action, for the cover of fog and the power of symbolism are powerful tools in the pursuit of these activities of governance.

4   Comparing the Theories

Figure 2 summarises some of the key differences between the theories.

Figure 2: Theories of e-governance at a glance

theory specific view	rationalisation	rationalisation at a price	loss of rationality	social shaping
information as	control (positive) integration	control (negative) integration	noise fragmentation	totem depends on balance of forces
public management planning style	anticipation	anticipation	resilience	depends on balance of forces
power shift	to policy makers	captured by special interests	undermining power	depends on balance of forces

Is a straightforward choice to be made between these theories? Or are they reconcilable perhaps by allocating them to different domains or else to different levels of explanation? As we have seen, each theory has some empirical support, although most empirical studies have been of rather limited scope and not in general designed to test, let alone falsify, these rival theories.

There are differences between theories in the explanatory level at which they work. Social science distinguishes between proximate variables - close to the phenomenon they purport to explain and distal variables at some explanatory distance, working at deeper levels, not necessarily directly observable. For example, the control theory works with proximate variables individual decision makers satisfaction, their sense of efficacy and control in their work, collective action capabilities of groups of decision makers. The noise theory is basically the converse of this focusing on decision makers sense of being overwhelmed. By contrast, social shaping or totem theory works with distal variables institutions, symbols, meanings, ritual formations, group identities and the ways in which they shape group interests. Indeed, social shaping theory can offer an institutional explanation of the phenomena to which the control, rationalisation at a price and noise theories point, as if they were data rather than explanations. Indeed, it suggests that the fears expressed in the price of rationalisation and noise theories are essentially resentments of particular forms of social organisation for which technologies are mobilised (Douglas, 1994). In this sense, e-governance technologies are no different from the development of governmental statistics in the eighteenth and nineteenth centuries as decision support tools (Hacking, 1990): there is nothing politically new in the e-governance debates.

Whereas the control and noise theories can be tested in large part through classical survey, interview and behavioural observation techniques, the totem or social shaping theory calls for quite different kinds of research to test it it would require ethnographic work of a high degree of sophistication. The rationalisation-at-a-price-theories are a mixed bag. Some are social shaping theories manqué, because they assert that social shaping by one group will dominate, no matter what counter shaping is provoked. Others such as governmentality theory or iron cage models that move beyond capture to look at whole society dynamics are closer to totemic institutionalist theories in their use of distal variables, but close to the control theory in their central claim that technology is itself a major causal force.

The central problem in using empirical studies to test the power of these theories, then, seems to be that if one sets the standards of what counts as control, noise and totem sufficiently high or low, then almost any empirical work one could design can be read as confirming any of the theories.

Although multi-theoretic approaches have their uses, especially for policy makers, it should be clear, however, from the foregoing discussion that I lean toward the totem or social shaping theory, partly on wider theoretical grounds such as a preference for distal variables (6, 1999b), and partly for reasons set out above about the inter-pretation of the empirical research data offered by the other theories. In the next section and the conclusion, I develop some of the main implications of the totem or social shaping theory for the uses of e-governance tools.

5   Technologies to Support Judgment and Appreciation in E-Governance

Judgment and appreciation (Vickers 1995) are the craft skills of governance and decision making (for an account of political judgment, see 6, 2000a). If tools of e-governance are used to economise upon or substitute for judgment, the consequences could be very damaging. One danger of rationalisation theories is that they can give legitimacy to uses of e-governance tools ways of streamlining and homogenising decision-making, when the political strength of many decision making systems is precisely their diversity and responsiveness. In the name of removing arbitrariness, information technologies can too easily substitute explicit and formal information for tacit and informal, and in consequence, lose proper discrimination, destroy knowledge and undermine judgment. The importance of the social shaping theory is its recognition that, more important than the design features of particular e-governance tools, ritual in judgment is often the way in which this tacit richness is encoded and applied, and through which technologies are domesticated . The challenge for policy makers is to develop norms, customs and rituals for the appropriate use of these technologies, which will help to sustain and cultivate judgment.

It is common in policy studies to be rather dismissive of ritual, on the grounds that ritual behaviours are supposedly sub-optimal, less than rational if not outright irrational: in mainstream policy sciences, it is often a debunking strategy to suggest that something is mere ritual or is symbolic (Edelman, 1985 [1964]). But this is inadequate (6, 2000c). Ritual is neither essentially irrational (as suggested by the Carnegie school, e.g. March and Olsen, 1989, 1995) nor insincerely and cynically conducted public ceremonial, as the Puritan tradition has misled us into thinking (and as many studies of political ritual suggest, e.g. Edelman, 1988, Kertzer, 1988): rather, it is the repeated enactment of social organisation and of settlement between rival and conflicting forms (Douglas, 1970, 1986). Anthropologists have long known that ritual is never empty, never formalistic, but endlessly inventive, and essential to the ways in which cultures, habits, expectation, solidarities are developed and judgment is practised, and to the social shaping and impact of technologies (Bell, 1992, Turner, 1974, 1982).

Rituals, institutions, customs and norms in the use of technologies govern expectations of speed and time (Adam, 1990; 6, 2000c). Many policy makers report that the impact of global media scrutiny and interviewing after events, of the culture of e-mail that has grown up on the Internet, and the customs of responsiveness associated with on-line voting press them to make decisions and respond at greater speed than permits the exercise of judgment. The effect can be to reinforce the sensibility that treats information as noise. Developing alternative customs requires more than simply assertion and effort: it requires work on institutionalised expectations and commitments among wider publics.

One of the customs and norms that we ought to expect in democratic societies is that the electronic tools of e-governance will increasingly be put into the public domain and be tested by experts and by ordinary citizens against a variety of assumptions, and against rival systems. Freedom of information should extend to public availability for all the models, simulations, problem structuring tools, geographical information systems and content analytic agents that policy makers themselves use (A recent report from the Performance and Innovation Unit (2000) in the British Cabinet Office has recommended this). This may not be appropriate for all models, such as those generated as normative heuristics in workshop settings, but is generally appropriate for most formal positive quantitative and qualitative causal models (except, of course, for those used in military contexts). For the aim, in a democratic society, of the cultivation of judgment in governance should not be the empowering of a political élite, but the strengthening of the competence, maturity and self-governing capabilities of the citizenry (Elkin and So tan, 1999). Indeed, every democrat must hold that in the medium to long run, only the robustness of the judgment capabilities of citizens can guarantee that those of policy makers will be similarly stout.

Similarly, the challenge to make e-governance tools serve the cultivation of policy judgment requires not only better designed software systems, but the institutional buttressing of the practice of judgment as the political settlement through ritual processes between rival forms of social organisation (6, 2000a,c). To this end, it would, at least in my view, be helpful to develop e-governance systems that explicitly modelled conflicts over policies as conflicts over forms of social organisation, and that related rival claims explicitly to the particular styles of organisation that they typically reflect.

Secondly, it should be a key element in the professional ethics of solution designers and system developers that their systems should make palpable to policy makers who use them, just what the political presuppositions of the systems under development are.

Thirdly, as politicians explain to their electorates why these systems justify the expense of investment, they need to make clear just how the central political virtues of judgment as settlement between rival forms of social organisation are being cultivated through the use of such tools. Only in that context, can we hope that e-governance tools will support democratic renewal.

References

Adam, B. (1990) *Time and social theory*, Cambridge, Polity Press.

Akrich, M. (1994) 'The de-scription of technical objects', in Bijker, W. and Law, J. (eds.) *Shaping technology / building society*, Cambridge, Massachusetts: Massachusetts Institute of Technology Press, 205-224.

Ballantine, J. and Cunningham, N. (1999) 'Strategic information systems planning: applying private sector frameworks in UK public healthcare' in Heeks R. (ed.) *Reinventing government in the information age: international practice in IT-enabled public sector reform*, London: Routledge, 293-311.

Bannon, L. J. (1997) 'A challenge to certain (G)DSS perspectives on the role of decisions, information and technology in organisations', in Humphreys, P., Ayestaran, S., McCosh, A., Mayon-White, B. (eds.) *Decision support in organisational transformation*, London: Chapman and Hall.

Barry, A., Osborne, T. and Rose, N. (eds. 1996) *Foucault and political reason: liberalism, neo-liberalism and rationalities of government*, London: UCL Press.

Bell, C. (1992) *Ritual theory, ritual practice*, Oxford: Oxford University Press.

Bellamy, C. and Taylor, J. (1998) *Governing in the information age*, Buckingham: Open University Press.

Berry, F., Berry, J. and Foster, S. (1998) 'The determinants of success in implementing an expert system in state government', *Public administration review*, 58, 4: 293-305.

Bijker, W.E. (1995) *Of Bicycles, Bakelites and bulbs: toward a theory of sociotechnical change*, Cambridge, Massachusetts: Massachusetts Institute of Technology Press.

Bijker, W.E. and Law, J. (eds. 1994) *Shaping technology / building society*, Cambridge, Massachusetts: Massachusetts Institute of Technology Press.

Borins, S. (1998) *Innovating with integrity: how local heroes are transforming American government*, Washington DC: Georgetown University Press.

Buckingham Shum, S. (1998) 'Negotiating the construction of organisational memories', in Borghoff, U.M. and Pareschi, R. (eds.), *Information technology for knowledge management*, Berlin: Springer-Verlag.

Bugler, D.T. and Bretschneider, S.I. (1993) 'Technology push or program pull? interest in new technologies within public organisations', in Bozeman, B. (ed.) *Public management: the state of the art*, San Francisco, California: Jossey-Bass: 275-293.

Burchell, G., Gordon, C. and Miller, P. (eds. 1991) *The Foucault effect: studies in governmentality*, Hemel Hempstead: Harvester Wheatsheaf.

Caiden N, 1998, 'A new generation of budget reforms', in Peters BG and Savoie DJ, eds, 1998, *Taking stock: assessing public sector reforms*, Montreal: Canadian Centre for Management Development, McGill-Queen's University Press, 252-284.

Carter, N., Klein, R.E. and Day, P. (1993) *How organisations measure success: the use of performance indicators in government*, London: Routledge.

Checkland, P.B. (1989) 'Soft systems methodology', in Rosenhead J. (ed.) *Rational analysis for a problematic world: problem structuring methods for complexity, uncertainty and conflict*, Chichester: John Wiley and Sons: 71-100.

Checkland, P.B. (1994) 'Systems theory and management thinking', in Blunden, M. and Dando, M. (eds.) *Rethinking public policy-making: questioning assumptions, challenging beliefs – essays in honour of Sir Geoffrey Vickers on his centenary*, London: Sage: 75-91.

Checkland, P. B. and Scholes, J. (1990) *Soft systems methodology in action*, Chichester: John Wiley and Sons.

Comptroller and Auditor General, 1999, *Government on the web*, HC 87, London: Stationery Office.

Conklin J. (1999) 'Seven years of industrial strength CSCA in an electric utility', <http://d3e.open.ac.uk/cscl99/Conklin/Conklin-paper.html>.

Danziger JN and Kling R, 1982, 'Computers in the policy process', in Danziger JN, Dutton WH, Kling R and Kraemer KL, 1982, *Computers and politics: high technology in American local governments*, New York: Columbia University Press, 136-169.

Dean, M. (1999) *Governmentality: power and rule in modern society*, London: Sage.

Dennis, A.R., Valacich, J.S., Carte, T.A., Garfield, M.J., Haley, B.J. and Aronson, J.E. (1997) 'Research report: the effectiveness of multiple dialogues in electronic brainstorming', *Information systems research*, 8, 2: 203-211.

Douglas, M. (1970) *Natural symbols: explorations in cosmology*, London: Routledge.

Douglas, M. (1986) *How institutions think*, London: Routledge and Kegan Paul.

Douglas, M. (1994) *Risk and blame: essays in cultural theory*, London: Routledge.

Edelman, M. (1985) [1964] *The symbolic uses of politics*, Urbana, Illinois: University of Illinois Press.

Edelman, M. (1988) *Constructing the political spectacle*, Chicago: University of Chicago Press.

Elkin, S.L. and So³tan, K.E. (eds. 1999) *Citizen competence and democratic institutions*, University Park, Pennsylvania: Pennsylvania University Press.

Finlay, P.N. and Forghani, M. (1998) 'A classification of success factors for decision support systems', *Journal of strategic information systems*, 7: 53-70.

Fox, N. and Roberts, C. (1999) 'GPs in cyberspace: the sociology of a "virtual community"', *Sociological review*, 4: 643-671.

Frissen, P.H.A. (1999) *Politics, governance and technology: a postmodern narrative on the virtual state*, Aldershot: Edward Elgar.

Frøkjaer, E. (1989) 'Controversial issues of expert systems in public administration', in Snellen, I.T.H.M., van de Donk W.B.H.J and Baquiast J-P. (eds. 1989) *Expert systems in public administration*, Amsterdam: Elsevier: 35-54.

Grønbjerg, K.A. (1993) *Understanding nonprofit funding: managing revenues in social services and community development organisations*, San Francisco, California: Jossey-Bass.

Hacking, I. (1990) *The taming of chance*, Cambridge: Cambridge University Press.

Hammer, M. and Champy, J. (1995) *Re-engineering the corporation: a manifesto for business revolution*, London: Nicholas Brearley Publishing.

Hasan, H. and Hasan, S. (1997) 'Computer-based performance information for executives in local government', *Australian journal of public administration*, 56, 3: 24-29.

Hayes, N. and Walsham, G. (2000) 'Competing interpretations of computer-supported co-operative work in organisational contexts, *Organisation*, 7, 1: 49-67.

Heeks, R. (ed. 1999) *Reinventing government in the information age: international practice in it-enabled public sector reform*, London: Routledge.

Heinrich, C. (1999) 'Do government bureaucrats make effective use of performance management information?', *Journal of public administration research and theory*, 9, 3: 363-394.

Hogwood, B.A., Judge, D. and McVicar, M. (1998) 'Agencies and accountability', paper to the Whitehall Programme conference, University of Birmingham, 17-19 December 1998.

Jones, M.R. (1994) 'Information technology for group decision support: beyond GDSS', *Journal of organisational computing*, 4, 1, 23-40.

Karagiannis, D., Radermacher, F.J., Teufel, B. and Wynne, B.E. (1994) 'Towards CSCW: meta-level environments for enhanced group and organisation effectiveness', *Journal of organisational computing*, 4, 4: 367-392.

Kertzer, D.I. (1988) *Ritual, politics and power*, New Haven: Yale University Press.

Klein, M., Roux, D. and Villedieu, T. (1991) 'Decision support for municipality financial planning in france: recent progress with "SIAD Mairie", a knowledge-based DSS' in Traunmüller, R. (ed.) *Governmental and municipal information systems II: proceedings of the 2ⁿᵈ IFIP TC8/WG8.5 Working conference on governmental and municipal information systems, Balatonfüred, Hungary*, Amsterdam: North-Holland: 117-130.

Kling, R. (1997) 'Multivalent Social Relationships in Computer Supported Workplaces', in Kiesler, S. (ed.) *Research milestones on the information highway*, Hillsdale, New Jersey: Lawrence Erlbaum.

Kraemer KL and Dutton WH, 1982, 'The automation of bias', in Danziger JN, Dutton WH, Kling R and Kraemer KL, 1982, *Computers and politics: high technology in American local governments*, , New York: Columbia University Press, 170-193.

Kraemer, K.L. and Dedrick, J. (1997) 'Computing and public organisations', *Journal of public administration research and theory*, 7, 1: 89-112.

Landsbergen, D., Coursey, D.H., Loveless, S. and Shangraw, R.F. (1997) 'Decision quality, confidence and commitment with expert systems: an experimental study', *Journal of public administration research and theory*, 7, 1: 131-157.

Lee, A.S. (1994) 'Electronic mail as a medium for rich communication: an empirical investigation using hermeneutic interpretation', *Management information systems quarterly*, 18, 2: 143-158.

Mackenzie, D. and Wajcman, J. (eds. 1985) *The social shaping of technology: how the refrigerator got its hum*, Buckingham: Open University Press.

March, J.G. and Olsen, J-P. (1976) *Ambiguity and choice in organisations*, Bergen: Universitetsforlaget.

March, J.G. and Olsen, J-P (1989) *Rediscovering institutions: the organisational basis of politics*, New York: Free Press.

March, J.G. and Olsen, J-P (1995) *Democratic governance*, New York: Free Press.

Margetts, H. and Dunleavy, P. (1995) 'Public services on the world markets', in *Missionary government, Demos collection*, 7: 30-32.

Massetti, B. (1998) 'An empirical examination of the value of creativity support systems on idea generation', *Management information systems quarterly*, 20, 1: 83-98.

Nedovic-Budic, Z. and Godschalk, D.R. (1996) 'Human factors in the adoption of geographic information systems: a local government case study', *Public administration review*, 56, 6: 554-567.

Mosier, J.N. and Tammaro, S.G. (1994) 'Video teleconference use among geographically dispersed workgroups: a field investigation of usage patterns and user preferences', *Journal of organisational computing*, 4, 4: 343-365.

National Audit Office (NAO) (1999) *Government on the web*, HC 87, London: Stationery Office.

Nidumolu, S.R., Goodman, S.E., Vogel, D.R., Dankowitz, A.K. (1996) 'Information technology for local administration support: the Governorates Project in Egypt', *Management information systems*, June, 20,2:197-225.

Niederman, F., Biese, C.M. and Beranek, P.M. (1996) 'Issues and concerns about computer supported meetings', *Management information systems quarterly*, 20, 1: 1-22.

Overman, E.S. and Loraine, D.T. (1994) 'Information for control: another management proverb?', *Public administration review:* 193-196.

Performance and Innovation Unit (2000) *Adding it up: improving analysis and modelling in central government*, London: Cabinet Office.

Portman, E.C.P. (1988) 'The Alvey DHSS large demonstrator project', in Duffin P. (ed) *Knowledge-based systems: applications in administrative government*, Chichester: Ellis Horwood, and London: CCTA: 76-88

Power, M. (1997) *The audit society: rituals of verification*, Oxford: Oxford University Press.

Pratchett, L. (1999) 'New technologies and the modernisation of local government', *Public administration*, 77, 4: 731-750.

Prinz, W. and Syri, A. (1997) 'Two complementary tools for the co-operation in a ministerial environment', *Journal of universal computer science*, 3, 8: 843-864.

Raab, C. (1997) 'Privacy, information and democracy', in Loader BD (ed.) *The governance of cyberspace: politics, technology and global restructuring*, London: Routledge: 155-174.

Ranerup, A. (1999) 'Internet-enabled applications for local government democratisation: contradictions of the Swedish experience', in Heeks, R. (ed.) *Reinventing government in the information age: international practice in it-enabled public sector reform*, London: Routledge: 177-193.

Reschenthaler, G.B. and Thompson, F. (1996) 'The information revolution and the new public management', *Journal of public administration research and theory*, 6, 1: 125-143.

Romm (Livermore) C.T. (1999) *Virtual politicking: playing politics in electronically linked organisations*, Cresskill, New Jersey: Hampton Press.

Rose, N. (1999) *Powers of freedom: reframing political thought*, Cambridge University Press: Cambridge.

Rosenhead, J. (eds. 1989) *Rational analysis for a problematic world: problem structuring methods for complexity, uncertainty and conflict*, Chichester: John Wiley & Son.

Scott, W.R. (1992) *Organisations: rational, natural and open systems*, 3rd edn, Englewood Cliffs, New Jersey: Prentice-Hall.

Shapiro, D., Hughes, J., Harper, R., Ackroyd, S. and Soothill, K. (1991) 'Policing information systems: the social context of success and failure in introducing information systems in the police service', in Traunmüller, R. (ed.) *Governmental and municipal information systems II: proceedings of the 2nd IFIP TC8/WG8.5 Working conference on governmental and municipal information systems, Balatonfüred, Hungary*, Amsterdam: North-Holland, 183-197.

Snellen, I.Th.M. (1998) 'Street level bureaucracy in an information age', in Snellen IThM and van de Donk (eds.) *Public administration in an information age: a handbook*, Amsterdam: IOS Press: 497-508.

Stevens, J.M. and McGowan, R.P. (1985) *Information systems for public management*, New York: Praeger.

Tapscott, D. 1997, 'The digital media and the reinvention of government', *Canadian public administration*, 40: 328-345.

True JL, Jones BD and Baumgartner FR, 1999, 'Punctuated equilibrium theory: explaining stability and change in American policy making', in Sabatier PA, ed, 1999, *Theories of the policy process*, Boulder, Colorado: Westview Press, 97-116.

Turner, V. (1974) *Dramas, fields and metaphors: symbolic action in human society*, Ithaca, New York: Cornell University Press.

Turner, V. (1982) *From ritual to theatre: the human seriousness of play*, New York: PAJ Publications.

van de Donk, W.B.H.J. (1998) 'Beyond incrementalism? redistributive policy-making, information systems and the revival of synopticism', in Snellen, I.Th.M. and van de Donk, W.B.H.J. (eds.) *Public administration in an information age: a handbook*, Amsterdam: IOS Press: 381-404.

Vickers, G. (1995) [1963], *The art of judgment: a study in policy making*, centenary edition, London: Sage.

Ward M, 1999, *Virtual organisms: the startling world of artificial life*, Basingstoke: MacMillan.

Watson, R.T., Alexander, M.B., Pollard, C.E. and Bostrom, R.P. (1994) 'Perceptions of facilitators of a keypad-based group support system', *Journal of organisational computing*, 4, 2: 103-105.

Weber, M. (1958) 'Bureaucracy', from *Economy and society*, in Gerth, H.H. and Mills, C.W. (eds. [1946]) *From Max Weber: essays in sociology*, New York: Galaxy / Oxford University Press: 196-245.

Weber, M. (1976) *The Protestant ethic and the spirit of capitalism*, London: Allen and Unwin.

Whitby, B. (1996) *Reflections on artificial intelligence: the legal, moral and ethical dimensions*, Exeter: Intellect Books.

Wiener, N. (1948) *Cybernetics: the emerging science at the edge of order and chaos*, New York: Simon and Schuster.

Wilson F. (1999) 'Cultural control within the virtual organisation', *The sociological review*, 4: 672-694.

Winner L. (1977) *Autonomous technology: technics-out-of-control as a theme in political thought*, Cambridge, Massachusetts: Massachusetts Institute of Technology Press.

Ytterstad, P. and Watson, R.T. (1996) 'Teledemocracy: using information technology to enhance political work', *Management information systems quarterly*, Sept, 20, 3: 347, full details at <http://misq.org/discovery.home.html>.

Zigurs, I. and Kozar, KA. (1994) 'An exploratory study of roles in computer supported groups', *Management information systems quarterly*, 18, 3: 277-298.

Zuurmond, A. (1998) 'From bureaucracy to infocracy: are democratic institutions lagging behind?, in Snellen, I. and van de Donk, W. (eds.) *Public administration in an information age: a handbook*, Amsterdam: IOS Press: 259-272.

6 P. (1997) *Holistic government*, London: Demos.

6, P. (1999a) *Morals for robots and cyborgs: ethics, society and public policy in the age of autonomous intelligent machines*, Brentford: Bull Information Systems.

6, P., (1999b) 'Neo-Durkheimian institutional theory', paper to the University of Strathclyde conference, *Institutional Theory in Political Science*, Ross Priory, 18-19.10.99.

.06, P. (2000a) 'Governing by technique: judgment and the prospects for governance of and with technology', paper to the Organisation for Economic Cooperation and

Development "Forum for the Future" conference, "21ˢᵗ century social governance: power in the global knowledge economy and society", 24-26 March 2000, Hanover, Germany.

6, P. (2000b) *London_Mayor@Your_Service: the prospects for digital democracy in the capital*, London: A New Voice for London.

6, P. (2000c) 'From affect to citizenship: the social organisation of emotion and ritual politics', paper to the University of East London seminar in the series "Affect, ethics and citizenship", 1.6.2000, Birkbeck College, London.

6, P., Leat, D., Seltzer, K. and Stoker, G. (1999) *Governing in the round: strategies for holistic government*, London: Demos.

6, P., Stoddart, P., Penston, N., Shire, C. and Laird, A. (2000) *If you're serious about modernising government...*, Cambridge: Smart Card Club.

6, P., Leat, D., Seltzer, K. and Stoker, G. 2001 forthcoming, *Toward holistic governance: the new agenda in government reform*, MacMillan, Basingstoke.

Chapter 3

Pluralising Teledemocracy. Not-for-Profits in the Democratic Polity

John A Taylor and Eleanor Burt

1   Issues, Orthodoxies and Boundaries

As we enter a new century, debates centring upon the state of health and vitality of contemporary democracy within the United Kingdom and Western Europe more generally, have been fundamentally limited by their pre-occupation with two particular orthodoxies. The first of these concerns the impact of the 'democratic deficit' upon the political process. The second derives from ungrounded and naive assumptions that networked information and communication technologies herald new opportunities for citizen participation in the form of direct involvement in the democratic process. Thus, on the one hand we have an ailing democratic system populated by a largely and increasingly disengaged citizenry. While on the other hand, the new electronic media are the trumpeted cure – the new techno-political recipe - that will see disengaged, disenfranchised, and disinterested citizens suddenly keen and able to (re)-engage in politics at all levels of society.

The debates that have emerged around the democratic deficit have had a largely mainstream focus. Their consuming concern has been with the mainstream institutions at the centre stage of democratic life – parliaments, councils, the relationship between Legislatures and Executives, voting, and citizen perceptions of politics and politicians. Linking this focus upon the mainstream institutions at the heart of the political arena are three distinct, but related trends. The first of these identifies the rapid reduction within the UK from the 1950s onwards, of active party memberships. Although surges in party membership are identifiable from time to time, such as at the height of the recent popularity of Britain's Labour Party, this membership is then shown to fall back rapidly to existing levels or even lower. The second trend associated with the focus upon mainstream political institutions concerns low electoral turnouts. Thus, for example, the last general election in the UK recorded the lowest turnout of any such event throughout the 20th century. Even for high profile local and regional elections in the UK the turnout is now regularly below 50%, and in decline. The third strand linking this focus on mainstream political institutions is the mounting evidence of reduced (and reducing) public trust in politicians and the institutions of government. Western politics is increasingly embroiled in scandal and corruption, minor and major. At the same time, and as significant in explaining citizens' disenchantment with politics, is the failure of politicians and governments to deliver on their electoral

J. E. J. Prins (ed.), Designing E-Government, 29–39.
© 2001 *Kluwer Law International. Printed in the Netherlands.*

promises. Thus, opinion polls and other research consistently reveal low trust amongst citizens of politicians and governments. A recent study (BT Government, 2000) which draws upon research findings from studies undertaken by the Henley Centre and the opinion polling company MORI, shows that public confidence in The Civil Service has fallen from 46% of respondents expressing confidence in 1983 to just 17% in 2000. In the same period, confidence in the legal system has fallen from 58% to 22%, and confidence in Parliament from 54% to 14%. The same report reveals that by using *predictive Internet segmentation* the deepest scepticism of established institutions of government and democracy lies in groups that are the highest users of the Internet – a finding to which we shall return at the conclusion of this chapter.

The second orthodoxy that has restricted the debate on contemporary democracy lies within the assumptive schemes of political scientists who focus upon 'electronic democracy'. Here, the paradigm that has shaped research and analysis has been that of 'direct democracy'. At the heart of this particular paradigm has been a set of ill-founded assumptions that the new electronic media will revitalise the democratic process by enabling the citizen to engage directly in the business of politics and government. From this perspective 'wired-up' citizens will be able to engage in a spectrum of activities which include at the less 'heroic' end of the spectrum relatively mundane activities such as accessing parliamentary papers on-line or emailing their parliamentary representatives upon issues of concern. Other commentators have envisaged an energised and politically active citizenry engaging politicians in electronic debates across the wires. Adopting a more 'heroic' position still, some commentators have predicted that 'connected' citizens will soon be enthusiastically voting on-line upon issues of the day. Accompanying this view has been the assumption that telecommunications-intensive voting must ultimately lead to the decline and dissolution of intermediated or representative systems of democracy as citizens establish a direct line to governance and the institutions of democracy. Journalists (and some politicians) sensing the 'sexiness' of these heroic viewpoints, have added to the hype surrounding electronic democracy. Whilst disintermediation perspectives continue to shape the discourse of electronic democracy, more considered commentaries acknowledge the potential to re-invent the democratic process, but perceive this to involve the gradual re-shaping of intermediated forms of democracy rather then their complete obliteration and replacement.

It is from these more evidence-based and reflective perspectives that the core argument of this chapter proceeds. Thus, the contention is that information and communications technologies (ICTs) are infusing all democratic impulses within the polity, whether those impulses are towards direct, representative, or pluralist forms of democracy. The new electronic media bring opportunities to re-shape (and possibly enhance and revitalise) democracy in all its forms. Rooted within the orthodoxies set out above, this perspective is deeply influenced by their focus upon the mainstream institutions at the heart of the formal political arena. Questions that this gives rise to are of the sort, 'how are parliaments as an expression of representative democracy using ICTs to establish their position in the democratic polity?' (Burt and Taylor, 1999c). 'Are parliaments deliberately employing new electronic media in ways that are designed to counter the democratic deficit?' Within this second strand of orthodoxy is scant acknowledgement of either the existence or role of non-mainstream institutions engaging in the polity. At the same time, there is little understanding of how institutions other than those in the conventional mainstream of the democratic polity are using ICTs to enhance their position as democratic actors. There are many such institutions that should be examined in this way if we are fully to understand the nature of modern democracy and the significance within it of ICTs, including media and tele-communications industries. The institutional type that we examine in this paper is the voluntary organisation, and, moreover, voluntary organisations of the type whose responsibility is to campaign on issues of concern to members and supporters. Some of these organisations have an explicit democratic mission. Our contention is that these organisations are beginning to use ICTs in ways that are strengthening their democratic role.

2 Voluntary Campaigning Organisations in the Information Age

Voluntary organisations are best known for their work as providers of a range of social and welfare services, both at home and abroad. With the exception of a few high profile organisations such as Greenpeace or Friends of the Earth their role in the political process is less well known. However, embedded within the economy, the polity, and civil society more generally, voluntary organisations are strategically situated to impact on the political health and direction of the nation and on the quality of life of citizens (Deakin Commission, 1996; Kemp Commission, 1997; Burt, 1998). Firstly, as mainstream service providers operating in the quasi-public sphere, voluntary organi-sations intersect with, and can influence, the governmental policy process. Secondly, as campaigning organisations engaging in process of public policy development they are able to engage with the polity as a set of political actors, actively seeking to shape social, economic, and environmental policies and legislation. Furthermore, at a time when so many citizens are disenchanted with, disinclined to participate in, or disenfranchised from, formal political processes, voluntary organi-sations can (potentially) provide an important alternative route through which ordinary citizens, including the most vulnerable in society, can make their voices heard within the formal institutions of parliament and government. They can both represent those citizens as intermediaries in the formal political arena, and empower individual citizens themselves to engage directly in the democratic process.

By contrast to the democratic deficit that afflicts the mainstream institutions of the democratic polity, citizen engagement and trust in voluntary organisations is high. For example, in research published recently by the National Council for Voluntary organisations 91% of respondents declared their trust in voluntary organisations (NCVO), 1998). While the research also demonstrates some scepticism on the part of respondents, particularly with regard to the relationships that exist between some voluntary organisations and the poorly trusted state sector, the high trust in the sector generally is in stark contrast to those findings that emerge from research into public trust in conventional institutions of democracy.

In research that we have recently completed as part of the Economic and Social Research Council's 'Virtual Society? Programme', we found evidence, particularly from our case studies, of this sector's growing use of ICTs to strengthen its influence both upon public policy discourse and on the day to day actions of governments. Three examples are illustrative here. Amnesty International, an organisation of international standing in the human rights field, is using ICTs to enhance the efficiency and effectiveness of its campaigns. Its reputation stands upon the quality of its research and information, while the capability to respond quickly (sometimes immediately) to changing global political situations and crises is essential to the effective achievment of its mission. With over one million members and more than four thousand local groups dispersed worldwide, ICTs are significant resources in the management and communication of its research and information. During the Kosovo crisis a field team despatched as observers to gather up-to-date local intelligence, was supported by a sophisticated technological mix involving groupware, laptops, cellphones, landlines and satellite transmissions. This enabled the rapid transmission of data to the organisation's research headquarters, in London. At the same time, the observers had access to the latest information about Kosovo coming into London from other sources, including the international press.

Electronic technologies also permit Amnesty International's members and supporters to be rapidly mobilised in emergency situations. For example, in a situation in which an individual's circumstances are undergoing rapid change, and in which interrogation or execution are imminent, email and fax transmissions are imperative. Utilising a recently developed database, 'case sheets' which detail the individual's situation together with details of government officials to contact on the person's behalf, can be circulated rapidly to thousands of members and supporters. Additionally, the case sheets can be targeted to suit the interests, expertise, and availability of individual members and supporters. Thus, some supporters will ask for appeals specific to women, the death penalty, or certain countries; some will be able to write fluently in a relevant language or will know something of the culture of the countries involved; and others will be known only to be able to respond to a specific number of appeals each year. Amnesty International believes that the ability to target appeals in this way lends both weight and effectiveness to urgent appeals.

Another example, this time at a policy development level, comes from the National Children's Bureau (NCB). NCB sits at the heart of a large and diverse population of organisations, interest groups, and individuals, whose aim is to promote the interests of young people through policy development and intervention. NCB believes that its effectiveness lies in its capacity to respond quickly to government proposals from a position of combined strength and expertise. ICTs are essential to its facilitative role within its own internal network, as well as within its wider external membership, with email particularly crucial and embedded. As well as using email to report issues emerging from conferences attended by individual staff members, thus permitting others to be kept aware of the most recent developments in their field, email also enables Government statements issued on the internet to be rapidly circulated around appropriate staff for discussion and formulation of response. Email has been found particularly useful in permitting controversial issues to be debated amongst the wider membership with a degree of candour difficult to achieve face-to-face. The 'email group' of which NCB is a part, can be activated by any member of the network, and used as an open or a closed forum to link to 'expert' groups on an informal and organic basis. Equally, where there is a tight window of opportunity in which to respond to Government policies and proposals, the network enables a high level of immediacy.

A final example from our case studies of the way in which voluntary organisations are playing out a broadly democracy-enhancing role comes from the environmental campaigning organisation, Friends of the Earth (FOE). Environmentalism has moved in recent years from concerns with 'discrete' issues such as the clearing of Rain Forests *per se* to a holistic perspective in which Rain Forests are understood to be part of a wider agenda. Thus, in this example, the loss of rare flora and fauna, the displacement of indigenous Forest people, and global climate change are all perceived to be vital facets of the same environmental challenge. At the same time, it has led to recognition that environmental issues are not 'localist' in nature, but span community, national, and global spheres. Together, these are profound imperatives for new participative arrangements within the environmental lobby, involving, in particular, information networking. Structured around a central office and some two hundred and fifty local groups throughout England, Wales and Northern Ireland, ICTs are fundamental to FOE's continued effectiveness within the environmental movement. Thus, whereas traditionally these local groups have campaigned independently on 'local' issues - specific forms of industrial pollution or the development of supermarkets on greenfield sites, for instance – now new technologies are enabling the groups to become 'information hubs' permitting 'intelligence', experiences, and expertise to be widely shared throughout the local group network. ICTs are also supporting FOE's explicit commitment to citizen empowerment in other ways. Factory Watch, a web-based geographical information system developed by FOE is one example. Using this system, members, supporters, and other citizens, have access to a wealth of data and information about, for instance GM test-sites, industrial pollution, and toxicity. By interrogating Factory Watch citizens can develop pollution profiles of their local area for independent presentation to their Member of Parliament.

3 Looking More Deeply

Those research findings that are set out in the previous section point to a range of contributions that are made by voluntary organisations to democratic activity in the polity. Taking this work further, five organisations were selected for a web-site study, each of which was primarily a high profile campaigning organisation in a field of activity in which there was a 'live issue' in April 2000. Table 1 below sets out the organisations concerned, alongside their field of activity and the live issue from April this year.

Table 1 Selected Voluntary Organisations by Field of Activity and Key Issue

Stonewall	Homosexuality/Civil Rights	Legal prevention of teaching of homosexual lifestyles
Compassion in World Farming	Animal Welfare	Export of live animals
Greenpeace	Environment	Genetic Modification
The Countryside Alliance	Business & Leisure in Rural Areas	Foxhunting
Charter 88	Democratic Reform	Freedom of Information

The web-site of each of these organisations was scrutinised against a common set of criteria. Collectively, these criteria reveal the extent of democratic engagement of these organisations. Key findings from this study were:

- Only one organisation, Greenpeace, explicitly pursued democratic objectives, though each was democratically active in a more objective sense.
- In general, organisation web-sites contained very high quality information on 'their' issue. The information was extensive in two senses. First, it was substantively extensive in providing a rich source on the issue in question. Secondly, it was extensive in allowing connections from the main site to other informative sites.
- The organisations generally provided contacts internal to the organisation for follow up information .
- Some provided detailed information and advice on how to campaign and who to lobby, including providing links to the parliamentary process.
- Both access to the site and navigation around the site were generally good.
- There was little 'direct democracy' on these sites. Views were not solicited, issue preferences were neither requested nor recorded, and only weak opportunities for discussion were available.
- Most surprisingly, some of these sites provided 'hotlinks' to independent and contrasting sources of information. Thus access to an abundance of information on the issue in question was being facilitated, without regard to whether that information was supportive or opposed to the policy preference of the organisation itself.

4   Parliamentary Web-sites. A Democratic Contrast

Having previously conducted extensive research on parliamentary web-sites for the new Scottish Parliament [Burt & Taylor, 1998,1999C] we are in a position to compare and contrast the democratic characteristics of those voluntary sector sites and those parliamentary sites. Before undertaking that comparison however we examine the characteristics of parliamentary sites at a general level, utilising the analytical categories listed below:

- The level of basic information provided about parliament
- The level of basic information provided about parliamentarians
- The extent of the electronic provision of services to the citizen
- The support and enhancement provided on the site for active citizenship
- Support on the site for electronic access for the citizen
- Forms of innovation in addition to those found in the categories above.

4.1   Basic Information about Parliament

This provision of basic information about parliament and government in the most general terms is a ubiquitous feature of the web-sites at which we looked.

Our main findings were five in number. First we found that the largest single informational component of parliamentary sites is in the form of general, 'educational' information, information that describes the activities and procedures of the chambers of the parliament. Secondly and linked to the first point these sites generally contained a large amount of historical material about parliament, with explanations about the origins and development of the particular parliament that will support a search for historical information by a school student, for example. Thirdly, we found that information about parliamentary committees, their working methods, memebership and timetable, is ubiquitous. Fourthly, although not as frequently found as the first three points, we found detailed budgetary information carried on some sites. Finally, many of these parliamentary sites provided hyper-links to government web-sites with those government sites then providing further and more extensive links to a wide range of agencies and organisations, including not-for-profits.

4.2   Basic Information about Parliamentarians

All web-sites that we looked at contained some personal and other details, such as personal political concerns and interests, about members of parliament. Amongst our main findings here was that most sites provided some CV and biographical material about members of parliament. Moreover, parliamentary sites in general offered access to Home Pages of Members that are part of the main site, though the quality of these Home Pages varies considerably. Furthermore, these home pages of Members of parliament are most often available only in the host country language. A further main finding under this heading was that occasionally there is an interactive facility on the site that allows the user to identify his/her local MP. Occasionally there is a register on the site of declarations of interests made by parliamentarians. Interestingly, most sites contained no links to political party sites, though some few did so.

4.3   Providing Citizen Services

Our main finding here is that the provision of services to citizens in not a strong feature of parliamentary web-sites. Occasionally, the ordering of parliamentary and government publications is enabled, either directly or indirectly and a very small number of sites provided details of student internship opportunities in Parliament.

4.4   Providing For Active Citizenship

A key element in our research into the content of parliamentary web-sites was the extent to which the site appeared to support active citizenship. Here we looked for evidence of the extent to which public participation in policy formation and feedback was being encouraged. We noted the provision of timetables for current parliamentary debates and opportunities within them for citizen involvement, and we noted too the development of discussion forums. We looked too for the identification on the site of current issues upon which citizen views were elicited. Ease of access to public policy and legislative documents was also noted as we searched these sites, as was the extensiveness of its provision. Finally we observed whether any form of voting facility was resident on the site.

Within this context our main findings are:
- A small number of sites explained how the citizen might best contribute to the development and formation of public policy.
- Most sites contain some information on the current parliamentary timetable.

- One site in particular, the Portuguese site, contains summaries of parliamentary plenary sessions and a search facility that allows the user to access topics of interest, where they have been the subject of parliamentary debate.
- A small number of sites offer hyper-links to news and discussion groups, eg the Australian parliamentary site.

4.5   Supporting Electronic Access

This part of our work was concerned to evaluate the sites themselves largely in terms of technical and design features. Here we looked for the provision of search engine facilities, of a site map and of a user help service. We looked too for the provision of instruction and advice on how the citizen might link electronically to the parliamentary web-site and at whether citizen users were able to identify where their nearest public access terminal is located. Our research into these sites also included whether they are supported in one or more language, whether there are touch-screen or voice activated facilities and whether there are additional facilities to support disabled access. We noted too the ease with which sites could be located and worked through, their general layout and the time taken to download material from them. Finally, we attempted to ascertain the frequency with which they are updated.

Here our main findings are:

- Help sections are often very supportive of users, though the nature of that support varies considerably from site to site.
- Most sites are presented in more than one language.
- Some sites offered text only versions, thus allowing for speedier access, because of the consequent omission of images.
- We found the updating of sites patchy with some frequently and regularly and others relatively neglected.

4.6   Innovative Features

In this section we note innovative features from the sites that we visited. We do so within an overall view that we formed that innovation on these sites was generally unadventurous.

Some innovative features that we found are:

- Many sites had a 'Parliamentary sites of the world' section e.g. France, Spain and Portugal
- The Irish Government site supported live 'chat' with the President of the Republic, and included transcripts of the conversations that took place. The German site gave access to a world directory of parliamentary libraries, including services provided and notes about how to access those services.
- The Belgian site contains a currency conversion table for all European currencies converting into Euros.
- Many sites had a European section including lists of Members of the European Parliament.
- On the New Zealand and Canada sites there is a screen that advises when parliament is not sitting.

- The Queensland and Quebec sites explicitly count the number of visitors they receive.

5   Teledemocratic Comparisons. Parliamentary and Voluntary Organisation Web-sites

Table 2 below juxtaposes these voluntary sector and parliamentary sites by reference to a combination of the core democratic values the sites express, the key characteristics through which those democratic values are expressed and the core content of the site in respect of those democratic values and that core content.

Table 2 Democratic Values, Characteristics and Content of Parliamentary and Voluntary Organisation Web-sites.

	Core Democratic Value	*Key Characteristic*	*Core Content*
VolOrg	Informative about organisation and its issue set	Deep substantive information	Knowledge development on issue
Parliament	Informative about the institution of parliament	Shallow substantive information	Little opportunity for knowledge development
VolOrg	Expressive	Engaged	Energy/vitality in presentation of information
Parliament	Educative	Disengaged	Good presentation of historical information. Otherwise low energy
VolOrg	Political	Advisory	Information on how to be heard
Parliament	Politically Neutral	Descriptive	Information about the parliamentary process
VolOrg	High level approach to knowledge development	'Hubbing'	Links to independent, issue relevant knowledge
Parliament	Low level approach to knowledge development	Self contained	Linkages to other parliaments and to libraries, and to government sites.
VolOrg	Activist	Empowering	Designed for active citizenship
Parliament	Passive	Sustaining the centrality of parliament	Designed for representative democracy

The comparisons provided for in Table 2 are striking. In terms of their core democratic values, we found voluntary organisation sites to reveal a desire to be broadly and extensively informative, expressive, political, concerned with the development of knowledge by the user of the site and activist in orientation. In sharp contrast, the democratic values that were deeply influencing parliamentary sites shaped them into being much more narrowly informative, educative rather than expressive, politically neutral, into having little concern for knowledge development and on the whole passive in their orientation.

The key characteristics of these sites adduced in Table 2, unsurprisingly given the context of those contrasting democratic values, are equally in sharp distinction. Where we found the provision of deep, substantive information on the voluntary sites, contrastingly we found relatively shallow information provided on the parliamentary sites. Where the voluntary sites are engaged with issues and offer advice to site visitors that allows further engagement, parliamentary sites by contrast exemplify a high level of substantive disengagement and little in the way of supportive advice. Where voluntary organisation sites enable the visitor to 'hub' to other linked sites, parliamentary sites are almost entirely self contained. And whilst voluntary organisation sites provide a sense of citizen empowerment, parliamentary sites sustain the power of the 'intermediator' [ie Parliament itself] rather than the citizen.

Finally the core content of these two types of site are equally striking in the contrasts that they bear. The content of voluntary sites supports the development of knowledge. It displays energy and vitality in the way it is presented and it provides information on how the citizen's voice can be heard. It provides links from which knowledge can be further developed and it is on the whole highly supportive of active citizenship. The content of parliamentary sites is once more in stark contrast. It contains little opportunity for knowledge development save for a better understanding of the workings and history of Parliament itself. That content is enhanced only modestly through linkages to governmental and other parliamentary sites, including those of parliamentary libraries. Finally, the core content of the parliamentary site is shaped by the imperatives of traditional parliamentary democracy rather than by any activist desire to engage the active citizen.

6   Conclusions

We began this chapter with a discussion of the so-called democratic deficit, a condition afflicting the mainstream political institutions of many Western polities. Our research evidence shows that far from this deficit leading to a desire to engage the citizen in new ways, Parliaments, as expressed through their web-sites, are locked in to a parliamentary model of democracy that prevents a more informative, expressive, political, knowledge developing and activist approach to relationships with citizens. The research findings presented here on voluntary organisations point entirely the other way. Here, in campaigning voluntary organisations we have found attachment to the development of the characteristics of 'strong democracy'.

We established earlier that those citizens most negative about contemporary democratic institutions are the heaviest users of the Internet. It follows from the evidence that we have presented here that those 'cyber-oriented' citizens are more likely to find democratic stimulation from the voluntary sector than they are from the time-honoured institution of parliament. In so-doing, will those citizens further contribute to the alienation of large sections of the populace with the formal processes of democratic involvement? Will the voluntary sector's contribution to the democratic process undergo some transformation, becoming more immediate and extending the scale and scope of its longstanding historical involvement? Will the voluntary sector provide ordinary citizens with more effective routes into the formal institutions and processes of parliament and government? These, and other equally fundamental questions must be asked and answered by all thoses with an interest in sustaining and enhancing the democratic process.

References

BT Government, *eGovernment. Ready or Not?,* Issue 1, July, 2000

Burt, E. (1998). 'Charities and Political Activity. Time to Re-think the Rules'. *In The Political Quarterly,* 69:1 pp. 23-30.

E. Burt & Taylor JA, Voluntary Organisations on the Net. Insights and Innovations. *The New Review of Information Networking.* December 1999 A.

E. Burt & Taylor JA *Information and Communication Technologies; Re-shaping the Voluntary Sector in the Information Age?* CSTAG, Glasgow Caledonian University. June 1999B

E. Burt & Taylor JA, Parliaments on the Web. learning through Innovation. *Parliamentary Affairs,* October 1999C

E. Burt & Taylor JA, *Telematics and the Scottish Parliament. Transferable Democratic Innovations.* 1998. HMSO, Edinburgh

Deakin Commission. (1996) *Meeting the Challenge of Change. Voluntary Action into the 21st Century.* National Council for Voluntary Organisations, London.

Institute for Volunteering Research, National Survey of Volunteering in the UK. 1997. http://www.ivr.org.uk/national survey.htm

Kemp Commission. (1997) *Head and Heart.* The Scottish Council for Voluntary Organisation, Edinburgh.

NCVO, Blurred Vision – Public Trust in Charities, Research Quarterly, January, 1998

Chapter 4

Electronic Service Delivery in the UK. Proaction and Privacy Protection[1]

Charles D. Raab

1   Introduction

In the private sector, the philosophy of 'relationship marketing' involves the increasingly intensive use of identifiable personal data to enable providers of goods and services to target prospective customers and to maintain relationships with existing ones. Customers are categorised and individually profiled in terms of their habits, tastes and characteristics. Information about individuals' current and past purchases is merged from different sources and oriented towards the making of future offers and the completion of future sales, often of very different kinds of goods and services.

In this way, both the customer and merchant are supposed to benefit. The customer's wants are said to be better catered for through the informed tailoring processes made possible through the mining and matching of personal data. The protection of these data for reasons other than proprietary ones - for example, for safeguarding customers' privacy - may play a part in this, as a practice and as a value; or it may not. Many companies understand that protecting their customers' information privacy can be worthwhile in terms of increased confidence and therefore increased profits. Gaining a reputation as an ethical business may be important to many firms, perhaps especially where data regarded as 'sensitive' are concerned: for instance, in the financial and health-care industries. But the connection is contingent and not always obvious; therefore, many firms pay as little attention as they can to complying with data protection requirements and principles, and some firms have little understanding of their legal obligations. In some countries, there are

---

1   This chapter is based on a paper given at the Conference on Electronic Government, Tilburg University, May 2000, and draws upon a paper given at the Conference on Public Management and Governance in the New Millennium, City University of Hong Kong, January 2000. I am grateful for comments received on these occasions and thereafter. I also acknowledge with gratitude the support of the Economic and Social Research Council of the United Kingdom for a project on Privacy Protection in the Virtual Society (grant no. L132251019), conducted within the Virtual Society? Research Programme.

J. E. J. Prins (ed.), Designing E-Government, 41–62.

no data protection laws covering the private sector as such, or the private-sector laws that do exist are only patchy in their scope and content.

In recent years, there has been a similar impetus in government to move towards the 'informatization' of public administration, involving increased processing of personal data for the provision of services and information to citizens. Governments have aimed to learn from, but also to modify, the customer-oriented use of information found in the private sector (Bellamy and Taylor, 1998). The United Kingdom (UK) is a case in point. The broader canvas for this public-sector initiative is the development and implementation of government modernisation as a whole[2] . This relies very heavily on flows of information and on information and communication technologies (ICT) to underpin an approach to governance that has important implications for government and other actors in promoting a more 'joined up' way of making policy as well as providing services. It was reported that at least £2 billion will have been spent on 'information-age government' (IAG) by 2004, a figure which does not include a sum for education and training[3].

One rationale for IAG is better, more efficient, more convenient delivery of services through the use of ICT and systems within a framework of 'modernising government'. The instruments for this will include digital signatures, smart cards, Internet websites, call centres and interactive TV. Different parts of government are expected to share information and to enter into partnerships with local authorities, the voluntary sector and private companies in a mixed pattern of public-service delivery. Government puts forward a user-friendly face to the citizen, re-defined as a 'customer' whose wants and entitlements will be met in better ways than before. Electoral consideration as well as reasons of efficiency, economy and effectiveness help to drive this agenda.

Here too, everyone is supposed to win. But it is noteworthy that the development of this elaborate vision includes an awareness that there are important issues of public trust and confidence to be tackled, of which some are privacy issues. Governments in many countries, including the UK, therefore propose practical ways of orchestrating a protective package that includes official regulation and law, codes of practice, privacy-enhancing technologies, and the establishment of a lawful basis for data-sharing for reducing fraud and improving services. The agenda of joined-up IAG therefore shapes a privacy protection agenda as well, but the latter sits precariously alongside the former and the relationship between the two is still in flux. The tensions inherent in this dual approach require discussion, because - as in the private sector - the connections, in theory and practice, are not necessarily compelling. Bellamy has drawn attention to the complexities of combining IAG practice with ethical considerations, including privacy, and has highlighted some issues (Government Computing, 2000a, p.6). The aim of this chapter is to examine further some of the thinking and activity that has been involved in this initiative. It pays particular attention to the question of privacy protection in the context of an electronic service

---

2   Cm 4310 (1999); http://www.citu.gov.uk/moderngov/whitepaper/4310.htm (accessed 27/10/00).

3   Government Computing (2000a), p. 6.

delivery (ESD) strategy in which government and its partners do not merely informatise the existing fragmented public sector, but seek to reshape it around the needs of the citizen.

2   IAG in the United Kingdom

In current UK developments, two significant elements of government strategy for electronic government can be highlighted. These elements are:
- the strategy for bringing to fruition the integration of service provision through re-organisation and cultural re-engineering to enable a more intensive and extensive use of ICT and information; and
- the attempt to establish a basis for public trust that personal information, which is vital for public services, will be handled in ways that protect individual privacy.

The first of these is outlined in this section; the second also requires fuller analysis, grounded in a discussion concerning privacy and strategies for its protection, and is taken up in the next section.

Both elements can be seen as proactive components of IAG, and at least in the current developmental phase they are innovative in terms of new kinds of relationships within government and between government and the public. In the UK, central government has been proactive in developing 'joined up' strategies for implementing ESD in ways that require it also to be proactive in developing strategies for privacy protection as an important dimension of promoting public trust. In both elements, the role of government itself at the centre is important in shaping the patterns of governance for the strategies concerned. But in both dimensions, government acts within complex relationships in governance networks that embrace other parts of the public sector and the private sector as well, giving a big role to technological industries. This has important economic implications, which are arguably among the most important drivers of change, and are not merely side-benefits that are expected and desired.

The electronic delivery of services to the UK citizen has been heralded in many policy documents and in current implementation work within central and local government (Bellamy, 2000). It is not a unique development; counterparts to this initiative can be found, in one form or another, in many Western countries in which the possibility of exploiting ICT and infrastructures has been married to an initiative for administrative reform and modernisation. The documentary history of the UK government's efforts to incorporate ICT in administrative modernisation and the delivery of services since 1996 requires a brief but selective review. It includes a rather technology-oriented Green Paper entitled *government.direct* (CM 3438, 1996) in 1996, followed by the more administratively contextual 1999 White Paper entitled *Modernising government* (Cm 3410, 1999), mentioned earlier. There has also been a host of developmental and strategy documents up to the present time, including the feasibility of, and policies for, portals and service-delivery channels. Most of these emanated from the Central Information Technology Unit (CITU) in the Cabinet Office[4] although there are detectable differences of emphasis between CITU and other central bodies within and outside the 'core executive'. An important output is CITU's e-government paper of April 2000[5], describing a strategic framework for public services in the information age, and a number of accompanying papers on specific topics produced by the welter of working groups that were set up in the previous year on such matters as smart cards, call centres, websites, digital TV, and data standards[6], in addition to work on channels and portals[7]. In 1999 and 2000, other important and lengthy reports came from another Cabinet Office player, the Performance and Innovation Unit (PIU). These included *e.commerce.@its.best.uk*[8] and e.gov[9], which contributed to the wider scope of 'information age' strategy that includes the commercial sector, with which electronic government bears a close relationship.

The agenda for government modernisation is vast[10], but the ICT-related items comprise a range of topics that concern the infrastructure of technical and administrative systems that will be important in modernising government, in joining up the fragmented parts of public-service provision, and in using electronic media. Under the IAG slogan are presented an ideology and a tool-kit for fundamental transformation, although the means for doing this are ostensibly gradual and incremental, prudently evolutionary rather than revolutionary. In practice, development has been marked by delays, reversals and postponements as well as achievements, as is indicated in the published and frequently updated 'Milestones Table' for the Action Plan[11]

3   IAG as a Governance Strategy

An interdependent 'governance' approach can be seen in the implementation of IAG. Close bilateral relations are envisaged between government and business as well as with other groups such as the Information Age Partnership, and with links created to the Government Secure Intranet (GSI) for local authorities, hospitals and post offices as agents in service-delivery. An IAG 'concordat' between central and local government, which was signed in July 1999, aimed at promoting co-operation and innovation, and improving technical standards. Perhaps the White Paper's most striking acknowledgement of the breadth of governance across sectors, levels and jurisdictions was that government was :

---

4   http://www.citu.gov.uk/index.htm; (accessed 27/10/00.)
5   CITU (2000); http://www.citu.gov.uk/iagc/strategy.htm (accessed 27/10/00).
6   http://www.iagchampions.gov.uk/iagc/guidelines.htm; (accessed 27/10/00.)
7   http://www.citu.gov.uk/channels/channelspolicy.htm;
8   http://www.citu.gov.uk/portals/portalmenu.htm; (accessed 27/10/00.) PIU (1999); http://www.cabinet-office.gov.uk/innovation/1999/ecommerce/index.htm (accessed 27/10/00).
9   PIU (2000b); http://www.cabinet-office.gov.uk/innovation/2000/delivery/intro.htm (accessed 27/10/00).
10   http://www.cabinet-office.gov.uk/moderngov/; (accessed 27/10/00.)
11   http://www.cabinet-office.gov.uk/moderngov/action/miles2.htm; (accessed 27/10/00.)

'talking to banks, the Post Office, supermarkets, accountants, interactive broadcasting companies, the information technology industry and others about how they can be partners in service delivery'(Cm 4310 1999, p.49).

In the 'joining-up' approach, technology was expected to:

'make it much easier for different parts of government to work in partnership: central government with local authorities or the voluntary sector; or government with third-party delivery channels such as the Post office or private sector companies' (Cm 4310 1999, p.46).

The centre was supposed to establish its objectives within the frameworks and approaches adopted across such an array, including the setting of performance targets and the monitoring of results. With more specific reference to ICT, a regulatory infrastructure was in formation for IAG-related transactions. Frameworks and laws were expected to contribute a degree of certainty and uniformity to the technical processes that occur among organisations and with the public. Areas to be included were data standards, digital signatures for identification and authentication, call centres, smart cards, digital TV and websites. This approach also involved government gateways or 'portals' to connect services and information in a common system, and better online information and registration services for businesses.

The government's implementation strategy, envisaged in earlier documents but now reinforced in the new corporate strategy, can be seen in 'governance' terms as the creation of a strong central steering capacity and an agreed mission or 'vision', along with the encouragement of action elsewhere in the networks for creating the infrastructures and later for service-related operations. Central government was given the role of setting the main objectives and standards, establishing frameworks, stimulating e-commerce through legislation, and enabling work to be done across departments, and even with local authorities, by means of the GSI.

The 1999 White Paper envisaged the Cabinet Office - part of the 'core executive' - orchestrating IAG developments through a corporate IT strategy in which government would set key objectives, create frameworks, promote e-commerce, and facilitate inter-departmental working through the GSI. More than thirty senior officials were appointed in 1999 as IAG 'champions' in their respective departments and agencies, with responsibility for developing a corporate IT strategy, working in partnership across the public as well as the private sector. Their role was to provide help in implementing and developing the strategy, in gaining and maintaining commitment to it across the public sector, and in identifying cross-cutting initiatives. They were to 'champion the delivery of departmental and sectoral e-business strategies' and 'sustain a network for sharing knowledge and experience in e-government programmes'(CITU 2000, p.23). The 'champions' initiative itself has created new intra-organisational networks for governance in the development of IAG, and has its own website[12].

---

12   http://www.iagchampions.gov.uk; (accessed 27/10/00.)

Central government's prominence was further emphasised by the appointments of Alex Allan[13] as the 'e-Envoy', a post created in September, 1999 and of Patricia Hewitt as Minister for Electronic Commerce, and by the involvement of Ian McCartney as Minister of State in the Cabinet Office. The e-Envoy and CITU were seen as crucial in this governance strategy; all lines seemed to lead to and from them as well as the two Ministers. According to the strategic framework, innovative leadership is required across the public sector: 'there is a need for strong central direction, but which recognises regional and local diversity' (CITU 2000, p.23).

The e-Envoy's Office and role are particularly significant. In a re-organisation of Cabinet Office forces early in the third quarter of 2000, CITU was re-positioned as the 'e-government' team, brigaded with two other teams, within the office of the e-Envoy[14]. With an Office having, reportedly, some 200 staff (Government Computing, 2000b, p.6), the e-Envoy was given ownership of the strategy on behalf of Ministers and was placed in charge of the whole programme, with implications considerably beyond that of ESD. Thus he was to lead the application of e-business thinking in government, play a major role in the 2000 spending review of the knowledge economy, and identify new opportunities for cross-cutting initiatives. He was also to prioritise work on infrastructure and policy issues, as well as speed up and co-ordinate ESD, and sponsor a semi-annual strategic review - firstly in December, 2000 - taking into consideration the spending review, CITU's report on IT projects, and the PIU's study of ESD. Lastly, he was to monitor implementation of the strategy and give progress reports to Ministers (CITU, 2000, p.23).

The role of CITU was seen as strategically very important in central activities; with its re-positioning, it is likely that its role is more closely integrated. Specifically, it had to develop, co-ordinate and monitor implementation of policies, standards and guidelines, to help departments develop e-business strategies, and collaborate with departments in developing shared infrastructures and applications. In addition, CITU was responsible for promoting cross-cutting services on the GSI and forging extranet links beyond the governmental part of the public sector. Finally, and of particular relevance to this discussion, it was to promote common information-management policies, including privacy (CITU, 2000, p.23).

However, progress towards putting the organisational and technical systems in place has been slow, and slower than expected. A report by the National Audit Office (NAO) at the end of 1999 (HC, 87, 1999) diagnosed and documented the sluggish pace of putting government on the Web, and of achieving joined-up activity. Early in 2000, the PIU reported critically on the management of cross-cutting policies and services, and contributed to the volume of exhortation for better performance (PUI, 2000a)[15]. Parliament entered the argument as well: focusing on the NAO's report, the Public Accounts

---

13   Alex Allan resigned as from October, 2000, for family reasons; see Government Computing (2000b), p. 4.

14   http://www.e-envoy.gov.uk/index.htm; (accessed 27/10/00.)

15   http://www.cabinet-office.gov.uk/innovation/2000/wiring/index.htm (accessed 27/10/00.)

Committee interrogated the e-Envoy and other senior officials and made many recommendations for improvement in its own report later in 2000 (HC 331, 2000).

It is plausible that the shortfalls that were identified and analysed indicate that central leverage has been insufficient to motivate significant change across government towards 'joining up' or delivering services online. Achievement has been restricted, owing largely to the strength of institutional, technological and cultural legacies in central administration. Yet, after some years of official inspirational statements about IAG, 'joined-up government', and the like, and despite the 'vision' chapter of the e-government strategic framework paper of April 2000 (CITU, 2000, pp.11-13), it is somewhat curious to find the e-Envoy saying that even the 'vision' was not yet in final form as of May 2000 (Allan,2000) . Nor, it seems, was there yet a 'road-map' of how to get to where government wanted to be, despite the many charts, diagrams, timetables, and other travel guides issued over this period. Once the vision and the map were in place, '[i]t will then be up to everyone in Government to study the vision and see if they can agree with it' (Allan,2000). This is a rather casual and non-directive turn of phrase, given the emphasis on creating powerful central drivers, although it is evident that efforts have long been underway to draw the maps and to engineer the consent. But already the journey towards 100 percent of services online by 2005 - a target that the Prime Minister brought forward by three years as recently as March 2000 - was then deemed by the e-Envoy probably to be unreachable with the current rate of 'joining up' and customer focus, although subsequent documents reasserted it as a goal (PIU, 2000b, p.8).

By September 2000, another influential quarter of the Cabinet Office took stock of the situation, giving a candid view of IAG development and of the obstacles. The PIU's September 2000 report on *e.gov* (PIU, 2000b) ostensibly intended to re-charge the batteries, and the Prime Minister's Foreword endorsed the strategy. Among the 43 Conclusions that were reached, stating tasks to be undertaken, no fewer than 16 gave the e-Envoy and his Office the lead responsibility; a further 11 saw them as key supportive players. Individual departments were enjoined to set ESD objectives and to sustain momentum. There was, however, a noticeable under-emphasis on the 'joining-up' part of the strategy. Although it remains a main objective, the difficulties in making significant progress towards it over the past few years are arguably reflected in the cooler approach to it, in contrast to the enthusiastic earlier vision set out in the earlier Green and White Papers.

4 Privacy as a Condition of IAG

Turning now to consider the place of privacy protection and public trust in these initiatives, three main and competing conceptions of it can be found in the UK discourse. One is that privacy or data protection is an obstacle or barrier to the achievement of the benefits of electronic government because it constrains the innovative possibilities of exploiting personal data in the provision of services. A second conception is that it is the lack of data protection and privacy that constitutes the barrier, and that this must be remedied as a precondition of IAG and ESD in order to enhance public confidence and trust in the necessary processing of personal data that is inherent in the provision of public services. The third position is that data protection - far from being an obstacle - is itself a valued objective of IAG, and not just a means to the end.

The first conception, and especially the second, have been far more prevalent than the third, but they have been at odds with each other and the outcome of any 'contest' hangs in the balance. Yet the second one has gained much ground as the conventional wisdom, at least in the planning of IAG if not yet in its implementation. The prevailing view in many circles is that the confidence and trust of the public is crucial if IAG - and indeed, electronic commerce as well - is to realise the benefits it promises (Raab, 1998). However, the third one, rather surprisingly, has been aired in policy documents and does not lack supporters, both within the IAG process and on its periphery, who are attempting to clarify its meaning and increase its potency. These alternative positions will not be systematically analysed here, but are important to be borne in mind in considering the unfolding of IAG policy as far as privacy is concerned. Each one has consequences for the extent and manner of privacy protection incorporated into the technologies, organisations and processes of IAG.

It is important, first, to place the question of public trust in information processes in the context of recent public events in the UK that shape the climate for the application of ICT to government. IAG launches itself in a climate of relatively low trust in government. A MORI poll for the Cabinet Office in January 1999 showed that fewer than 25 per cent of respondents trusted Ministers to tell the truth, and that they were the least trusted to advise on the risks of pollution and bovine spongiform encephalopathy (BSE); scientists and academics were trusted most (Cited in HC 570-II ,1999 42).

There have been many public issues in which Ministers and officials were shown, in official reports and in the media, to have been less than candid (or, as has sometimes been said, 'economical with the truth') about public safety, including matters to do with biotechnological and nuclear technological danger. In many domains of policy, safety has become a major issue in public policy debate and in media discussion, and a major value amongst sections of the public. Risk, its assessment and its reduction or management have become preoccupations in these discourses. In the second half of 2000, the climate of public trust in government appeared demonstrably less favourable in the UK, with the eruption of furore over a 'cover-up' concerning scientific advice and government (in)action over BSE in the previous years, and over the safety of railways under the privatisation schemes of recent governments. The reputation of the UK government as a purveyor of reassurance has been tarnished by the hesitant, ambivalent or evasive accounts given by itself or by other organisations concerning safety issues more generally; these range from BSE to genetically modified foods to nuclear waste disposal and to the health risks of mobile phones.

Government's responsibilities for reassuring the public on the basis of well-founded evidence, for telling the truth, and for transparency have been at the focus of attention and criticism. So, too, has been the question of the proper stance to be taken towards innovations by government and its watchdogs when the risks are unknown or unknowable. The reputation for safety of government's use of information technology may arguably suffer as well if, as is likely, the public does not clearly differentiate amongst branches of technological application when government takes the floor to perform, with its critics, the familiar dance of risk, reassurance and revelation. Low levels of trust in ICT may also result more directly from the highly damaging, albeit non-privacy-related calamities that have befallen large-scale and extremely expensive projects in the UK, such as air traffic control systems, ambulance services, and the computerisation of social security.

Privacy protection and information security are integral parts of the trust dimension, but they are not the only elements that are felt to be important for public trust and confidence in ESD. For example, the efficiency and accuracy of the new service systems are vital to their success, and those two functional criteria may well conflict with the establishment of high levels of safeguards for confidentiality and privacy within new IAG processes. That is an unresolved complexity in terms of the objects of public trust. It is certainly possible that the public are more interested in whether the systems 'work' properly and provide them with the services to which they are entitled, speedily and conveniently, than they are in high levels of privacy protection for their personal data. However, such evidence as there is suggests that it would be rash to assume that this holds generally across the population, or to assume that any unconcern about privacy is a stable position that will remain unchanged in future, especially in a future in which online communication will be prevalent. It would also be unwise to assume that the public does not include privacy protection as part of their conception of 'working properly'. There are good reasons for supposing that large proportions of the public are anxious about potential threats to the privacy of their information, as surveys have indicated. Moreover, there are laws as well as other policy instruments that require to be complied with in order to ensure that, as far as possible, privacy is protected. In any case, the technical reliability of networks carrying personal data, as well as verification and authentication methods and the question of legal liability, are compatible with personal privacy and may have positive value for protecting it.

It is worth noting that the development of electronic government parallels the more prominent development of electronic commerce, and that many of the same considerations apply to the latter, especially concerning trust and confidence. Questions appropriate to both the public and the private sector concern the meaning of 'trust', and how much of it is necessary. These cannot be dealt with here, but the application of the concept of trust to developments in public administration has been discussed elsewhere (Raab, 1998), and there is empirical evidence as well as conceptual analysis concerning the relationship of privacy to the shaping of trust in both sectors (6, 1988). However, the line between e-commerce and e-government is, in fact, blurred, both in discourse and in the practical application of instruments and strategies that embrace both kinds of transaction, such as encryption tools and electronic signatures, and also laws. Moreover, inasmuch as ESD is expected to involve implementation and delivery relationships between government and 'partners' in the business and voluntary sectors, the blurring of the line has practical consequences which have not been clearly addressed in IAG development materials.

While CITU has been heavily involved in developing the IAG infrastructure, the governmental stimulation of electronic commerce has taken place partly through a legislative and promotional route involving the Department of Trade and Industry (DTI), but also through the involvement of the PIU. These activities indicate that the UK definition of e-commerce by now embraces public-sector e-government transactions as well. This has been evident in discourse and in the materials related to proposed legislation establishing technical, legal and confidence-related infrastructures which go in tandem with those for IAG. Government also intends to play the leading role in the governance strategy for promoting e-commerce, not least as an exemplar, transforming its own procurement approach, its internal processes, and its delivery of information and services to the public. As already mentioned, a new Ministerial post has been created to co-ordinate and implement strategy at the central level, and the e-Envoy was given a wide and roving brief within and outside government.

There are ample indications in the documents, discourse and developments of the IAG programme that privacy, and the trust and confidence associated with its protection, are taken seriously, and that efforts are being made to build it into the plans and systems that are emerging. Policy actors themselves are increasingly claiming that there is an important relationship between modernisation and privacy, and they seem to be trying to engineer trust into the agenda of IAG. The 1996 Green Paper clearly indicated the necessity to address the question of promoting public confidence in the information systems that are intrinsic to the back-office as well as the government-to-citizen sides of the modernisation programme. It said:

> 'The strategy should safeguard information collected from citizens and businesses and be seen to do so. The customer should be able to understand how this is achieved, should have access to their own data, and should be confident that personal and other sensitive information is protected, and is kept and used in accordance with the principles of data protection law' (Cm 3438, 1996, p.13).

The danger lurking in the background arose from the desirability of sharing personal data across government and integrating them in relation to individual citizens in dealing with their benefits, applications, or other transactions. This integrated service is the heart of the proactive attempt to cater to the needs of the citizen more efficiently and effectively, built around an analysis of important 'life events' in which a number of public agencies at different levels are involved, and eventually reaching out to bring in the public through many kinds of interface. There are efficiency gains envisaged from this linking of the 'silos' of single-service provision, as well as greater convenience for the citizen in approaching the bewildering structure of government at central and local levels. But it entails the availability across organisational boundaries of citizens' personal information, and the terms on which this is enabled require careful specification. Some years ago, the Data Protection Registrar, who is responsible for enforcing the Data Protection Act 1998 and encouraging good information-privacy practices within its scope, had this to say about these practices:

> 'Sometimes public officials...assume that because information is held in one part of the public sector or for one...function it can be used and shared for any public function. This is a fundamental misconception. Information held by one public body...for a particular function

is generally limited to use for that function only and it is not open to the public body to share it...' (ODPR, n.d.., p.9).

Later on, the Registrar's response to the 1999 White Paper drew attention to the need for a lawful basis for data-sharing, which the White Paper also recognised. She emphasised the legal requirements for other kinds of data processing in which, for example, data collected for one purpose are then used for another purpose (HC 575, 1999, p.81). In a general review of public-sector privacy issues in 1999, the Registrar reminded readers of her remarks on data-matching made in previous years, and drew attention to the IAG agenda and the governmental impetus towards data-matching and data-sharing for anti-fraud and public-order purposes. Expressing her anxiety about the National Fraud Initiative and the workings of the Crime and Disorder Act 1998, she considered that codes of practice were essential, and to that end she urged their further development. The involvement of invasive data practices in the field of immigration and asylum also provided her with an occasion to make representations to government departments to limit the purposes of such sharing (HC 575, 1999, pp. 20-3).

In face of the discourses that reflect the first two conceptions of privacy within IAG, the White Paper took bold steps. Its strategy included the aim to 'strengthen the protection of privacy and human rights while providing a clear basis for sharing data between departments', and, especially, it emphasised in particularly strong terms that 'data protection is an objective of information age government, not a obstacle to it' (Cm 4310, 199, pp. 47, 51) . It thus acknowledged - possibly for the first time - an appreciation of the value of privacy that places it even somewhat beyond the second conception, depending upon how the declaration is interpreted in practice. Further 'third conception' thinking could also be found in a CITU paper on channels for ESD, which went slightly further and noted that 'data protection is a product and objective of better government, rather than an obstacle to it'. It also argued that 'information age government should not only deliver services more efficiently and conveniently but should also protect and, where possible, enhance, the privacy of the individual'[16] .

These declarations are somewhat ambiguous, but could be seen as hinting at a more proactive approach to promoting privacy as a value that must be achieved, and not merely as asserting that protecting it had instrumental values for IAG or that its absence would interfere with government plans. This approach may well have reflected the direct influence of the Registrar on the formulation of government policy. The Registrar was quick to cite, with approval, this emphasis on 'objective, not obstacle' in her published comments on the White Paper and looked forward to co-operating in the search for organisational and technical methods to achieve it. She embraced the recognition of this new perspective in her response to the White Paper and in other remarks on the use of ICT and information systems, including the innovations of governmental modernisation (HC 575, 1999, pp.

---

16   http://www.citu.gov.uk/moderngov/cpintro.htm (accessed 27/10/00), para. 17 of the outline, and ch. 9, para. 2; emphases added.

20,47, 74-6), although disbelief should perhaps not be suspended until the practical realisation of IAG is further advanced.

In a number of the more recent documents emanating from the centre of government, there has been further and more specific emphasis on devising not only the ICT mechanisms for use in governance, but also on devising the governance techniques for controlling the use of those ICT devices in the interest of privacy. Many indications have been given that the conception of privacy as a barrier to the economic, governmental and public-order policy aims has been put into some doubt by the official endorsement of the view that privacy protection may actually be conducive to the achievement of these aims, and that therefore privacy protection should be taken seriously as a reinforcer of public trust. CITU's own survey and focus-group research (CITU, 1998) highlighted the considerable extent of public worry and scepticism about technology and about invasions of privacy. When a Deputy Director of CITU wrote of the great benefits of joined-up services, he added:

> 'While the customer sees this as a benefit if you are doing it for him or her, there is a well developed suspicion of big brother in this country and the customer is very wary of what Government might do to him or her.
> For this reason it is essential that the system is subject to rigorous external audit do that the customer can have complete confidence in the probity and accuracy of the new types of transactions which become possible' (Gladwyn, 2000, pp. 6-7).

The PIU's in-depth report of 1999 (PIU, 1999) bears analysis for its thinking about central strategies that also have implications for ESD and for the privacy agenda. Whilst hinting at a 'barriers' approach to privacy (PIU, 1999, p 4), it was concerned about gaining business and public confidence and trust in e-commerce (PIU, 1999, pp. 69-87). Action was recommended for implementing technical standards for encryption and smartcards, for enforcement activities including the use of electronic signatures, and for education towards better understanding of intellectual property matters and for content-filtering. There were many issues that bore upon the willingness of business, government and individuals to engage in online transactions: the PIU enumerated fraud, privacy, content, liability and redress. These are controversial, because they open up conflicts of interest and of rights in the information age. Not the least of these controversies has been broached in the UK by the strong intervention of law-enforcement priorities in a climate where trust itself, as well as utilitarian values inherent in ICT, might be compromised if the technical and legal arrangements were so influenced by these priorities as to cast doubt on the security of transactions or the protection of free speech. Conflicts over the use of public-key encryption and over legislation concerning the interception of electronic communication have highlighted these issues in the UK and elsewhere. On the other hand, without certain initiatives to combat fraud and other criminal activity, e-commerce and e-government as trusted environments might be threatened from the opposite direction. This is a serious political dilemma in a liberal-democratic system.

From the standpoint of privacy protection's place within the agenda for trust, the report gave conspicuously thin and incomplete treatment of the main issues and of the ways in which they were being, or might be, handled through governance. The PIU's identification of spamming, hacking, and the use of information gathered from the Internet for marketing purposes hit upon important problems. However, they constituted a relatively meagre inventory of data-protection issues and regulatory responses, and little was said with specific respect to how privacy, in the broad human-rights terms in which it is now coming to be conceptualised in some quarters, might be affected by online ICT developments. For example, the report envisaged important uses for multi-functional smartcards, perhaps incorporating biometric means of identification. Yet, in its lengthy discussion of these (PIU, 1999, pp. 79-82), it gave no indication that identification systems are one of the most contentious areas in which personal information is used. There have been, and may continue to be, serious public concerns about the implications of these technologies for privacy which implementation must address if there is to be broad public acceptance. It did, on the other hand, hint at the sensitive issue of whether smartcards could be used as identity cards, and it urged the early involvement of the Registrar in the design of smartcard systems for use in public or private applications. The Registrar's Office, in fact, has played a part in the IAG champions' smartcard working group.

The PIU also saw the collaborative government-industry development of 'TrustUK'[17], a non-profit organisation which is endorsed by government. Its 'hallmark' for websites is intended as a means whereby Internet users can be reassured of the trustworthiness, security and authenticity of traders. These are important benefits, if such a branding scheme can be made to work; but current initiatives emanating from, for example, the USA and Japan, have not yet inspired great confidence. Moreover, in its 1999 report, the NAO's normative idea of an 'active Web site' (HC 87, 1999, p.7) excluded any mention of security, confidentiality, or privacy, or of the desirability of giving reassurances about these to citizens when they visit a site. Data protection is but one element in the TrustUK 'seal', as is shown in a DTI White Paper of 1999 (Cm 4410, 1999)[18], which advanced the idea of codes of practice for consumers, developed by business under the accrediting aegis of the Office of Fair Trading (OFT). The DTI emphasised the strategy in which government sets the policy framework and business develops market solutions, which was seen as ideal for e-commerce. However, its remark that consumers 'want to know that there is *reasonable* privacy about the records of what they buy or look at'(Cm 4410, 1999, p.30; emphasis added) was less than a clear declaration of support for strong data protection, given the language of debate and discourse within the privacy policy community.

In sum, the approach taken by the PIU's 1999 study recognised privacy protection as one element in underpinning trust, but implicitly and even explicitly at times seemed to construe it as more of an obstacle than an objective of e-commerce. Perhaps this reflected the commercial, rather than government-use thrust of the report as against the clearer public-sector context of the CITU's documents. But, as mentioned earlier, the sectoral differences are not rigid and the technologies as well as the systems involved in both are not

---

17   http://www.trustuk.org.uk/; accessed 27/10/00.
18   Cm 4410 (1999); http://www.dti.gov.uk/consumer/whitepaper/wpmenu.htm (accessed 27/10/00), ch. 4.

wholly distinct or different. Perhaps it also reflected a differential involvement of privacy-protection discourse and influence in the plural arenas from which reports, policy proposals and practical initiatives have emanated. In any case, the Prime Minister praised the PIU report fulsomely in accepting all its 60 recommendations[19], and endorsed its self-regulatory approach for business.

5   The Privacy 'Mix'

Enjoining a practical and equivalent concern for data protection across a wide landscape of organisations and processes may pose a test to the governance of ICT and to IAG itself. There may be pressures in the other direction that prove to be irresistible given the higher-profile governmental 'mission' to make the UK a good place to conduct e-commerce and to create e-government to a tight schedule, whilst necessarily involving a vast array of participants, including 'partners' across the central/local government divide and across the public/private boundary. The level of Parliamentary pressure to build data protection into IAG can perhaps be gauged by the fact that the question of privacy was not raised in the evidence given by officials to the Public Accounts Committee in 2000, nor was it mentioned in the Committee's recommendations.

It is important to mention that another area of policy towards business is concerned with de-regulation or 'better regulation'. It is possible that the strong emphasis placed on reducing the burdens of regulations and controls on the business sector, and now on the public sector itself, will affect the climate for applying data-protection regulations in given situations. It may at least be expected to affect the philosophy and modes of privacy protection, moving them away from reliance on statutory regulation and closer towards self-regulation and technological solutions. With regard to e-commerce, for instance, the Prime Minister stated in his Foreword to the
PIU's 1999 report:

> 'the Government alone cannot drive forward the development of e-commerce. What is needed is a sustained joint campaign between Government and business....Similarly, Government cannot simply regulate to achieve its aims....This report, therefore, recommends a light regulatory touch. Enough to build confidence...' (PIU, 1999, Forword).

Most significantly for the governance of ICT, especially in terms of Kooiman's (Kooiman, 1993) perspective, the report strongly emphasised a 'co-regulatory' approach, a partnership between government and business, which would supersede traditional approaches as a response to the dynamism of e-commerce. This approach was seen as more flexible and adaptable to the pace of technological change than the slow processes of legislation. It would rely more on self-regulation by the business sector within a framework of state regulation which can be brought to bear to keep self-regulating firms in check. Trust was

---

19   http://www.number-10.gov.uk/news.asp?NewsId=405; (accessed 15/5/00.)

an important ingredient, along with greater understanding of opportunities and greater access of the public to e-commerce interactions. All these would rest on a foundation consisting of a competitive and innovative environment, co-ordination and focus across government, monitoring and evaluation, and tax and regulatory frameworks agreed internationally. While much of this would depend upon the market, there would be important roles for government initiatives in steering, in stimulating, and in removing obstacles.

A 'light regulatory touch' is consistent with the emerging conventional wisdom about data protection which says that legislation and its enforcement is too clumsy and long-winded as a privacy protection strategy, unless as a framework within which other tools are integrated and perhaps orchestrated as a package or 'mix'. The tools include laws, self-regulation by organisations through codes of practice, 'privacy-enhancing technologies' (PETs) including encryption, smart cards and biometric devices, and individual self-protection through better awareness and market arrangements made with those who collect and process personal data. Taken together, these comprise an overall governance strategy in which government policy-makers and their creatures, the regulatory agencies, set the ground rules and steer, deter or facilitate the actions of others, but remain interdependent with these other actors (Raab, 1993; 1997a).

Elements of the package were reflected in the PIU's 1999 e-commerce study, as has been shown. Recent IAG developments provide further evidence of the embryonic formation of a privacy-related governance regime for ICT in both e-government and e-commerce. Public-sector movement in the direction of more open government, as well as the spread of ICT into domestic and other everyday domains may be expected to underpin public education, awareness and confidence, but may also raise public expectations of better privacy protection. The IAG strategy says little about individual self-protection except in the context of the usefulness of technological instruments in the hands of individuals, and of privacy 'seals' on websites, which will be discussed below. Market solutions cannot be expected to play a large role given the nature of transactions with the state as contrasted with commercial suppliers of goods and services. As for laws, the Data Protection Commissioner (formerly entitled the Registrar) pointed to the Data Protection Act as an 'enabler', defining standards, indicating the issues that must be addressed, and creating enforceable rights (HC 575, 1999, p.82). This gives some indication of the way in which the mix of privacy strategies works together, even across a dispersed array of participants in the system who are responsible for different elements.

Organisational self-regulation, including codes of practice, is seen as a particularly important component of IAG, and requires some explanation. This preference is evident, for example, in the CITU's work on channels, where the interconnection of electronic transaction channels between the private and the public sector is seen to need explicit service agreements that include a range of industrial codes of practice among a host of other requirements, including data protection and security[20]. Within the IAG strategy, there is

---

20   http://www.citu.gov.uk/channels/channelspolicy.htm; (accessed 27/10/00.)

particular emphasis placed on developing codes throughout the public sector to provide a common understanding and common practice, based on the law, and sufficient to sustain the new information practices including data-sharing. In the CITU's 'channels' document, the government undertook to promote specific data protection codes departmentally or inter-departmentally; it 'will expect that all organisations involved in service delivery will adopt as robust an approach'[21]. As cited in the PIU's report, the 1999 DTI White Paper was based on the continuing collaborative work of the DTI and the Alliance for Electronic Business (AEB), a consortium founded by five leading 'peak' associations in the UK electronics and marketing industries. An AEB paper of 1998 (Alliance for Electronic Business, 1998) sought to strengthen data protection through voluntary codes of practice, but observed that current website practices of indicating companies' privacy policies left something to be desired. It therefore advocated better technical methods and self-regulatory 'teeth', although the details of this regulatory dentistry were not elaborated; beyond these, it was a matter for individuals to take the necessary precautions.

The Commissioner has an important interest in privacy codes as well as a statutory responsibility for promoting them; she has elaborated a three-tier architecture of codes (HC 575, 1999, pp. 77-79). First was a high-level, government-wide tier, based on the Data Protection Act 1998, the Human Rights Act 1998, and Freedom of Information proposals, but augmented by the privacy commitments in the White Paper. At this level, there would be a consistent standard embodied in a code that would be produced by CITU and the Commissioner and 'owned' by Government. The second tier was envisaged at departmental or interdepartmental level and 'owned' by them. These codes would be produced by the IAG 'champions' and would specify many elements, such as the legal basis of the processing, the locus of responsibility for trans-institutional processing tasks, the applicability of the requirement that data be fairly obtained, security features, how individuals are to be helped in exercising their rights, the procedure for complaints, and the penalties for breach. The third tier would be a supportive one at the level of operating procedures, and would include training and the monitoring of compliance.

The IAG 'champions' were expected to have a major role in the production of data-protection codes of practice for their departments, and in being responsible for their practical implementation. This poses a potential dilemma, because they are supposed to be 'champions' of IAG and of government modernisation in general. It is not at all clear whether the conceptualisation of privacy as an objective rather than an obstacle will be robust enough to withstand a softening of the privacy side of their role in favour of meeting performance targets or achieving the other 'milestone' objectives of service delivery and joined-up government. The incentives to produce IAG are greater than the incentives to protect privacy, if it comes to a conflict of aims. It is worth noting that the NAO's study of government on the Web had little to say about the question of privacy protection beyond noting that only a small proportion of government chief executives saw the inability to guarantee privacy as a barrier to the development of Web-based communications between

---

21 http://www.citu.gov.uk/channels/channelspolicy.htm, ch. 9, para. 3; (accessed 27/10/00.)

government and citizens (HC 87, 1999, Figure 19 and para. 1.36). Any 'balance' to be struck between conflicting objectives is thus potentially a de facto one, and not necessarily a reasoned, deliberative outcome. Work on codes is in its infancy, however; therefore, judgements are premature. But it is worth noting that privacy protection is identified as a 'milestone' to be reached by March 2001 as part of the common policies on the management of information.

The inclusion of PETs as an important element of privacy protection indicates, first, that technological solutions for privacy problems are an 'idea in good currency' and are perhaps the leading edge in international data protection circles. This raises important questions about the future place of privacy, and of thinking about privacy, in a hypothetical world in which certain levels of privacy protection are automatically designed into technical information system. But, second, the intention of government and the Commissioner to integrate technical solutions into a wider structure of policy instruments, without which the design of PETs might take place uninformed by wider or overarching data-protection principles and criteria, serves to steer technological design and to subject it to broader scrutiny from perspectives that are arguably more in touch with political and social currents. The latter indicate the importance, for example, of collecting as little identifiable data as possible, and of setting the rules for transmission.

Meanwhile, although the framework document produced in April 2000 on privacy and data-sharing ran only to two pages[22], it said that CITU was establishing a working group to develop guidelines by March 2001. Its terms of reference were the well-known data protection principles that form part of the Data Protection Act 1998. There are important developments in OECD thinking and in the privacy sector - the Platform for Privacy Protection (P3P)[23] for online privacy protection, to which the privacy and data-sharing paper referred. But these developments are still embryonic and very controversial; the gestation of P3P has been very long and it is not yet an operative system. The paper also drew attention to the involvement of the Commissioner in developing the guidelines, to the wider framework of information policies that includes Freedom of Information and Human Rights legislation, and to the British Standard BS7799 for information-system security as a tool for '[s]trengthening the public's trust'[24]. The gaining of consent for data sharing remains a key issue, especially in the light of survey evidence on the public's worries about information misuse.

The paper also drew attention to the more technical questions of authentication and security systems, about which there are much more elaborate framework documents that bear scrutiny. The authentication paper[25], in particular, is of interest. It was concerned to show the relationship between transaction-related authentication procedures and levels and the public's trust and confidence in e-government, and to enjoin upon departments that they

---

22   http://www.citu.gov.uk/iagc/pdfs/privacy.pdf; (accessed 27/10/00.)
23   http://www.w3.org/P3P/; (accessed 27/10/00.)
24   http://www.citu.gov.uk/iagc/pdfs/privacy.pdf, para. 7; (accessed 27/10/00.)
25   http://www.citu.gov.uk/iagc/guidelines/authentication/approach.htm; (accessed 27/10/00.)

comply with authentication procedures in the interest of data protection. It identified several 'trust levels' which tailor requirements, or 'profiles', for the proof of identity, to the consequences or risks involved. This approach broaches some interesting issues concerning trust and risk that cannot be explored here, but the work being done on authentication could go some distance towards fulfilling the remit to protect privacy. The smart cards paper[26] is also relevant in this connection. It noted the importance of early consideration of data-protection issues in regard to the introduction of smart cards, both in order to comply with laws and 'to maintain public confidence....particularly... where perceived or actual risks to data protection may be heightened by the deployment of unfamiliar technology'[27]. Yet it is important to recognise that technical system solutions only speak to certain aspects - although these are important - of the privacy, confidentiality and trust issues.

More recently, the PIU's report of September 2000 gave a prominent place to articulating the obstacles facing the implementation of the IAG 'vision', and to designing strategies for overcoming them. Among the issues taken up at some length was the question of public trust and confidence in electronic service transactions, and specifically the question of the extent to which privacy will be protected. Conclusion 12 dealt with this: by June 2001,'the Office of the e-Envoy should develop a Trust Charter for government ESD in co-operation with the Data Protection Commissioner'(PIU, 2000b, pp. 55, 98) .

6   Conclusion

In the policy process, there are apparent tensions between advocates of 'strong' and 'weak' versions of data protection as part of a governance strategy for ICT, but the nature of a resolution of any disagreements cannot be confidently predicted. Be that as it may, government can be expected to be concerned to develop, and to be seen to develop, what they regard as adequate measures of privacy protection, and to embed them in organisational and technical infrastructures. It will also aim to take the lead in enjoining these safeguards upon the diverse array of implementation agencies involved in the programme. Some of these measures will be described later; however, it is difficult to evaluate their ultimate effect on both the modernisation of government and the protection of privacy. How far, and how rapidly, this construction of privacy protection will proceed is a relevant question. So, too is the question of who in government 'owns' this objective sufficiently to ensure that proactive, joined-up mechanisms are put in place to achieve it.

A caveat can be entered to these expectations, for their fulfilment may turn on the meaning of 'adequacy'. This is both a contested concept within the world of data protection and a focus for highly conflictual political negotiation. There is a cautionary history, in the UK and abroad, and in both the private and public sector, of privacy and data protection falling off the bottom of the agenda or being 'balanced' out of existence in favour of the

---

26   http://www.citu.gov.uk/iagc/guidelines/smartcards/summary.htm; (accessed 27/10/00.)
27   http://www.citu.gov.uk/iagc/guidelines/smartcards/privacy.htm, p. 17; (accessed 27/10/00.)

achievement of other competing policy objectives. This reflects our first conception, and perhaps a certain settlement within the framework of the second. Within the UK's IAG repertory of conflicting pressures, there remains a distinct possibility of privacy's relegation, although such an outcome would not be unique to the UK.

This paper has mainly described developments and commented on them piecemeal in respect of what they tell us about the place that privacy protection holds within the UK government's plans for electronic government, and concerning the mixed, perhaps pluralistic modes, of governance for both e-government and for privacy protection. Joined-up, proactive government requires joined-up, proactive data protection. The latter would be reflected not only in a consciously integrated version of the privacy 'mix', but also in co-ordinated privacy protection across the public sector and between it and its service-delivery 'partners' in the private and voluntary sectors. Both IAG and privacy protection require proactive approaches to put together the pieces. Proactive service delivery anticipates needs and packages solutions in ways that shape those needs. Proactive privacy protection anticipates privacy invasions and impacts, and seeks to put safeguards in place rather than leave everything to individuals in the pursuit of their rights.

In the IAG developments, one can see the intersection of the two sides, such that the modernisation of government and ESD take on board a proactive approach to privacy protection in order that these governmental objectives can be more successful. In turn, proactive privacy protection is enhanced by its integration into some of the leading edges of the relation between government and the citizen, giving it a higher profile and moving it closer to the centre of policy. But this is theory; reality may well differ, the pace of change is likely to remain slow, and the winds are not too favourable for realising the aims of IAG and 'joined-up government'. Nor, for that matter, might be the prospects for joined-up, proactive privacy protection, according to some observers; after all, are we not told that 'privacy is dead, and we may as well get used to it'?

The legitimisation of the construction of privacy as going with the grain of 'modernising government', rather than cutting across it, provides a platform for requiring more emphatically that data protection be a hallmark of the new developments. How sturdy the platform is may depend on the way IAG is arbitrated in the implementation networks. A stronger emphasis on privacy protection may be the more achievable to the extent that the Commissioner is involved, as her office continues to be, in the further development of IAG strategy and implementation. Among the gainers are likely to include technology providers, given the recognition of the efficacy of technological solutions to some privacy problems, but they are also likely to include regulatory organisations and the wide penumbra of consultants, lawyers and activists who have a material and ideological stake in the elevation of privacy's status in public policy initiatives.

Although it can only be noted here, it is interesting to observe that this proactive promotion of privacy protection construes it as a public good, to be provided for all citizens through the technical and administrative systems for public services, and not only as an individual benefit whose protection is tailored to a person's particular preferences or level (Regan, 1995; Schoeman, 1992; Raab 1997b). That said, an element of custom-building could be included in certain technologies, such as smart cards. In all this, an important new plateau appears to have been reached, on which there is something of an attempted paradigm shift in the depiction of the relationships between privacy protection and the purposes of government. The conventional wisdom on this relationship, whether in the private sector or the public sector, has portrayed an adversarial situation in which efficiency, effectiveness, economy and the other desiderata of public administration confront the tender-minded concern for civil liberties and human rights, including privacy and public access to information. Leaving the latter aside in this discussion - although it is far from a negligible question - the mantra intoned by all except perhaps the civil libertarians and privacy advocates is that a 'balance' must be struck between the two competing sets of values. This doctrine has been criticised elsewhere (Raab, 1998), but it is likely to continue to prevail.

However, there is one indication, in current UK discourse, of a new perspective on it that may give rise to more searching questioning of the appropriateness of the 'balancing' paradigm or at least of its application in practical decisions. This is the emphasis on human rights that is now more evident in privacy discourse in the UK, even in the world of regulatory policy. The concept of a legal 'right to privacy' has been anathema to British jurisprudence, and 'data protection' has had to serve as a pale reflection of the policy assumption that privacy is the aim of such legislation. The Data Protection Commissioner has for several years emphasised this, and gradually the idea that privacy may be an enforceable right has gained ground. It has been boosted by the passage of the Human Rights Act 1998 which allows the rights enshrined in the European Convention on Human Rights, including privacy, to be pursued in British courts. The Commissioner was quick to welcome this development as providing a new context of rights within which data-protection adjudication will now develop[28]. Although that would not challenge the paradigm as such, it would at least affect the nature and location of the 'balance' that might be struck between privacy and other interests or values. Government's attempt to cope with the question of privacy protection and data-sharing will remain under investigation well into 2001[29]. Whether it moves closer to recognising a 'rights' conception as an ingredient in the criteria of what is permissible remains to be arbitrated by that time, and further into the future.

---

28   HC 910 (1998), p. 3.
29   http://www.cabinet-office.gov.uk/innovation/2000/privacy/datapress.htm; (accessed 27/10/00.)

References

6, P. (1998) *The Future of Privacy* (2 vols.), London: Demos

Allan, A. (2000) 'Why we need a strategy', *Government Computing*, 14, 4 (May), Supplement

Bellamy, C. & Taylor, J. (1998) *Governing in the Information Age*, Buckingham: Open University Press

Bellamy, C. (2000) 'Implementing Information-age Government: principles, progress and paradox', *Public Policy and Administration*, 15, 1, pp. 29-42.

CITU (1998) *Electronic Government: the view from the queue*, London: Cabinet Office

CITU (2000) *e-government - A Strategic Framework for Public Services in the Information Age*, London: Cabinet Office

Cm 3438 (1996) *government.direct,* London: The Stationery Office

Cm 4310 (1999) *Modernising government*, London: The Stationery Office

Cm 4410 (1999), *Modern markets: confident consumers*, London: The Stationery Office

Gladwyn, M. (2000) in *Government Computing*, E-government Supplement, May

Alliance for Electronic Business (1998) *Electronic Business - Leading Britain towards Greater Competitiveness,* London: Alliance for Electronic Business

Government Computing (2000a) 14, 8 (September)

Government Computing (2000b) 14, 9 (October)

HC 87 (1999) *Government on the Web - A Report by the Comptroller and Auditor General*, Session 1999-2000, London: The Stationery Office

HC 331 (2000) Select Committee on Public Accounts, *Twenty-First Report, Session 1999-2000*, Government on the Web, London: The Stationery Office

HC 570-II (1999) Select Committee on Public Administration, *Third Report, Session 1998-99, Freedom of Information Draft Bill*, Vol. II - Memoranda of Evidence, Memorandum 7, submitted by the National Consumer Council, London: The Stationery Office

HC 575 (1999) *The Fifteenth Annual Report of the Data Protection Registrar*, Session 1998-99, London: The Stationery Office

HC 910 (1998) *The Fourteenth Annual Report of the Data Protection Registrar*, Session 1997-98, London: The Stationery Office

Kooiman, J. (ed.) (1993) *Modern Governance*, London: Sage.

ODPR (n.d.) *Private Lives and Public Powers - A Guide to the Law on the Use and Disclosure of Information About Living Individuals by Public Bodies*, Wilmslow: Office of the Data Protection Registrar

PIU (1999) *e-commerce@its.best.uk London*: Cabinet Office

PIU (2000a) *Wiring It Up - Whitehall's Management of Cross-Cutting Policies and Services, London*: Cabinet Office

PIU (2000b) *e.gov - Electronic Government Services for the 21st Century, London*: Cabinet Office

Raab, C. (1993) 'The Governance of Data Protection', in J. Kooiman (ed.) (1993) Modern Governance, London: Sage

Raab, C. (1997a) 'Co-Producing Data Protection', International Review of Law, Computers and Technology, 11, 1, 11-24.

Raab, C. (1997b) 'Privacy, Democracy, Information', in B. Loader (ed.), *The Governance of Cyberspace*, London: Routledge

Raab, C. (1998) 'Electronic Confidence: Trust, Information and Public Administration', in I. Snellen and W. van de Donk (eds.), *Public Administration in an Information Age:* A Handbook, Amsterdam: IOS Press

Regan, P. (1995) *Legislating Privacy*, Chapel Hill, NC: University of North Carolina Press

Schoeman, F. (1992) *Privacy and Social Freedom*, Cambridge: Cambridge University Press

Chapter 5

Broadening the Concept of Electronic Government

Klaus Lenk and Roland Traunmüller

1 Broadening the Concept of Electronic Government

All too often, Electronic Government is perceived in a very narrow way. The view is limited to phenomena like 'Electronic Service Delivery', 'Electronic Democracy' and to issues like security, reliability, data protection or access to information, which concern the infrastructure of an 'Information Society'. Such issues are easier to understand for a larger public than the wider perspectives of Electronic Government, which concern the use of IT to support the actions of public administration as well as political processes.

A first attempt to broaden the concept can be found in definitions which are based on a matrix listing all possible 'x-to-y' (or 'x2y') relationships, e.g. government to citizens and vice versa, government to government, government to suppliers, to the non profit sector, etc. (von Lucke and Reinermann 2000). In this way the attention is drawn to several fields where better communication yields important effects of rationalisation or service quality improvement. Examples include Electronic Procurement or better co-operation among government units over distance; especially the latter holds a huge potential to step up intergovernmental relations.

Yet such a definition of Electronic Government which unfolds a communication matrix falls short of revealing the full potential of information technology which is behind it. This potential can be used for increasing the effectiveness and efficiency of governance and public administration and for attaining wider goals of transparency, of enhanced democratic participation of citizens and of accountability. Making good use of Electronic Government, beyond some early showcase projects which helped to exploit the Internet fascination politically, depends on a thorough understanding and engineering of the processes which produce public services, regulations and interventions.

In a comprehensive view, taking our start from the presently observable functions and institutions of government, we can say that Electronic Government relies on a fundamental redesign of the different types of interactions just mentioned. This is coupled with a reorganisation of the business processes within public administration. We insist on the fact that the chances which such a combination of external and internal aspects holds can be fully exploited only if the special features of the work of government including public administration, as well as those of political processes, are taken into account. Careful analysis of the different functions which governments

J. E. J. Prins (ed.), Designing E-Government, 63–74.

perform is required. Unfortunately, many proponents of Electronic Government are not very well aware of these manifold functions, let alone of the different ways in which they are accomplished and which are due to the history of national governmental and administrative systems.

Four perspectives will be developed in order to gain a clearer view on the future shape of an Electronic Government. This view should inform efforts, both incremental and momentous ones, to move into a direction which, to our feeling, is made mandatory by the thrust of many problems of our evolving societies. Suffice it to say here that governments will in the future be obliged to perform their core tasks with only a fraction of the efforts involved in them today. This is a. o. due to a growing discrepancy between the (decreasing) costs of industrial production and the (rising) costs of service production and informational work performed by human beings. Moreover, there is a growing unwillingness to finance public services through taxes.

These four perspectives are:

- the addressee's perspective where the citizen interface of administrative work is particularly prominent;
- the process perspective in which re-organisation of processes making use of all kinds of human-machine synergies is paramount;
- the co-operation perspective which complements the process perspective especially through insisting on ubiquitous (tele-) co-operation and on collaborative efforts like meetings, negotiations or deliberations which do not follow a clearcut process model and which cannot be fully standardised beforehand;
- the knowledge perspective which highlights the management of information and knowledge as the major asset in many work situations in the public sector.

We will address each of these four perspectives separately before addressing some of the possible consequences of Electronic Government for the modernisation of the state.

2 The Addressee's Perspective: Integrated Access Management and Single-window Service

Perhaps the most salient characteristic of modern IT is the ease with which people, data, and processes can now be brought together over distances. An infrastructure of 'Digital Nerves of Government' is emerging. People can be reached everywhere and processes can be started from anywhere and anytime. Data, which used to be hidden in masses of paper, or of which we were not even aware of, can be located and accessed. Such a quantum jump in availability will spur change.

A striking example is Electronic Service Delivery using innovative modes of communication between administrative agencies and citizens. The major innovation consists in a simple organisational trick. Service production is split up between a front office and a (distant) back office. This helps to create a totally new scheme for bringing administrative services and their addressees into contact. Whilst in a classical administrative agency, the citizen has to appear at fixed hours in an office, he or she may now go to a multifunctional front office. Besides obtaining access to the service actually needed, citizens can perform all other communications and transactions with public administrations through it. Commercial services, too, may be accessed through the same 'single-window' front office. Alternatively, a 'virtual' front office in the internet may offer part or all of the same conveniences.

In this way, 'service retail shops' can be set up to make service available at one location in the neighbourhood or in any case easy to reach. Today, in accessing services - both public and commercial - we still act as if we would go to a farmer to buy eggs or to a mill to buy cereals, instead of shopping in a neighbourhood shop or supermarket. A new type of service retail shops in the public sector is now becoming possible by combining the 'Digital Nerves of Government' with a front office / back office architecture.

This situation calls for conceptual efforts to create reference models for such multifunctional service shops and for new ways of producing and rendering basic services. The challenge consists in inventing an integrated access structure which takes advantage of all possible types of organising the front office as a single-window service. Some people may access it in the presently dominant written mode over the Internet, asking for information or triggering a transaction. Others may use the telephone, so that the front office, in their view, amounts to a joint Call Centre serving the public sector as a whole. Others, finally, may wish to expose their problem personally to a service worker in a service shop located in the neighbourhood of the citizen. The French expression 'service de proximité' is particularly apt at designing this access mode. As a matter of course, traditional forms of access: directly going to the back office in charge, writing letters or making telephone calls, will persist.

An 'Administraton à accès pluriel', as the Rapport Lasserre (Lasserre, 2000) calls it, is needed now to take full advantage of potential of the Internet. This potential should not only serve those which have access to the Internet from at home and are skilled enough to interact with public bodies in a competent way. People should be able to choose the access 'channel' which suits them best, without incurring financial disadvantages. Having embarked on one of these, they should be able to switch, e.g. from an Internet-based communication to a personal visit in the service shop. Here, they could get access over distance, via desktop video and document sharing, to a competent person in the relevant back office. Also, the integration of these access channels will soon make progress, first with Computer Telephony Integration (CTI), and later with reliable video communication over an upgraded Internet guaranteeing the required quality of service.

One-stop access, important as it may be, is only one aspect of the entire interaction process which accompanies any service delivery. Other functions include:
- Citizen pre-information at various stages and in various depths,
- Help in filling in forms etc., if necessary,
- 'Translating' the demand for a service (a license, etc.) from the citizen's life-world to legal-administrative jargon,
- Matching of the demand with the jurisdictional structure (competencies in the legal sense), routing the citizen demand to the relevant back office (which may also be a completely automated process),
- Keeping track of the process, handling 'Freedom of Information' requests and other 'due process' requirements.

Many projects are already focusing on improved citizen service. But unlike in Electronic Commerce, the market test is usually lacking. So we only begin to realise that an 'Administration à accès pluriel' will have to replace a one-sided reliance on the Internet which is driven by considerations of bringing as many 'users' as possible to the Internet. Giving in to the tendencies to propagate Internet use at any rate is not conducive per se to better service. It may even jeopardise the improvements in service quality which are possible now, shifting many burdens to the addressee. Especially the 'translation' effort required when contacting an agency for a service, which is not frequently asked for, should not be left to the citizen, since a failure to understand the 'official' terminology may result in useless contacts or in a wrong framing of the demand.

Taking into account the entire process of service delivery, not just problems of citizen access, means that the external perspective has to be complemented by three further perspectives that all address the less visible parts of the machinery of government.

3   The Process Perspective: Redesigning Organisations

Restructuring the business processes is unavoidable if these processes will increasingly be spanning the boundaries between a front office and one or more back offices. As an example, in a one-stop-shop, multimedia technology may be used to operate an on-demand link between the service outlet staffed with one or two persons, and back office personnel competent to answer any difficult question arising in connection with production and delivery of a determined service.

A point which is often overlooked is that the design of business process in the public sector has to take into account an enormous multitude of different processes which often involve complex decision making activities. Therefore the established view on process re-engineering, which follows the model of industrial engineering, is only partly adequate. In a production chain, each activity is intrinsically related to preceding and succeeding ones, so as to make synchronisation a major issue. This Tayloristic model is suitable for well-structured business processes like conventional ordering, invoicing, or registering. Strict co-ordination of the single steps in these processes is required to make them reliable and efficient. Modelling therefore can closely follow what is known from industrial engineering.

The consequence to date has been that the overwhelming number of methodologies and tools for modelling, implementing and executing business processes have closely followed the model of an industrial plant. The conveyor belt is at the heart of the workflow. Compared with earlier office automation systems, Workflow Management Systems (WFMS) have achieved a big leap forward, as they focus on the entire business process, instead of on the individual task. Most WFMS have been successful in providing support for streamlining and synchronising work processes which are amenable to a closely defined procedural approach. In the work of August-Wilhelm Scheer (Kraemer et al., 1998), this perspective of industrial engineering is developed into a coherent model which is at the root of ERP (Enterprise Resource Planning) software which aims at comprehensive support of all (routine) functions in a plant or an office. This incurs the danger of strictly sequencing many work processes which exhibit some degree of informality and of more or less openly acknowledged discretion.

Efforts to transplant this type of WFM via reference models to public administration draws the limitations of the underlying Tayloristic model into the limelight. Especially for the higher echelons e.g. in a ministerial department, strict co-ordination of workflows is a minor concern. Strict co-ordination such as embodied in first-generation WFMS represents only one end of a continuum with respect to the structuring of work. Its counterpart at the other extreme is collaboration, which designates persons working together without any previous external co-ordination. Self-coordination as an important element in the work of public administration has been recognised quite early (Traunmüller, 1992; Shapiro and Traunmüller, 1993). The tendency towards promoting self-organisation, also in work situations where a more standardised way of proceeding would be feasible.

For this reason, business process reengineering in the public sector has to take into account the co-operation perspective which will be dealt with in the next section. But there are additional elements which have to be mentioned first. In order to achieve a reorganisation of the business processes of public administration one has stress in which respect these are different from processes in the private sector (Lenk, 1997).

Administrative processes are characterised by three factors: law, politics, and information as a resource.

- They are partly, but to varying extents, structured by legal rules which, however, often demand interpretation and allow for some amount of open or hidden discretion.
- They are subject to political influences and bargaining, although considerations of justice and equity would often plead against taking those influences into account.
- They draw on information which is not consumed in the process but can be reused, and furthermore the experience gained in carrying out processes adds to the asset of knowledge available.

We will shortly address here the legal and the political aspects. Taking a closer look on administrative decision processes (such as police work, internal revenue, determining a construction license etc.), one will find the following schema of steps (Lenk and Traunmüller 1999, p. 57ff.):

Observation and Information: Information has to be gathered form various sources. The behaviour of the society or a group of citizens is observed. Such observations can be made for specific purposes (e.g. by the police authority) or for general planning purposes.

Substantiating facts: The material gained from such observations is combined with facts of the case.

Decision to act: When enough material is collected and combined to facts, administrators have to take a decision for action; this decision can be seen as the final result of the information processing.

Intervention: In a typical administrative act, the results of the decision-making process are simply communicated to the addressee. Equally, also physical-technical actions can occur, e.g. arresting a person, paying a sum of money, setting up of roadblocks, closure of a bridge.

Execution: If some addresses do not comply with the orders, an execution of the order may become necessary. A common example is the forcible way of tax collection.

Evaluation: In the last step it has to be checked whether the aim of had the intended effect concerning the influence on the society. The results of the evaluation should be used to compare the plans and the actual results. Sometimes they may be employed to reorganise the preceding steps.

Not all observable decision processes correspond to this schema. In administrative practice, their basic structure is often hidden:

- Many observing and information gathering activities take place without producing any tangible results. The collected information may never be used directly but it may contribute to organisational learning within an agency.
- Actions can be taken without any incoming external information.
- Administrations also have to maintain their organisation and supportive activities have to be taken that do not produce any output.

Another aspect which in public administration is governed by legal rules are organisational structures and administrative procedure. Process reorganisation may often not dispose of established structures. Administrative structures have many functions: protecting the rights of citizens; ensuring procedures bound to the rules of law. An important aspect of government action is a division of labour which is often congruent with a division of jurisdictions. The latter tends to delimit separate information domains within government, thereby often protecting against unwanted intrusion by an omniscient government. Various forms of co-ordination constitute the reverse side of this division of labour. They include more or less formalised workflow processes as well as a multitude of teamwork, negotiations, collaborative decision making and managerial co-ordination instruments like supervision or inspection rights. All this cannot be sacrificed for the sake of process optimisation. Some of these functions will be implicitly dealt later with from a co-operation and a knowledge perspective.

Also for reasons of the political nature of many activities in the public sector, the structuring of processes has its limits. Processes often need to be very flexible in order to allow for political considerations.

4   The Co-operation Perspective: Sustaining Collaborative Decision-Making

For the reasons set out above, process structure should not be taken as the only perspective when discussing the changes which happen in the inner workings of the public sector. Of equal importance are two complementary perspectives: collaboration and knowledge as the main asset from which an information processing organisation draws its strengths.

This leads to telecooperation as a holistic vision whose focus lies on work aiming at the support of computer-mediated co-operation in a comprehensive sense. Telecooperation covers the whole fan of work activities of government agencies or firms. It also allows for spanning organisational boundaries and involving the suppliers and customers of processes outside the organisation by opening up e.g. EDI (Electronic Data Interchange) or common work platforms. Spatially unconstrained telecooperation is the decisive technological concept for a global society. This is mirrored in expressions like Global Office, Telepresence (of actors), Tele-Administration. In the last-mentioned field, 'quasi-face-to-face-encounters' with specialists operating in back-offices located anywhere in the world are increasingly becoming possible. In the longer run this will affect the traditional organisation of the public sector profoundly, by loosening territorial constraints and enhancing the effectiveness and the quality of the services and interventions produced.

Human work is at the centre of telecooperation. Hence procedural and collaborative work converge, also including the management of documents and other tools for knowledge management. Real office situations require the integration of procedural and non procedural work such as reassigning work, overriding missing approvals, seeking amendments of incomplete work etc. Especially for the higher ranks of bureaucrats, strict co-ordination ceases to be the prime mode of action; it is collaboration that becomes prevalent.

The concept of co-operation spans both, strictly co-ordinated work and collaboration work. As a pure type, collaboration designates persons working together without any external previous co-ordination. The round table is an adequate metaphor. Particular mechanisms have to be provided for sustaining collaborative work. Key requirements are the following ones:

- Sharing of objects has to be supported
- Integration of individual and co-operation tasks is necessary
- Domain directories manage users and objects
- Sharing and access policies have to be determined.

The co-operation perspective is of special importance to activities related to complex decision making, negotiation and in general policy formulation. Policymaking is normally taking place through multiple processes of negotiation among actors based in different organisations. The theory of 'policy networks' takes into account a variety of structures of policy networks, even beyond the classical 'policy triangles' involving parliamentarians, administrators and field representatives. The negotiated character of policymaking permeates all phases of the policy process. It is perhaps not so visible in early phases of policymaking like information collection and analysis. During these phases, divergence of interests and positions do not yet reveal themselves very clearly. On the other hand, agreeing on some kind of information and demarcating the search space for further information may pre-empt substantial decision making which characterises the following phases of agreeing on some policy and of implementing it.

Most important to policymaking activities are meetings. In order to achieve adequate support environments one has to blend conventional data and decision support with collaborative functions to a set of highly-modular components, comprising scheduling of the overall negotiation procedure; clarifying procedural questions; scheduling of meetings and implied sub-activities; supporting the agenda setting for all these activities and pre-discussing agendas; supporting communication among participants to the meeting (same place or different place), drawing on supplementary information, commenting on that information, spotting experts, structuring issues, summing up results; documenting of processes and results.

5 The Knowledge Perspective: Managing Distributed Domain Knowledge

The Tayloristic model of business processes as some sort of production chain not only neglects the co-operative aspects of many activities and difficulties of casting them into a process format. It also overlooks the fact that information and knowledge have other characteristics than matter and energy which are transformed in material production processes. Information and knowledge can be shared and given away while still be retained by their original holder. They can be used ubiquitously, with costs of transmission in sharp decrease. But most importantly, information and knowledge are not only embodied in 'storage bins' outside the minds of individuals. These individuals may even not be conscious of the fact that they hold 'tacit' information which directly informs their decisions and actions. And it is the combination of much explicitly and implicitly held information by several individuals which may create important synergies.

So the knowledge management perspective is extremely important in understanding administrative work in such a way as to be able to redesign it without incurring major losses of skill, expertise, know-how and goodwill. In many ways, the output of this work influences society or engenders other outcomes in conformance to legal rules or political expectations. Its effectiveness critically depends on administrative knowledge of different types:

- knowledge about the policy field to be influenced
- knowledge about the effects of previous actions
- knowledge about legal rules, standards, political attitudes of stakeholders and other political conditions commanding and constraining action
- knowledge about one's own capabilities to act.

Max Weber, one of the founding fathers of administrative science, lumped these types of knowledge together in his notion of 'service knowledge' (*Dienstwissen*). This is a hard-to-define amalgam of different types of knowledge: explicit and implicit knowledge are closely intertwined. In the English translation of his bureaucracy theory, these aspects almost got lost, but for him they constituted one of the most decisive characteristics of bureaucracy. Further, there are overlapping realms of knowledge, according to whether the operational layer is concerned or the higher echelons. Often domain knowledge might not be perceivable at routine work; yet in the case of exceptional events or in emergencies its importance becomes apparent. So it becomes evident that one cannot reduce administrative skills to a 'McJob' level. Although obvious, this statement has to be made explicitly. There are too many naive beliefs nurtured by eager advocates of reengineering in the Tayloristic tradition. Not only heedless reorganisation, but also fluctuations of personnel may result in losses of knowledge assets.

Knowledge management comprises several steps which are of importance in dealing with information: information gathering, its transformation into knowledge, availability and (re-) use of this knowledge, as well as the regulatory framework in which all this takes place. Due to inadequate technological support, it is still in its infancy.

The most pressing problem with knowledge is how to spot it. Even where it may be explicit in the mind of a member of the organisation, it may be hidden from an organisational standpoint. Previous experiences get lost, scientific results are not used.

Moreover information and knowledge might be concealed deliberately. No wonder that enterprises and agencies are eager to invest huge sums into their organisational knowledge. It is of paramount importance to facilitate and systematise the use of existing information and knowledge, to transform private knowledge into structural knowledge and to support the development of new knowledge. It becomes more and more important to solve such issues: as finding the right expert, securing the acquired expertise, managing intellectual property or accessing the institutional knowledge potential. The challenge is to build an organisational culture in which knowledge has a high importance and in which the estimation and position of each individual is mainly driven by his or her contribution to the corporate knowledge.

Building up institutional memories is an old dream that has gained actuality. Enterprises and agencies invest more and more in the establishment and maintenance of their intellectual property and in accessing the institution's knowledge potential. But all too often a static view of storing information in data bases prevails, in combination with a 'plumbing system' which can be tapped by organisation members looking for information. Unfortunately, good support for organisational learning cannot be achieved in such a simple manner. The institutional memory of an organisation is retained in many places and also in artefacts: individuals, organisational culture, organisational structures and standard operating procedures, internal information repositories, and external archives (Walsh and Ungson, 991). As far as information dissemination is concerned, information users and information producers can conceivably be brought together on electronic markets.

Adequate technical support for knowledge management is becoming increasingly important. Beyond tools like electronic document management systems, collaborative tools such as Lotus Notes, argumentation systems such as Issue-Based Information Systems (IBIS) and knowledge based techniques, further complex support tools have to be developed e.g. for ordering and retrieval: indexing, categorising, semantic correspondences, definition of hyper-structures, fuzzy retrieval, case based search etc.

6   The Future Shape of Electronic Government

Redesigning citizen access structures, processes, co-operation and knowledge management will eventually lead to rethink and restructure government and its work in a very fundamental way. This redesign is only at its very beginnings. Predictions as to its speed and pervasiveness are almost impossible to make. In any case, the cultural change which New Public Management brought to many branches of public administration will put its stamp on further developments. It has already brought a shift from institutional considerations towards the final outcomes which have to be produced by government action, regardless of current functional and organisational boundaries and of the spatial distribution of agencies and individual agents. But Electronic Government is clearly transcending New Public Management in that it implies new bold and comprehensive approaches to administrative modernisation, beyond managerialism and a few theories borrowed from economics. Moreover, it is directly acting upon the production processes in which administrative services are generated, and not only upon better ways of managing these processes.

Restructuring government with the tool-set, which the four perspectives on

Electronic Government will soon put at our disposal, will have to overcome much institutional inertia and deeply ingrained habits of 'public sector politics'. Many students of public administration therefore doubt that significant changes will occur in the near future (Bellamy and Taylor, 1998). Existing institutions of social and political life exert strong influence in shaping behaviour and organisational culture. The latter can be circumscribed as 'the ways we do things here'. These ways cannot be changed easily through re-engineering. The institutional setting influences the nature of innovation in government and it determines its pace and selectivity .

But this opinion has to be evaluated in the light of the sweeping changes which Electronic Commerce has already wrought in the private sector. There are good reasons to believe that the public sector cannot stay aloof as commercial business is undergoing deep changes. The technology potential itself changes widely-held fundamental conceptions of good practice. Beyond its actual effects it creates expectations of various kinds, e.g. about offering new types of services, or improving the effectiveness of existing ones.

In our book (Lenk and Traunmüller, 1999) we discuss the relative merits of increased co-operation between administrative agencies

- over distances,
- across organisational boundaries
- across hierarchical echelons (e.g.: European Union - National - State - Regional - Municipal levels),
- between public and private organisations, especially with a view to Public Private Partnerships.

Advantages of this co-operation include a better distribution of workloads, access to remote specialists, broad implementation of single-window services for citizens and for small and medium enterprises. The overriding aspects seems to be that we are entering an age of co-operation, as far as the public sector is concerned: co-operation to share workloads, co-operation with remote specialists, co-operation across organisational boundaries and especially with private actors in public-private partnerships. But - after preaching the gospel of competition for some time now - the spirit of co-operation has first to be instilled in the public sector, where fragmentation and a narrowly conceived optimisation of the results of smaller units now prevail.

The immediate effects of increased co-operation and of new architectures like an 'Administration à accès pluriel' relying on new types of multifunctional service front offices will become visible only after massive investments in new Electronic Government structures. But beyond them, already now the perspective of a 'virtual' administration appears. Especially the consequences of new structures of service delivery are likely to affect the organisation of the public sector. The fragmented and multi-layered character of present public administration will be concealed behind access structures which no longer follow the instrinsic needs of service production but rather concepts of whole-person or life-event oriented service delivery.

It is still an open question whether, in the long run, improved citizen service, better engineered processes, ubiquitous co-operation and knowledge management will only result in hiding the existing complexity from the eyes of the beholder, or eventually amount to a profound restructuring entailing a substantial reduction of the ever-increasing complexity of the public sector.

Also, the vision of a 'seamless government' is very fascinating. But due to what has been said about the functionality of existing administrative structures in the light of Rechtsstaat requirements, it cannot be developed without a re-assessment of the goals and instruments of the European type of 'data protection' and of other 'informational guarantees'.

The prevailing patterns of using IT are far from exhausting the potential. It is an urgent task now for the research community to develop reference models inspired by visions of a modern public administration and of the potential of IT. Combining the four perspectives developed here, one should be able to devise bold solutions. Basic notions like administrative jurisdiction and the territoriality of public administration have to be questioned. In the long run, a radical overhaul of the 'machinery of government' in the spirit of Electronic Government will lead towards sustainable institutions which are able to face the challenges of the future.

References

Bellamy, C. and Taylor, J.A., *Governing in the Information Age*. Open Univ. Press, Buckingham, 1998.

Kraemer, W., Köppen, A., Scheer, A.W., „Industrielles Produkt- und Prozessdesign für Verwaltungs-Dienstleistungen", in Budäus et al. (eds), *New Public Management*, de Gruyter, Berlin, 1998, pp 217-253.

Lasserre, B., L'Etat et les technologies de l'information. Vers une administration à accès pluriel. Rapport du groupe présidé par Bruno Lasserre. Paris : La documentation francaise, 2000.

Lenk, K., *Business Process Re-Engineering in the Public Sector: Opportunities and Risks*, in Taylor, Snellen, Zuurmond (eds.), *Beyond BPR in Public Administration*. Institutional Transformation in an Information Age, IOS Press, Amsterdam, 1997, pp. 151-163.

Lenk, K. and Traunmüller, R. (eds.), Öffentliche Verwaltung und Informationstechnik - Perspektiven einer radikalen Neugestaltung der öffentlichen Verwaltung mit Informationstechnik, Decker, Heidelberg, 1999.

Shapiro, D. and Traunmüller, R., *CSCW in Public Administration. A Review*, In Bonin (ed.), Systems Engineering in Public Administration, North-Holland, Amsterdam, 1993, pp 1-18.

Traunmüller, R., 'Rechnergestützte Teamarbeit im Kommunalbereich: Stand, Perspektiven und Scenarien des CSCW', Wirtschaftsinformatik, Vol. 33, No. 6, December 1992.

Traunmüller, R. and Lenk, K., *New Public Management and Enabling Technologies*, *Proceedings of the XIV. IFIP World Computer Congress*, Chapman & Hall, London, 1996, pp 11-18.

Von Lucke, Jörg, and Heinrich Reinermann, Speyerer Definition von Electronic Government. Ergebnisse des Forschungsprojekts *Regieren und Verwalten im Informationszeitalter.*http://foev.dhv-speyer.de/) (2000).

Walsh, J.P. and Ungson, G.R., Organizational Memory, *Academy of Management Review*, Vol. 16, No 1, 1991, pp 57 - 91.

Chapter 6

Designing Electronic Government Around the World. Policy Developments in the USA, Singapore, and Australia

Miriam Lips[1]

1   Introduction

A rumor circulated in Washington DC that every head of state who visited President Clinton at the White House was guided downstairs at the end of their meeting and then met by Vice President Gore who showed them a huge scale model of the Internet. After having explained the American government's policy programs regarding the Internet, the following message was conveyed by the vice president to the honourable guest: 'this is the way you should develop your national information infrastructure'.

Since the Americans opened the Internet in the early 1990s to everyone in the world, the Internet has indeed been acknowledged in many countries as an important infrastructure enabling various interactions to be redesigned in their society. For instance, the Internet is widely perceived as a medium to enable the transformation of government and its relationship with society. Consequently, visions of a new government of the future, a so-called 'e-government', appeared in various policy documents around the world. Some of these visions and their related policy programs are explained in other chapters of this book, most of them can be located in Europe. In this chapter, a brief exploration of e-government developments in other parts of the world will be made. Widely acknowledged leading countries such as the USA, Singapore, and Australia which have been eager to take up new ICTs like the Internet, will be quickly scanned on their national policy developments with regard to e-government.

Bearing the above-mentioned rumor in mind, the question arises as to whether these three countries are heading in a similar direction as regards building a new government by means of ICT. To what extent can we perceive similarities in e-government developments around the world? Can we expect to have a single model of e-government in the long run, or are national governments around the world too different from each other, in spite of using the same kind of ICT-infrastructure as a major change agent for government? After having looked at e-government developments at the

---

1   The author would like to cordially thank Vivian Carter for her assistance in checking the English and Prof. Corien Prins for her invaluable comments

J. E. J. Prins (ed.), Designing E-Government, 75–90.
© 2001 *Kluwer Law International. Printed in the Netherlands.*

national level in successively the USA, Singapore, and Australia, some answers to these questions will be provided in the last paragraph of this chapter.

2   The United States of America

As said before, the United States of America (USA) has been one of the first countries in the world where new ICTs like the Internet were perceived as an important means to transform government and its relationship with society. As early as 1993, Clinton and Gore announced during their election campaign the development of an 'information highway' which would no longer be exclusively accessible to universities and companies, but could be used by everyone at any place and any time. As part of the broader reinventing government framework of the National Performance Review (NPR), the newly elected Clinton-Gore administration published in September 1993, a policy document entitled 'Reengineering Through IT'. Perceiving ICT as the essential infrastructure for the government of the 21st century, Clinton and Gore presented a policy agenda in this document to build the government of the future: the electronic government. In their vision, this electronic government. '...overcomes the barriers of time and distance to perform the business of government and give people public information and services when and where they want them. It can swiftly transfer funds, answer questions, collect and validate data, and keep information flowing smoothly within and outside government'.[2]

With this aim, an efficient, customer-oriented electronic government was envisaged. By putting this vision into practice, the purpose was not to automate traditional working processes of government through ICT, but to fundamentally rethink how people in government work and how to serve customers. The interaction between government and citizens would be transformed with the goal to provide better access to government services. Or, as it was stated: "it's all about putting people online, not in line".

To implement the vision of electronic government the following seven initiatives for further action were proposed (Lips & Frissen, 1997, p.118):
- to implement nation-wide, integrated electronic benefit transfer;
- to develop integrated electronic access to government information and services;
- to establish a national law enforcement / public safety network;
- to provide integovernmental tax filing, reporting, and payments processing;
- to establish an international trade data system;
- to create a national environmental data index; and to plan, demonstrate, and provide government-wide electronic mail.

It is important to be aware of the fact that Clinton and Gore could only propose a policy agenda which would be limited to the US federal level, and those policy areas in which the federal government has authoritative powers. In the USA, states and local governments have their own autonomy to develop e-government initiatives. This also applies to the proposed policy actions in the'Reengineering through IT'-document to

---

2   Office of the Vice President, Reengineering Through IT, September 1993, NPR Report. Available at: http://www.npr.gov/library/reports/it.html

establish necessary support mechanisms for electronic government. Among the proposed policy actions were the development of a coherent government information infrastructure, the development of systems and mechanisms to ensure privacy and security, the training and technical assistance in ICT to federal employees, and the provision of incentives for innovation within government (Lips & Frissen, 1997, p.119-120).

The NPR-policy program was continued in 1997 under the name of 'Access America'. A blueprint for further development of the federal electronic government program was published which, in fact, slightly differed from the original 'Re-engineering through IT'-policy agenda. The objective formulated under the new' Access America' policy program was to allow every American citizen to transact business with the government electronically, and to do so easily and quickly. At present, the various policy initiatives as described in the blueprint and the earlier policy agenda have been put into practice. Some projects are being further developed, partly on the basis of new technological facilities since 1993 (for instance, the possibility of using smartcards). In addition the NPR-program has been renamed. To particularly emphasize the participation of parties outside the federal government, such as the Postal Service, Internal Revenue Service, and Social Security in the reinvention program, it was decided to change the name from the National Performance Review into 'National Partnership for Reinventing Government' (NPR).

As a result of the US Paperwork Reduction Act, the federal government was obliged to offer all federal services and transactions online by 2003. Therefore, in late 1999, president Clinton issued a series of directives, which are referred to as the so-called 'e-gov' framework. Three main strategies formed the basis of this framework, viz. to ensure privacy and security, to increase agency use of automation to transact services, and to adopt cross-cutting electronic government initiatives.[3] More specifically, the heads of the federal government's executive departments and agencies were directed to take the following actions:[4]

- to promote access to government information organized not by agency, but by the type of service or information that people may be seeking; the data should be identified and organized in a way that makes it easier for the public to find the information it seeks;
- to make as far as possible the forms needed for the top 500 government services used by the public available online by December 2000;
- to promote the use of electronic commerce for faster, cheaper ordering for federal procurements resulting in savings to the taxpayer;
- to continue to build good privacy practices into their web-sites by posting privacy policies and by adopting and implementing information policies to protect children from viewing information unsuitable for them on web-sites which are otherwise dedicated to children;

---

3   Access America: E-Gov, 'Electronic Government', July 2000. Available at: http://www.npr.gov/initiati/it/index.html.

4   The White House, Memorandum for the heads of executive departments and agencies, 17 December 1999, Office of the Press Secretary. Available at: http://www.npr.gov/library/direct/memos/elecgovrnmnt.html

- to permit greater access to agency officials by creating a public electronic mail address through which citizens can contact the agency with questions, comments or concerns. Also, to provide access to federal web-sites for people with all kinds of disabilities;
- to conduct a 1-year study by the National Science Foundation examining the feasibility of online voting;
- in the policy area of benefits assistance, to make a broad range of benefits and services available through private and secure electronic use of the Internet;
- to develop private, secure, and effective communication across federal agencies and with the public, through the use of public key technology. In light of this goal, agencies are encouraged to issue, in coordination with the federal General Services Administration, a government-wide minimum of 100,000 digital signature certificates by December 2000; and
- for each agency to develop a strategy for upgrading its capacity for using the Internet to become more open, efficient, and responsive, and to more effectively carry out its mission. At a minimum, this strategy should involve:
  a) expanded training of federal employees;
  b) identification and adoption of'best practices' implemented by leading public and private sector organizations;
  c) recognition for federal employees who suggest new and innovative agency applications of the Internet;
  d) partnerships with the research community for experimentation with advanced applications; and
  e) mechanisms for collecting input from the agency's stakeholders regarding agency use of the Internet.

To help meet the goal of online federal service provision and transactions by 2003, the new NPR in partnership with the Council for Excellence in Government started the'E-government Initiative'. Leaders from government, business, non-profit organizations, and the research community are participating in this initiative to produce an alternative, unified vision of e-government and to discuss current challenges and barriers to accomplish this vision. So far, several principles have already been acknowledged to guide this e-government vision. These principles are for instance to be citizen driven and user-friendly (for instance: one stop access), responsive and results oriented (for instance: citizens having the opportunity to complete transactions and receive services online), universally accessible, cost effective, and to use high standards for privacy, security, and for authentication (for instance: smart cards, digital certificates).[5]

Also within the framework of the E-government Initiative, four areas were identified as critical for the implementation of e-government. First, transformation rather than just the automation of government, was perceived to be an important principle for making e-government a reality. Second, to achieve e-government both

---

5   McGinnis, P.,'E-Government Testimony', May 2000, Statement of the president and CEO of the Council For Excellence in Government before the Subcommittee on Government Management, Information, and Technology of the Committee on Government Reform US House of Representatives. Available at:
    http://www.excelgov.org/techcon/news/testimony_mcginnis.htm

public and private organizations were perceived to be needed. This brought up the question as to how these organizations could work together and what roles they respectively need to have in such an e-government. Infrastructure to ensure privacy and security for electronic government was identified as a third critical area. And finally, the area of information was identified. Here, the content, format, architecture, and accessibility of information and transactions in an e-government environment were seen as important issues. Around these four areas, working groups were organized to further develop the e-government vision and the way it could be implemented. The release of a new blueprint for e-government has been announced for late 2000, after the presidential elections.

In his first webcast to the American people 24 June 2000 address, president Clinton announced new policy initiatives '...*to give the American people the "information Age" government they deserve'.*[6] Goals of these initiatives were to cut red tape, improve the responsiveness of government towards citizens, and expand opportunities for democratic participation. For these purposes, the following three initiatives which are to be accomplished by the end of the year 2000 were presented:

- citizens will be able to search all online resources offered by the federal government from a single web-site called "firstgov.gov";
- citizens, small businesses and community groups will have 'one-stop' access to roughly US $500 billion in grants and procurement opportunities; and
- citizens, students, researchers, and government employees will be able to compete for a new US $50,000 prize for the most innovative idea for advancing e-government.

After making basic government information available on the Internet, the next step of the US federal government towards e-government will be to give citizens the opportunity to conduct all government transactions online. The objective is to offer citizens integrated services across different federal agencies so they can tailor government to their specific needs.[7] Therefore, services have been grouped on websites targeted on specific groups of customers, such as students, seniors, entrepreneurs, and workers. Projections are that by the end of 2000, approximately 40 million American citizens will do transactions with the federal government electronically.[8] Besides by then, people will have the opportunity to access federal government information to solve problems themselves through the Internet, via telephones, and through neighborhood kiosks.

However, to see how Americans perceive the federal e-government developments today, a study was conducted for the Council for Excellence in Government in August

---

5   The White House, 'President Clinton and vice president Gore: major new E-Government initiatives', 24 June 2000, Press Release. Available at:
    http://www.whitehouse.gov/wh/New/html/e-government.html

7   Access America: E-Gov, 'Electronic Government', July 2000. Available at:
    http://www.npr.gov/initiati/it/index.html.

8   Access America: E-Gov, 'Electronic Government', July 2000. Available at:
    http://www.npr.gov/initiati/it/index.html.

2000.[9] The study included three surveys of 150 government officials, 155 business and non-profit leaders, and 1003 members of the general public, respectively. The results of the study[10] showed that all groups of respondents perceived e-government to have enormous potential. According to them, e-government can improve citizen participation in government and make government more accountable to citizens. For instance, high marks were awarded to websites that allow citizens to look up voting records, comment on federal legislation, and monitor public hearings. Sixty-five per cent of the respondents however, indicated to want e-government to be developed slowly, because of their concerns about security, privacy, and the fact that many people do not have access to the Internet. Besides, 59% of the respondents perceived limits to e-government and were opposed to voting over the Internet.

3   Singapore

Although it is not well-known in the western part of the world, Singapore launched its IT2000 Master plan in 1992 even earlier than the USA. Committed to making ICT a way of life and exploiting new technological developments to the fullest, Singapore indicated that it wanted to develop into an'Intelligent Island'. Actually by means of this Master plan, and because it had a small domestic market and few technological resources of its own, Singapore tried to encourage foreign technology suppliers and lead users to transfer their technologies as well as to bring regional market business to Singapore (Wong, 1997, p.26). The IT2000 Master plan started as a broad vision for which hardly any details were worked out. At that time, the following strategic objectives for a nationwide ICT infrastructure were identified: developing a global hub, boosting the economic engine, enhancing the learning potentials of individuals, linking communities locally and globally, and improving the quality of life of Singaporeans (Wong, 1997, p.33-34). One of the elements of the IT2000 Master plan was a blueprint for the use of ICT in nearly every government department.

The Singapore national government launched in 1996 its 'Singapore ONE'-initiative, the implementation of a nation-wide high-capacity network infrastructure to which all Singaporeans are connected. The introduction of this national multimedia broadband network was acknowledged as being crucial to realize the IT2000 Master plan and, as such the essential infrastructure of the Intelligent Island. At present, for instance, the Singapore national government provides public services to its citizens through the Singapore ONE-network. Furthermore, it also uses the Internet and public kiosks for information and service provision.

With regard to the Internet however, a clear policy decision of the Singaporean Minister of Information and the Arts was needed to be able to broadly encourage Internet use and information abundance in Singapore. Although Singapore was one of

---

9   Intergovernmental technology leadership consortium, 'Public sees Internet as a Positive force in negotiating the web of government, new poll finds', 28 September, 2000, press release. Available at: http://www.excelgov.org/techcon/media/pr9_28.htm

10   Hart-Teeter, E-government: the next American revolution, September 2000, The Council for Excellence in Government. Available at:
      http://www.excelgov.org/egovpoll/report/contents.html

the first countries in Asia to adopt the Internet[11], this was initially only accessible to the Research and Development community. At the end of 1994, the Singapore government finally decided to promote the Internet more broadly and to stimulate Internet penetration into businesses and households. This delay in widespread Internet take up had to do with the promotion of a communitarian ideology by Singaporean political leaders, who unlike politicians in western social democracies, prescribe the restriction of individual freedom of expression in the public domain and control over freedom of the press (Wong, 1997, p.26). For instance, the Singapore government maintains tight control over newspaper publishing and broadcasting, and has a strict ban on pornography and satellite receiving dishes. This rigorous attitude of the Singapore government towards what they perceive as 'information pollution' has not changed in the Internet era, although the increasing difficulty of controlling information distribution through the Internet has been acknowledged. For instance, the Singapore Broadcasting Authority (Class Licence) Notification 1996 indicates the following categories of content, to which Internet providers have to block access for Singaporean citizens: general security and national defence, racial and religious harmony, public morals, and certain other content (Koops et al, 2000, p.164). In addition, cross-border Internet traffic is directed through a limited number of proxy servers, where content is filtered (Ibid.).

So far, the IT2000 Master plan has been largely implemented. For ICT-policy initiatives aimed at reforming national government departments and agencies, the Infocomm Development Authority (IDA) can be seen as the responsible government agency. General tasks of IDA are to articulate ICT-policies and standards for the Singaporean civil service, to identify appropriate ICTs for experimentation and exploitation within government, and to manage government-wide ICT-initiatives.

Among other things, IDA established a multi-layered government-wide ICT Infrastructure and made extensive use of Internet technology and applications to improve communication and transactions between the Singapore national government and its citizens. Examples of the latter are a one-stop shop Government Internet Website set up in 1995, and an eCitizen Center where people obtain 'one stop, non-stop' online services and information. In providing services and information to citizens, the eCitizen Center has adopted the metaphor of a citizen travelling through life: going through certain events and having to complete certain tasks. Services and information of various government departments have been integrated into so-called 'service packages' that connect with these life events. Easy descriptions have been chosen for these service packages to every citizen such as: 'move house', 'attend primary school', 'look for a job'. These packages are offered, as far as possible in chronological order through the stages of life of an average Singaporean.

The Singapore national government set a target in 1998, to make all key public services electronically available by the end 2001. The Electronic Transaction Act 1998 supports this goal in establishing a uniformity of rules, regulations, and standards regarding the authentification and integrity of electronic records in Singapore (for example: the use of digital signatures). Generally under Singaporean Law, electronic

---

11   The National University of Singapore was among the first in Asia to introduce WAIS and Gopher servers in 1992 and the World Wide Web in 1993 (Wong, 1997, p.45)

records and digital signatures enjoy the same status as traditional records and signatures by virtue of the principle of non-discrimination (Nicoll, 1999, p.128). Presently, about 130 public services are now being delivered electronically through the eCitizen Center. From the perspective of new ICT opportunities, it is remarkable that the Singapore national government explicitly emphasizes its 'one-stop, non-stop' electronic government service delivery as being beneficial to *all* Singaporeans, including those who live abroad.

In June 1999, the Singapore national government presented the successor of the IT2000 Master plan, the so-called 'ICT2' Master plan. A basic blueprint 'ICT21' was published to develop Singapore into a leading ICT-hub in Asia. Measures to establish this leading position were for instance the liberalization of Singapore's telecommunications market from 1 April 2000, helping Singaporeans to go online, developing ICT manpower and talent, building Singapore's ICT industry, and gearing Singapore up to be a leading e-government.

The Singapore national government presented its 'eGovernment Action Plan' on 6 June 2000, through which it wants to become '..a leading e-government to better serve the nation in the digital economy'.[12] For this purpose, the national government has allocated US $ 900 million over the next three years. According to the Singapore national government however, more important than funding for the Action Plan is the mindshift needed to push Singapore forward in the new economy. To achieve the Singapore e-government vision the following five strategic thrusts were presented in the Action Plan:[13]

- *Delivering integrated electronic services*: to establish an e-based society in the digital economy, the Singapore government wants to play a catalist role by means of developing electronic services in an integrated and customer-oriented way;
- *Using ICTs to build new capability and capacity*: government agencies have to move beyond productivity gains and create new value to customers through re-engineering traditional working processes. Consequently, civil servants will be equipped with the necessary skills, tools, systems, and infrastructure to make them effective workers in the digital economy. For instance, the Singapore Government Network (an Intranet facility) will be broadband-enabled in early 2001. A new network architecture and security framework will be implemented to allow over 30,000 civil servants to access systems and information at any time, anywhere;
- *Innovating with ICTs*: the Singapore government has to be prepared to experiment with new ICTs to learn and develop capabilities for the digital economy. According to the national government, this new economy demands a 'creative destruction' approach towards existent policy making traditions, regulation and working processes. Consequently, government agencies need to experiment with, for instance, interactive broadband multimedia to provide a superior online experience

---

12 IDA, 'Singapore gears up to be leading government to better serve the nation in the new digital economy', 6 June 2000, press release. Available through: http://www.ida.gov.sg/

13 Speech by Dr Tony Tan Keng Yam, acting Prime Minister and Minister for Defence at the eGovernment Action Plan opening ceremony of Communicasia 2000 held on Tuesday 6 June 2000 at 10.00AM at Singapore Expo, Hall 1. Available at: http://www.gov.sg/mcit/s_00_06_06.html and IDA, The Singapore e-Government Action Plan, 2000. Available through: http://www.ida.gov.sg/

in comparison with the online performance of the private sector. Also, experiments with wireless technologies are needed to be able to provide more convenient access to government services;

- *Being pro-active and responsive*: like the private sector, government agencies will need to adopt a fast 'sense and respond' approach to be able to keep up with new trends. This means that public services must be delivered at Internet speed and continuously have to be fine-tuned to respond to customer needs and feedback.'Time to market' for new public services is perceived to become an
- equally important standard as the quality of public services. ICTs will be used to enhance policy development, simplify regulations, and improve service levels;

Reinventing government in the digital economy: civil servants need to get a better understanding of the impact of ICTs on the economic and social landscape to be able to continue to make meaningful policy decisions. Therefore, civil servants will be equiped with the necessary knowledge and skills to use ICT-systems and applications effectively.

The following six strategic policy programs were identified to support the above mentioned strategic thrusts:[14]

- knowledge-based working places for civil servants: civil servants at all organization levels must be ICT-literate and exploit the power of ICT to improve working processes, public service delivery, and teamwork;
- electronic public service delivery: all public services which are suitable for electronic delivery or can be improved by means of ICT, should be re-engineered accordingly;
- ICT experimentation: the government's capability to adapt to rapidly changing ICT trends should be enhanced. Also, the probability of committing large investments in the wrong decisions should be reduced;
- operational efficiency improvement: up-to-date hardware, work engines and data processing are acknowledged to be the backbone of an efficient and effective government;
- adaptive and robust ICT Infrastructure: a well-designed, reliable, and scalable infrastructure is seen as critical for supporting e-Government initiatives and will therefore be implemented;
- ICT education: these education programs will go beyond learning about technical systems and applications and will teach civil servants how to use technology to improve working processes and public service delivery.

The Singapore national government will implement these policy programs in the next three years.

---

14 IDA, The Singapore e-Government Action Plan, 2000. Available through: http://www.ida.gov.sg/

4   Australia

Australia is one of the leading countries in the world in terms of per capita use of the Internet just behind countries like the USA and Finland. Therefore, it is not surprising that in Australia the Internet is nowadays perceived as an important means for government to transform its working processes and to improve information and service provision to its citizens. For the first time in history, the Internet enables the Australian federal government to provide the same quality of public services to Australians living in rural areas as for those living in bigger Australian cities. E-government has therefore become an important policy vision for the Australian federal government to accomplish.

The first traces of an e-government vision and related activities in Australian federal policy can be found in 1995 in a report of the Minister of Finance's IT Review group called *Clients First. The challenge for Government information technology.* This Review Group came to the conclusion that there was room for reform in how the Australian federal government used IT to develop policy and conduct its administration, identifying the greatest potential for the government in transforming the quality, range, and relevance of its service delivery to all kinds of customers. For this purpose, the Review Group's recommendations to the government were for instance to develop a service vision.'...that puts clients first', to provide a blueprint for public service delivery, and to draw IT and corporate planning processes closely together in order to enable government reform by the use of technology. Also, the Review Group recommended a more vigorous pursuit of the benefits of cross-agency uses of IT to establish greater efficiency in government activities and better service delivery to customers.[15]

Within the Australian federal Department of Communications, IT and the Arts a special Office for Government Online (OGO) was created to deal with all kinds of questions regarding the development of e-government at the Australian federal level. Recently, OGO became part of the National Office for the Information Economy, an executive agency within the Department of Communications, IT and the Arts. This new executive agency has been given direct responsibility for the development and coordination of advice to the Australian federal government on information economy issues (including issues related to technology and industry convergence and the regulatory and physical infrastructure needed for online services and e-commerce), the application of new ICTs to government administration, information and service provision, the assistance to business and government agencies to deliver services online, the consistency of the government's position relating to information economy issues in relevant international forums, and the promotion (both nationwide and internationally) of the benefits of and Australia's position in the information economy.[16]

The Australian Prime Minister emphasized in 1997 the importance of the information age for his country in a policy statement In 1997 In 1997 'Investing for Growth'. He presented the various ways in which the Australian federal government

---

15 Department of Finance and Administration, Clients First. The challenge for Government IT, 1 March 1995, Report of Minister of Finance's IT Review Group. Available at: http://www.dofa.gov.au/pubs/itrg/itrg-tc.html

16 Http://www.govonline.gov.au/

was supporting the uptake of ICT-developments. An important role of the Australian federal government in this respect how well the federal government itself could make the online transition. This was acknowledged to have a strong demonstration effect to other parties in Australian society. This is why the federal government committed itself and showed leadership by adopting new ICTs and improving service delivery and business practices. More specifically, the following commitments were made in this policy statement:[17]

- to have all appropriate federal government services available online by 2001, complementing - not replacing- existing written, telephone, fax, and counter services;
- to establish a Government Information Center through the Office for Government Online as a main point of access to information about government services;
- to establish electronic payment as the normal means for federal payments by 2000; and
- to establish a government-wide Intranet for secure online communication.

The Australian federal government further emphasized in 1998, the importance of its leadership role in adopting new ICTs. In the policy statement *A Strategic Framework for the Information Economy* ten national priority areas were identified to make Australia a leading player in the global information economy. One of these key strategic priorities was to implement a '...world class model for the delivery of all appropriate government services online'.

For the (further) development of online service provision, the Australian federal government has recognized the major importance of resolving security issues. For this reason, OGO developed the 'Gatekeeper'-framework for the federal government, which addresses the needs of government agencies for public key technology to support authentication and identification in government online transactions. OGO's ambition has been to establish a government-wide framework to provide interoperability, integrity, authenticity, and trust for both government agencies and their customers. All federal government agencies are expected to use the gatekeeper framework by 2001.

To manage the Gatekeeper Government Public Key Infrastructure (GPKI) and supervise the accreditation of certification authority service providers and their public key technology products, the Australian federal government created a Government Public Key Authority (GPKA). This Authority determined the following criteria for allowing the supply of public key technology products: compliance with the federal government's procurement policy, security policy and planning, physical security, technology evaluation, certification authority policy and administration, personnel vetting, legal issues, and privacy considerations.[18] In September 2000, 15 organizations applied for Gatekeeper accreditation, with one company fully accredited and two with entry-level accreditation.

---

17 Department of Communications, IT and the Arts, Government Online. The Commonwealth Government's Strategy, April 2000. Available at: http://www.govonline.gov.au/projects/strategy/GovOnlineStrategy.html

18 Office for Government Online, Commonwealth Government Online - progress report, December 1999, Department of Communications, IT and the Arts. Available at: http://www.govonline.gov.au/projects/strategy/ProgressReport1999.html

The first large-scale introduction in Australia of digital certificates was carried out in June 2000 under the Gatekeeper framework. As a result of a taxation reform in Australia, a special Australian Business Number was introduced for Australian companies. The Australian federal government developed a common digital signature certificate to be linked to this Australian Business Number. This enables businesses to deal with the Australian federal government in a secure and authenticated online environment.

Agreement to common standards has been acknowledged as another key development towards online integrated public services. An important project in this respect has been the development of the Australian Government Locator Service (AGLS) metadata standard. This standard makes it possible for government agencies to describe and label public information and services in a standard way and will therefore assist customers to easily find government information across government agencies. Another key enabler for customers to quickly find government information and services at one online public service counter, has been the implementation of a cross-jurisdictional Government Electronic Resources Network (GOVERNET). This network has been established under the auspices of the Australian Online Council, a council composed of all federal, state, and territory ministers with responsibility for online issues.

To be able to establish electronic payment as the normal means for federal payment by 2000, the federal government introduced its 'e-Procurement Strategy'. This strategy consists of a framework of e-commerce standards for procurement and a series of projects and activities to implement electronic procurement. Aims are to have 90% of all government departments and agencies to electronically undertake 'simple procurement transactions' by the end of 2001 and to pay all suppliers electronically by the end of 2000. The idea behind this strategy is to, as a government, 'lead by example' in the field of e-commerce. Expectations are that this strategy will have significant influence on the economy-wide development of e-commerce in Australia.

The Australian federal government passed the Electronic Transactions Act in November 1999. This Act gives government agencies the opportunity to accept online communications as written communications for most purposes.[19] Although this Act will formally be effective from July 2001, special clauses have been provided for to make it possible for some agencies to take immediate advantage from enactment.

To fulfil the government's commitment to have all appropriate government services available online by 2001, the Australian federal government presented its 'Government Online'-strategy in April 2000. The aim of this strategy for the federal government is to become more accessible, flexible, and responsive to every Australian citizen:'..people don't want, or need, to know how government is structured. They want to access the services they need, easily and safely'.[20] At the same time, the Australian federal government perceived new opportunities through ICT to provide a direct channel between government and the citizen. Australian citizens could get a greater

---

19 Office for Government Online, Commonwealth Government Online - progress report, December 1999, Department of Communications, IT and the Arts. Available at: http://www.govonline.gov.au/projects/strategy/ProgressReport1999.html

20 Department of Communications, IT and the Arts, 'Government Online - A Strategy for the Future', 6 April 2000, Media Release. Available through: http://www.dcita.gov.au/

familiarity with government policy and programs through their ability to customise their online channel with government. To emphasize the aim of the GovernmentOnline strategy, the strategy itself was constructed online and in an interactive way with the Australian public. Also after publication of the strategy on 6 April 2000, an electronic feedback service was offered at the government online website.

The GovernmentOnline strategy of the Australian federal government consisted of the following elements:[21]

- improving public access to a wide range of government services, especially by people who live in regional, rural and remote areas or older Australians and people with disabilities. Here, the ambition is to break down the barriers of distance or mobility that some Australian citizens face;
- providing access 24 hours a day, seven days a week;
- reducing the cost of delivery of some government services;
- increasing efficiency-saving tax payers' funds;
- reducing bureaucratic and jurisdictional demarcation to provide unified services based on user requirements. Australian citizens no longer will need to understand the structure of and distinctions within the Australian government as a whole. Also, multiple approaches to accessing information and services will be designed for different categories of users; and
- encouraging growth of e-business (both business to business and business to government), and associated opportunities.

To meet the objective of providing access to government information services without the need to understand structures within government, a single entry point for the Australian federal government (the 'Australia Entry Point' at www.fed.gov.au) has been developed and managed by the 'Australian Department of Finance and Administration'.

To further understand the use of the Internet in public service delivery, the Australian federal government adopted an agency-based approach to best suit the needs of that agency's clients and explore the possibilities for quality service provision. Accordingly, each government agency had to develop and publish an Online Action Plan by September 2000. This Online Action Plan had to be based on a comprehensive audit of the agency's information, transactions, purchasing and other external arrangements; it had to be related to the agency's customer service charter and had to identify all functions which potentially can be made available online; it had to identify services which can be coordinated with services of other agencies; it had to identify an indicative time frame for implementing the Online Action Plan; and finally it had to indicate the barriers which need to be removed to achieve the 2001 target to have all appropriate services available online.[22] Also, a government agency was obliged to address a number of specific issues in the Online Action Plan, such as legislative issues, costs and benefits of Internet service delivery, and risk control strategies for electronic service provision.

---

21 Ibid.
22 Department of Communications, IT and the Arts, Government Online. The Commonwealth Government's Strategy, April 2000. Available at:
    http://www.govonline.gov.au/projects/strategy/GovOnlineStrategy.html

As in Australia all federal information principles are equally applicable to the online environment as to traditional forms of information provision, the federal government announced to implement Online Information Service Obligations (OISO) for agencies in a staged manner. These OISOs need to ensure the online availability of a minimum, common set of information about agencies and their services and of any information released to the public in printed form. By December 2000 for instance, all forms for public use must be available online, to be downloaded and/or electronically completed. Wherever possible the Australian federal government intends to apply the principle of storing information once but linking to this information from multiple sites. Besides, the federal government requires agencies to comply their online activities with the Australian Privacy Act 1988 from 1 June 2000. To assist agencies in this process, the Australian Privacy Commissioner published special guidelines covering issues like openness, collection of personal information, security of personal information, and publishing personal information.

To be able to monitor agencies' progress towards the 2001 target, all government agencies have to report twice a year to OGO. On the basis of this reporting OGO will also monitor on progress of cross-agency and/or jurisdiction integrated service provision. Besides, in partnership with agencies, OGO is in the position to identify areas of potential cross-agency collaboration. The reporting process will enable agencies to benchmark their online activities and to identify best practices.

Results of the first round of reporting in July 2000 show that 91% of agencies are expecting to meet the 2001 target. At that time, already 526 of the 714 identified services were provided online.[23] Other key findings in this first round of reporting were the following:[24]

- 90% of agencies have a website and offer information and services to customers;
- 85% of agencies will have an Online Action Plan by the end of September 2000;
- 96% of agencies pay a portion of their suppliers electronically; and
- 79% of agencies expect to implement authentication and/or encryption technologies by the end of 2002.

5   Comparing E-government Developments Across the World: Towards a Single Model of E-government?

Looking at e-government developments in the three countries, we can see a number of similarities between the national policy programs. For instance, the principle not to automate traditional working processes in government, but to fundamentally rethink the way government could work, seem to be an important guide in designing e-government in the three countries. In the USA, Australia, as well as in Singapore, the e-government of the future first of all seems to be a government which puts customers first. Better access to government information and services for all citizens equally (including those who are disabled, who live in rural areas or even abroad), can be seen as the main

---

23 The Office for Government Online, GovernmentOnline. Round One Survey Results. Executive Summary, September 2000. Available at:

http://www.ogo.gov.au/publications/GovernmentOnlineRoundOneSurveyResults.htm

24 Ibid.

motive for the implementation of e-government in the three countries. So far, 'one stop, non-stop' access to government has been a major, general remedy to accomplish this goal. People in these three countries no longer need to know how government is structured to be able to find government information or apply for public services. Additionally, all three countries set targets to have full key public services electronically available in the next couple of years.

In addition, the e-government of the future in all three countries is being designed to be cost efficient and to use high standards for security and authentication. Technical standardization together with the development of common standards are important means to accomplish these shared objectives. In all three countries, public key technology (for example: digital signatures) is used or will be used in the short term to establish secure and effective communication with or within government.

However, all three countries acknowledge that the future design of the new e-government is still vague. Governments, but also other parties in society, are perceived to need to broadly experiment with new ICTs to learn and develop capabilities for the innovation of government activities. With that, a 'creative destruction' approach toward current policy making traditions, regulation, and working processes is observed to be required. Besides, as the Australian federal government shows, the national government may choose to provide a leadership role in the online transition of actitivities in its society, with the aim to stimulate public awareness of new opportunities through ICT.

The vague borders of a potential future e-government design are further unclear at the present because of specific cultural barriers within the countries under study. The restricted authoritative powers of the American federal government resulting in a limited policy implementation of e-government together with indispensable partners, and the strong censorship of the Singapore national government toward 'information pollution' leading towards restricted online information and service provision, are both good examples of the culturally dependent developments of e-government in each country. But also the resistance of American citizens against online voting opportunities can be seen as an example here. Besides, differences in national government traditions with regard to the reporting of effects of policy programs may further muddy the view on potential characteristics of an e-government model on the short term.

Therefore, we may conclude for the moment that although a number of similarities undeniably exist between e-government developments in the three countries under study, it still seems to be too early to acknowledge the presence of a single, worldwide model of e-government. However, if we take into account the speed of Internet developments, we need not be surprised to find such an e-government model sooner than expected.

References

Koops, B.J., J.E.J. Prins and H. Hijmans (eds.), *ICT Law and Internationalisation*, 2000, Kluwer Law International, The Hague

Lips, A.M.B., and P.H.A. Frissen, *Wiring Government*. Integrated public service delivery through ICT, 1997, ITeR-series No.8, Samsom Bedrijfsinformatie, Alphen aan den Rijn.

Nicoll, C.C., 'Singapore: The Intelligent Island', in: *The EDI Law Review*, 1999, Vol.6, Nos 2-3, pp.123-141, Kluwer Law International, The Netherlands.

Wong, Poh-Kam, Implementing the NII Vision: Singapore's Experience and Future Challenges, in: B. Kahin and E.J. Wilson III (eds.), *National Information Infrastructure Initiatives. Vision and Policy Design*, 1997, The MIT Press, Cambridge, Massachusetts.

Chapter 7

Electronic Government. From an Organization Based Perspective Towards a Client Oriented Approach

Koen Zweers and Kees Planqué

1   Introduction

As has been mentioned in previous chapters of this book, the United States was the first country to introduce a national information and communication technology policy aimed at e-government. In 1993, the federal government set ambitious goals to provide electronic access to all government information enabling the public to perform all major transactions online. In order to determine the extent of the accomplishment of these goals, there are some questions which should be answered. These are:
Which goals are pursued when implementing e-government?
How well do governmental agencies adapt to e-government?
What infrastructure requirements are necessary for e-government?
Which information and communication technologies does e-government require?[1]

Analyzing the US situation in light of these questions, can provide valuable insights into national and international governmental initiatives because of the major advances which have been made and it also provides the opportunity to learn about the practices there. This chapter aims at gaining these insights. In order to give an accurate summary of the current situation in the US, different government levels will be addressed separately. The federal level on policy and legislation will be addressed first. In continuation an analysis of state web sites will be discussed. Thirdly, several case studies on all government levels will be discussed. Developments in the private sector will be discussed in Section 4. The last subject concerns Internet usage in the US.

---

1   Introduction to Electronic Commerce. Available at:
     http://wwwhome.cs.utwente.nl/~grefen/Teaching/ec/Lecture1b.pdf

J. E. J. Prins (ed.), Designing E-Government, 91–120.
© 2001 *Kluwer Law International. Printed in the Netherlands.*

2   Electronic Government Defined

E-government definitions are scarce in contrast to those defining e-commerce. E-government is often thought to be synonymous to the provision of government services to citizens through electronic means. A comprehensive definition has nevertheless been found:

Electronic government = electronic commerce + customer relationship management + supply chain management + knowledge management + business intelligence + collabora-ive technologies (Baltius, 1999).

This definition shows that e-government is more than just providing electronic services to citizens. E-commerce is part of this definition. More specifically:
- Business-to-Government e-commerce: the government acting as a customer in electronic purchasing processes;
- Government-to-Consumer e-commerce: electronic services to citizens;
- Government-to-Government e-commerce: internal electronic services.

Customer Relationship Management (CRM) is part of the definition too. CRM comprises the systems, methods, software products and Internet technologies, which can help an organization to do business with its clients in a structured way. Supply Chain Management concerns the integration of all processes in the production chain, starting with the supplier and ending with the client. Integration is an important aspect when implementing electronic services. Knowledge Management is defined as using existing knowledge to create new knowledge and transferring this in a meaningful way[2]. Understanding one's business is decisive to accomplish the right service levels. Finally, collaborative technologies are part of e-government.

Using the mentioned concepts as a foundation, the following more specific definition can be derived:

Electronic government concerns providing or attainment of information, services or products through electronic means, by and from governmental agencies, at any given moment and place, offering an extra value for all participating parties.

Digital Democracy is not part of this definition. This is considered a possible consequence of current and future Internet developments. However, it does not fit in with the description of the current state of e-government.

---

2   What is Knowledge Management? Available at:
       http:///www.sveiby.com.au/KnowledgeManagement.html

3 The Federal Government. Policy and Initiatives

President Clinton describes the role of government in the information age as follows:
"*I believe in the information age the role of the government is to empower people with the tools to make the most of their lives, to tear down the barriers of that objective, and to create conditions within which we can go forward together.*"

The US federal government clearly intends to act as an initiator, coordinator and leader in integrating information technology within governmental agencies, in the interest of citizens. The National Performance Review report (1993) is a first elaboration of this role[3]. This report extensively discusses the supporting mechanisms for e-government. The Access America report (1997) sketches the outlines for an e-government, focusing on providing services to citizens, on partnerships between governmental agencies and on the use of technology to integrate information of various agencies [4]. Recent memorandums further specify the role the government wants to play now and in the near future. These will be addressed in the following pages.

3.1 Federal Government

a. Electronic government
In the memorandum "Electronic government" dated December 17, 1999, President Clinton expressed his concern about the organization of the online information of the federal government. Most federal services can only be performed through non-electronic forms. Processing can take several weeks. Few government initiatives have been undertaken to structure government information category-wise instead of agency-wise. Efforts to create one-stop-shopping access to information on agency web sites have been unsuccessful as a result. Citizens are obliged to determine which agency provides a service, before being able to use this service.

To help citizens gain one-stop access to existing government information and services, and to provide better and more efficient government services and increased government accountability to citizens, President Clinton directed the officials of governmental agencies, to take the following actions:
- Agencies that support the shift towards an electronic government, should support access to government information in a question-oriented manner;
- Governmental agencies shall make available online, by December 2000, the forms needed for the top 500 government services used by the public;
- The heads of agencies shall promote the use of electronic commerce, where appropriate, for faster, cheaper ordering on federal procurements;

---

3 From Red Tape to Results - Creating a Government that Works Better & Costs Less.
   http://www.usgs.gov/public/npr/nptoc.html
4 http://www.accessamerica.gov/docs/access.html

- Agencies shall continue to build good privacy practices into their web sites by posting privacy policies in so-called privacy statements;
- Each agency shall create a central e-mail address through which citizens can contact the agency with questions, comments, or concerns;
- The feasibility of online voting shall be examined in a one-year study;
- Agencies that provide benefit assistance to citizens shall make a broad range of benefits and services available through private and secure electronic use of the Internet;
- IT-related agencies and organizations shall assist agencies in the development of private, secure, and effective communication across agencies and with the public;
- The heads of agencies shall develop a strategy for upgrading their respective agency's capacity for using the Internet to become more open, efficient and responsive. At a minimum, this strategy should involve:
  - Expanded training of federal employees;
  - Identification and adoption of "best practices" implemented by leading public and private sector organizations;
  - Recognition for employees who suggest new and innovative agency applications of the Internet;
  - Partnerships with the research community for experimentation with advanced applications;
  - Implementing mechanisms for collecting input from the agency's stakeholders regarding agency use of the Internet.

b. Use of information technology to improve society

The Clinton administration has taken specific initiatives to improve society using information technology. On December 17 1999, President Clinton issued the memorandum "Use of Information Technology to Improve our Society". In this memorandum the following guidelines are issued to government officials:

- Adopt policies that will remove barriers to private sector investment in Internet applications;
- Explore partnerships with companies, state, and local governments, and other entities, such as nonprofit organizations and universities;
- Explore innovative mechanisms for fostering a national discussion on the potential of the electronic society;
- Consider other policies to promote the electronic society, such as the establishment of national goals.

These measures should make sure that new technological developments are used to create an e-government, in which everybody can participate.

c. Closing the digital divide

The Office of the Press Secretary of the White House defines the digital divide as follows:

"The digital divide is the gap separating individuals and communities with access to Internet applications and those without."

The inequality in access is correlated to disparities in income, education level, age, family situation, geographic area and ethnic origin. Nowadays, the digital divide is seen as a major problem, especially since it grew in the past years. President Clinton has therefore unveiled a program to bridge the digital divide and create a new opportunity for all Americans. Access to computers and Internet should be as universal as the telephone is today. To accomplish this objective, three main goals are set:

1   Broaden access to technologies such as computers, Internet and high-speed networks;
2   Provide people with skilled teachers and the training they need to master the information economy;
3   Promote online content and applications that will help empower the people to use new technologies to their fullest potential.

The following specific proposals have been announced to accomplish these goals:
- $ 2 billion in tax incentives over the next ten years to encourage private sector donation of computers, sponsorship of community technology centers and technology training for workers;
- $ 150 million to help train all new teachers entering the workforce to use technology effectively;
- $ 100 million to create 1,000 Community Technology Centers in low-income urban and rural neighborhoods;
- $ 50 million for a public/private partnership to expand home access to computers and the Internet for low-income families;
- $ 45 million to promote innovative applications of information and communication technology for under-served communities;
- $ 25 million to accelerate private sector deployment of broadband networks in under-served areas;
- $ 10 million to prepare the Native Americans for careers in information technology and other technical fields.

By means of these actions, the Clinton administration wants to transform the digital divide into a digital opportunity: improved possibilities for participation in America's economic, political and social life through an effective use of technology. The federal government's policy concerning a number of the mentioned actions and initiatives taken to accomplish the proposed goals are discussed in the following section.

3.2   National Partnership for Reinventing Government (NPR)

NPR is a federal activity aimed at increasing efficiency and restoring the trust of the American people in government. The program has been developed in 1993 on initiative of President Clinton and Vice-President Gore. NPR's mission is to make the government more efficient: "doing more with less". A number of strategies has therefore been contrived.

Developing and implementing e-government initiatives is part of this. The aim is to provide Internet based government services, covering subjects that are of interest to the public, at any given place or time. Conditions are:

• Presenting information in a well-organized and user-friendly way;
• Providing online services and transaction performing possibilities.

The 1997 Access America report outlines the e-government. One of the first aims is to create a number of question-oriented public counters. These counters will be focused on separate audiences, for example students, workers, seniors, and businesses. The scope of the developed counters varies from a portal site linking to existing information to a site containing new information, applications and transaction performing possibilities. An example of an integrated counter is Students.gov, aimed at the needs of students. Students.gov will be discussed in the "Case Studies" paragraph.

Providing a citizen-centric service shall be achieved by offering Internet-based services in agencies with a high degree of client interaction. Some initiatives have already been taken. A non-exhaustive list:

• "America's Job Bank", developed by the Department of Labor, provides persons seeking employment with a job database. Employers can place openings and search a nation-wide database with tens of thousands of resumes[5];

• The *"International Trade Administration"* of the Department of Commerce provides information on international markets and treaties through the Internet. It also provides the opportunity to file complaints about unfair competition and violation of treaties online [6];

• The US Customs Service has implemented the *"Automated Commercial System"* as an aid to track, check and process all commercial goods imported into the United States[7];

• The Department of Defense (DoD) has created the *"DoDBusOpps.com"* web site. Through this portal site sellers are able to do business with DoD accessing several services and agencies, which can all be reached at one central point. The response time has decreased; the negotiating process has been streamlined and less paper is spilt. All this leads to significant cost savings[8];

• The *"United States Postal Service"* has developed the *"StampsOn-line"*, *"Postmark America"* and *"SuppliesOn-line"* virtual stores to give customers the opportunity to order mail products online[9];

• *"Recreation.gov"* is a web site aimed at providing information about all federal recreation areas in a quick and simple manner. Through this site recreation areas can

---

5   http://www.ajb.dni.us/
6   http://www.ita.doc.gov/
7   Automated Commercial System. Available at: http://www.customs.gov/imp-exp2/auto-sys/acs_ci.htm
8   http://dodbusopps.com/
9   http://new.usps.com/cgi-bin/uspsbv/scripts/front.jsp

be searched by state, activity, agency or map. The site also provides the opportunity to reserve camping spots in national parks[10];

The NPR pays much attention to the *"Smart Community"* concept. A Smart Community (SC) is a community in which information and services are made available and accessible by means of well-directed application of (information) technology. *"Smart"* means: "Services through Multiple Accessible Responsive Transformative communities":
- Services should be accessible for everybody;
- Technologies and applications must be used to help satisfy community needs;
- Transformation is the objective of a SC – a community that uses powerful technology to realize positive change.

A SC spans a limited geographic area. The SC concept is important, because most interactions between citizens and the government take place at the state and local levels. Citizens desire universal access to information, wherever this information is coming from (which level or sector), during these interactions. A SC can also help bridge the digital divide, because all citizens are given equal access opportunities. An example of a SC is the *"Public Access Network in Seattle"*, Washington.

The Public Access Network - Seattle, Washington
Seattle's *"Public Access Network"* (PAN) consists of a web site and e-mail list server allowing Seattle citizens to communicate with City officials and obtain City information and services electronically. The primary purpose of PAN is to serve as an electronic City Hall. In addition, PAN hosts other content, particularly useful to Seattle citizens, communities, visitors, and businesses alike. PAN hosts the following "Smart services":
- *"Keeping the Streets Lit at Night"*: on-line forms to report broken streetlights;
- *"Tracking Building and Construction Permits"*: the status of a permit application can be checked online, without mediation of government employees;
- *"City Directory On-line"*: to increase the involvement of citizens in government and policy making, government employees engaged in citizen-relevant cases can be reached electronically. In April 2000 twenty percent of the citizen-government communication took place by way of e-mail.

PAN uses questionnaires and recommendations from a committee appointed by the mayor and city council to improve its services[11].
    In the year 2000 government budget, a substantial amount of money has been set aside for creating Community Technology Centers (CTC) in rural and urban areas with low average incomes. This initiative aims at giving Internet and 'information age' access to communities, which cannot afford computers [12].

---

10 http://www.recreation.gov/
11 http://www.cityofseattle.net/html/pan.htm
12 http://www.ctcnet.org/

3.3   Government Coordination of E-government Initiatives

The coordinating role of the government comes to the foreground in the establishment of the Government Information Technologies Services Board (GITS Board) and the CIO-Council. Vice-President Gore established the GITS Board in 1993. De GITS Board workgroup coordinates efforts to apply information technology within government agencies and has been given the task to implement information technology initiatives, described in the National Performance Review report. In short, the role of the GITS Board is to speed up the development and implementation of e-government [13].

The Chief Information Officers (CIO) Council leads and directs the strategic management of federal information technology resources and serves as a focal point for coordinating challenges that cross agency boundaries. The Council also partners with other councils to address management challenges that require multidisciplinary solutions. In addition, the council wants to establish an image as the leader in the information technological community within the federal government. In general, it wants to improve the outcomes of information technology.

The CIO-council is responsible for developing, maintaining and providing the conditions for implementation of reliable and integrated information technology architectures. The principal roles of the council are:

1   Developing recommendations for information technology management policies, procedures, and standards;
2   Identifying opportunities to share information resources (interoperability);
3   Assessing and addressing the needs of the federal government's information technology workforce[14].

The council has issued a list of committee objectives:
*   Lead the establishment of integrated, government wide information technology guidelines, best practices, tools, training, and proposed policies in areas of privacy, critical infrastructure, and security;
*   Promote the effective implementation of IT management and its integration and alignment with agencies' missions and processes;
*   Facilitate the government information technology infrastructure;
*   Support collaboration and resource sharing (improving interoperability);
*   Develop government wide architecture and technology strategy;
*   Develop and implement strategies for recruitment, retention, and development of information technology professionals and to upgrade skills of current workforce;
*   Create high-leverage partnerships with international, federal, state, and private sector information technology leadership groups.

---

13 http://www.gits.gov/
14 http://www.cio.gov/

A high-priority initiative in the field of interoperability and emerging information technology is the support for a common physical and web accessibility solution, using a Public Key Infrastructure smart card. The council will particularly direct its attention at the infrastructure component of the project[15].

3.4 Private Sector Partnerships

Private sector partnerships were rare in the past. The lead of the private sector considered, giving serious thought to such partnerships is useful. By mobilizing public and private stakeholders to take initiatives, more extensive and advanced solutions can be implemented and systems compatibility is fostered.

An example is the partnership between the United States Postal Service (USPS) and IBM on the implementation of a Point-of-Service solution. IBM provides the technical knowledge and educates USPS instructors, who subsequently educate their own employees. USPS also works together with Microsoft to make 170 of its existing applications Windows compatible.

a. Shift from an organization-oriented to a question-oriented approach
Explaining why the organization-oriented government model is still the most popular one is simple. Budget allocation takes place on an agency basis. Within Congress, committees also direct their attention at individual agencies. The government as a whole is organized around in principle independent agencies. Four interrelated problems delay the development of an e-government:

1   Congress lacks resources to create a government wide perspective. As a result of this, interagency initiatives often do not come to anything;
2   Government employees see the world through 'agency-glasses'. This makes it difficult for them to create question-oriented e-government solutions;
3   At present, each government agency has an individual information technology plan, which in most cases has been drafted without paying attention to interagency applications;
4   There is a lack of competition, in contrast with the private sector. This makes the need for change less evident.

The shift to a question-oriented organization of government services has to be imposed from above. The political support for e-government initiatives is particularly absent within congressional committees. The administration has set progressive goals and has started projects, among which those mentioned in the NPR program. Despite Vice-President Gore's mandate the NPR has not always been given the support needed to achieve the desired results. According to the Progressive Policy Institute[16] the Office for Management and

---

15 http://www.cio.gov/files/stratplan2000.pdf
16 http://ww.ndol.org

Budget, responsible for allocating budgets, has not been an advocate of e-government, resulting in limited resources for significant e-government implementations within agencies.

b. Use of information technology to improve social quality

Restoring trust of citizens in government is a main objective of e-government, along with effectiveness and efficiency of services. To achieve this, e-government has to offer the customer an added value over conventional government services. Values of importance are the protection of privacy, safety and equality.

The government wants to catch up with the private sector, by entering into (already mentioned) partnerships. In this field the government deviates from the leading and initiating role. This development is currently visible in distance learning and telemedicine: using information and communication technology to provide health care when physician and patient are geographically separated.

c. Customer protection

Customer privacy has not always been a spearhead of government policy. An example is selling a database with driver license data to a third party. The Supreme Court has ruled this to be illegal. President Clinton has recently issued a memorandum that directs agencies to exercise good privacy measures on their web sites, by enclosing a privacy statement. Without a healthy privacy policy the trust of citizens in government will decrease instead of increase.

The federal government has an important role to fulfill in the field of safety. It has to provide safety systems that protect the integrity of information from hackers and other threats from the outside.

d. Use of information technology for strategic innovation

E-government is often seen as a means to automate routine tasks. Its potential is much bigger. It can be used to simplify government processes, stimulate internal change, and reorganize the government.

Strategic innovation can be accomplished by separating service providing from the structure of the providing organization. This separation between front office and back office is necessary to automate in a client-centric way. At the front office side the client has a central position, while on the back office side an as efficient as possible organization structure is the focal point. This approach is used in the state of Massachusetts, where integrated and consistent services are replacing the organization-oriented approaches. More information can be found in the paragraph *"Case Studies"*.

e. The government purchasing process

The 'Electronic Commerce for Buyers and Sellers' e-commerce strategy plan dated March 1998[17] argues for exploring the application of commercial e-commerce technologies to

---

17 Electronic Commerce for Buyers and Sellers available at:
    http://policyworks.gov/org/main/me/epic/ecplan.pdf

improve the federal purchasing process and payment operations. The ultimate goal is that all federal agencies will support their programs by making available customer-friendly electronic purchasing tools integrated with end-to-end commercial electronic processing of payment, accounting and performance reporting information[18]. To accomplish this goal, a series of actions has been defined:

1 Managing the transition from paper-based to electronic processes by fostering partnerships with affected stakeholders within government and with industry;
2 Reengineering and integrating buying with end-to-end ordering and payment processing for low priced, high volume buying activities;
3 Reengineering additional buying and paying functions as promising technologies emerge.

Government agencies made 28 million purchases in 1998. About 98 percent of these transactions was valued at $25,000 or less. Applying electronic purchasing processes can therefore lead to substantial cost savings. The Department of the Interior has already realized cost savings of $ 120 per purchase. The Office of Management and Budget states that these savings primarily concern high-volume (and in general low-value) transactions.

The Administration has stimulated the use of purchase cards in streamlining the purchasing process since 1993, the year the NPR was established. Purchase cards are easy to use and suitable for end-to-end electronic processing. They are well suited to purchasing from electronic catalogs. Purchase card usage in the government is expected to increase to $18 billion in 2000, contrasting $ 0.5 billion in 1993. Purchase cards are more than upgraded credit cards and have evolved into multifunctional smart cards.

Apart from transactions between the private sector and government, internal government transactions are an important subject for electronic initiatives. The Electronic Privacy Information Center[19] has established the Intra-Governmental Transfer System, to facilitate the processing of payment transactions between federal agencies. A team of financial and purchasing experts has been composed, supplemented by bank representatives to implement this system. Research of an inter-organizational task force showed that an adapted version of a commercial purchase card suited most internal government transactions. After analyzing the functional requirements and services the banks were able to provide, it became evident that an adapted version of the commercial purchase card was difficult to implement and financially not feasible. On account of this the decision was taken to implement a conventional credit card mechanism.

Using the Internet to acquire government contracts resulted in the emergence of electronic catalogs, which buyers can browse using their www-browsers. Electronic catalogs realize substantial time and cost savings, improved accessibility and an increased flexibility.

---

18 Electronic Purchasing and Payment in Federal Government available at:
   http://policyworks.gov/org/main/me/epic/ecreport.pdf
19 http://www.epic.org/

The General Services Administration (GSA) provides federal staff supporting services, products and solutions. It has developed an electronic catalog, through which buyers can place orders, using their smart cards [20]. To improve accessibility and user friendliness of the catalog, GSA has taken the following actions (among others):

- Ease the burden on sellers, by copying information from sellers' web sites and making it available and accessible on GSA servers;
- Online interactive help function, for example for order status information via e-mail or telephone;
- A back-up server to guarantee 24/7 availability;
- Improved interfaces to purchasing and payment systems of government agencies.

Creating a central index is another initiative necessary to guarantee fast and simple access to existing catalogs for inter-organizational use. An example is the NASA Consolidated Contract Initiative (CCI), a web site presenting current NASA contracts and other governmental contracts that may be of use for NASA[21] [21]. The CCI made it possible to make us of existing contracts, saving the time usually needed for the acquisition process. Attunement between government agencies has been made easier and double contracts occur less frequently.

Ten agencies, including GSA, NASA, and DoD, working with an industrial partner, undertook a pilot in 1998 to create a search environment and demonstrate that buyers could search across multiple existing electronic catalogs for items and obtain consistent results, without having to perform a search in the different catalogs and manually compare the answers. Agencies worked with vendors to standardize the content and structure of information concerning a select group of items. The eXtensible Markup Language (XML) was used to organize and tag the information. The pilot demonstrated the ability to successfully search across multiple seller databases based on one set of parameters. For buyers, the results point to greater potential efficiency in conducting market research. Vendors do not need to present their wares to each customer in a unique way anymore and can reach out to new markets instead.

f. eXtensible Markup Language (XML)
XML is a language for documents that contain structured information. Structured information contains the content as well as an indication of the role of that content. XML offers a way to label information. Users have the possibility to search different web-based information sources and to obtain consistent search results, because XML puts structural relations between the labels[22].

---

20 GSA Advantage. Available at https://www.gsaadvantage.gov/cgi-bin/advwel
21 NASA Consolidated Contracting Initiative. Available at
    http://ec.msfc.nasa.gov/hq/cci/first.html
22 XML in 10 points. Available at http://www.w3org/XML/1999/XML-in-10-points

g. Infrastructure improvement

An expansion of the infrastructure is deemed necessary to be able to give all Americans access to government information and to provide them with the opportunity to perform all major transactions online in 2003.

Broadband Internet access is more and more seen as a necessary condition for future participation in the economy. Broadband access in rural areas remains behind by that in urban areas. Underlying reasons are:

- The costs for connection in rural areas are an obstacle to implementation;
- The costs for services to customers increase accordingly as distances between customers are bigger;
- Competition that stimulates installation of broadband services in urban areas is absent in rural areas;
- Most common broadband technologies are only feasible in urban areas.

The Digital Subscriber Line and Cable Modem are two emerging broadband technologies. President Clinton emphasizes that private sector initiatives for broadband Internet access in rural areas are necessary. MCI-WorldCom, Qualcomm Inc., Bellsouth, Sprint en GTE have already taken initiatives.

4   The Federal Government: Legislation

The leading and initiating role the government has adopted, is reflected in legislation in the past few years. Two laws will be mentioned here.

4.1   Paperwork Reduction Act

President Clinton signed the (adapted) Paperwork Reduction Act into law on May 22, 1995. The objective of the law is as follows: 'To further the goals of the Paperwork Reduction Act to have federal agencies become more responsible and publicly accountable for reducing the burden of federal paperwork on the public, and for other purposes."

One clause in the law lays down the responsibility of a government agency to spread information. An agency must make sure that every citizen has access to public information. To prevent people from gaining access to such information is deemed illegal. The law demands that an agency that provides electronic information also makes accessible the underlying data. Citizens are therefore entitled to access data, which they provided themselves, and which is not publicly accessible. Finally, the law requires an agency to adequately mention the start, change, or stop of significant information services. Significant means that the supply, change or stop of information services is of importance to citizens and/or private sector.

In short, this law demands efforts from government agencies to publish information (online), whilst putting the interests of citizens in first place.

4.2   Electronic Freedom of Information Act

The Electronic Freedom of Information Act (EFOIA) aims at free electronic availability of information. An agency should respond to a request for information within twenty days, unless special circumstances apply. Much requested information should be made accessible directly through electronic means.

The EFOIA stimulates the development of e-government initiatives and puts demands on electronic service providing. Customers benefit and the use of e-government is stimulated.

5   Electronic Government on State and Local Levels

As a result of the smaller scale of the political apparatus, the 50 state governments are able to manage change faster than the federal government can. State governments have taken advanced e-government initiatives. Local governments enjoy the same advantages as state governments.

The contents of the information and (transaction) possibilities offered on state, county and city web sites will be discussed next.

5.1   Information and Services Provided by States

States offer a considerable amount of information and services through the Internet. To be able to make an estimate of the quality of government services at the state level, a number of representative state web sites has been analyzed. The extent, to which these sites are question-oriented, has been the focal point.

To be able to determine the extent to which sites are question-oriented, four characteristics of web sites have been analyzed.[23]
1   Organization of services and information;
2   Approach of the user;
3   Service level;
4   Democratic level of information.
The following three categories have been added:
5   Compatibility of the site;
6   Search options;
7   Measurement of the number of mouse clicks needed to download a form or read a publication.
The organization of services and information analyzes fragmentation, concentration, integration, and standardization. The approach of the user is reactive, responsive, or pro-active. Services can take place at the information (one-way), intake (options for service requests), or transaction (two-way) level. Information providing cannot be divided in

---

23   These characteristics are, for example, mentioned in the "One public counter on the Internet" report of the Dutch "Public Counter 2000" initiative. See Chapter 12 in this book.

separate levels, but is related to the phase of the policy-making process. These phases are policy execution, decision-making and policy-making.

When analyzing the web sites, it is striking that the differences between sites are considerable. Noteworthy is however that all analyzed web sites have passed the reactive approach level. Services are at least offered at intake level. State web sites do not only serve an information function, but also offer services to go along with the wishes and demands of citizens. Services have often been separated in services for citizens and for businesses.

The most substantial differences have been found in the organization of services and information, approach of the user and service level categories. The higher scoring sites are in general highly question-oriented, have a standardized layout, go along with the needs of their intended audience, and offer opportunities to perform transactions online.

Quantifiable differences have been found in a comparison of the number of mouse clicks needed to read a publication or download a form. This ranges from one to seven clicks to download a similar tax form. Table 1 presents the rating of the analyzed web sites.

Table 1
Rating of a selection of state web sites, Source: (Zweers, 2000).

State	Rating (0-125)	State	Rating (0-125)
Virginia	98	Colorado	55
Massachusetts	97	Maryland	53
Texas	91	North Dakota	51
Georgia	86	Montana	50
Pennsylvania	85	South Carolina	48
Washington	79	Nebraska	48
North Carolina	78	Mississippi	48
Florida	70	Oklahoma	40
California	59	New York	38
Oregon	57	Maine	37

Along with the state web sites a central state news portal has been developed: Stateline.org. This site has been established to inform journalists, policy makers and involved citizens in a better way about state politics. All fifty states can be accessed through this portal. Every state has a standardized web site. On each site a biography of the governor can be found, as well as information on the political structure and a schedule of upcoming political sessions. The sites also present economic and demographic information and options to compare this data by state. Finally, a standardized search form can be used to request documents.

5.2 Information and Services Cities and Counties Offer Online

The web sites of the larger cities and counties are in many respects similar to the covered state web sites. Information about the various departments, local politics and government officials can be found. Citizens can pay parking violations and other fees online, as well as file taxes, request permits, look for a job, get new license plates and perform small purchases. Web sites of smaller counties usually only offer a description of the area, some general information about administrative issues and links to adjacent (and larger) counties. Some sites appear to be a private initiative. The differences between county web sites are huge compared to those between state web sites, because of the larger scale differences.

6   Case Studies

In this paragraph a number of case studies on federal, state, and local levels will be addressed. Case Study Federal portal – Students.gov – http://www.students.gov Students.gov (Figure 1) has been developed by a partnership of the Department of Education (DoE), the Department of Veterans Affairs and the Department of Labor. NPR initiated it. DoE had the final responsibility and was also sponsor of the project. The site has been designed as a portal for students to the federal government.

Figure 1. The Students.gov web site

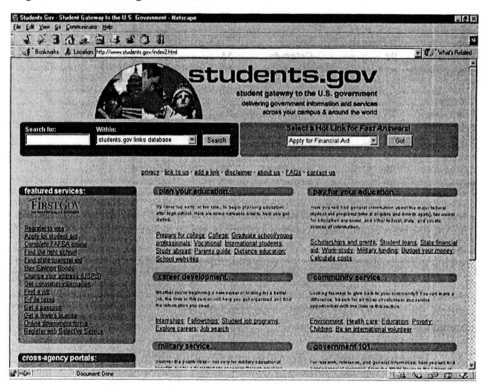

The site does more than just link to other agencies. An important application is the 'Student Account Manager' (SAM). This system gives students one point of reference for information, financial statements and customer service concerning their Federal Students Financial Assistance (FAFSA), consisting of loans and grants from several programs and funds. The system offers educational agencies a standardized method for handling requests for financial aid. The agencies in turn are provided with a review of the finances provided through SAM.

The application uses a Public Key Infrastructure to provide a digital signature, which enables the student to sign legal documents online with an 'Education PIN'. For other users a valid combination of a unique username and password is required to gain access. Security was important at the time of implementation, because the application processes and stores sensitive information. The liability of the government is not limited in case of fraud, as is the case in the private sector. Damage claims are therefore a serious threat.

The designers' team consisted of less than ten people from several organizations. Three individuals and a contracted software company did the actual programming. The first phase in the development process consisted of interviews with schools, universities and students. These interviews resulted in requirements of agencies and students. For several weeks research was done on the Internet and useful information categorized and documented. This information was used to develop a prototype of the site. Applications, which offer transaction-performing possibilities, have been developed and implemented gradually by the involved departments.

The development costs of students.gov were low. In the first year $100,000 was spent, in the second year (2000) so far $175,000 to $200,000. These however are only the costs of web design and implementation of the portal site. The development and implementation of the SAM application for instance has already cost $5,000,000. The savings are estimated at this amount many times over. Savings are especially big with the SAM application, which will end once and for all the inefficient distribution of loans and funds through schools.

A number of lessons have been learned during and after implementation of the web site. A general summary is given here, to give something to hang onto when developing and implementing government web sites:

1   There should be one agency with a dominant position for making decisions;
2   Acknowledge that the chosen solutions are a reflection of the dominating agency or the sponsor of the development;
3   There should be an external independent project coordinator overseeing the project, who can function as the leader of an inter-organizational steering committee to curb the influence of the dominating agency;
4   Emphasize that each participating agency should give up some autonomy in the interest of successful development and implementation;
5   Pay attention to marketing: the legal possibilities for government agencies are limited. The same goes for the budget;
6   The private sector is in most cases more technologically advanced than government. If there are useful industrial applications, these should be applied instead of trying to reinvent the wheel. Partnerships can provide new perspectives.

Case Study Montgomery County web site – http://www.co.mo.md.us
Montgomery County (MC) is located north of Washington DC in the state of Maryland. MC has a population of 840,000. The average income is approximately $ 100,000 per household, making it one of the wealthiest counties in the US. The level of education is high. The inhabitants demand high quality e-government and are politically educated. This is reflected in over 900 committees, actively involved in governing and decision-making.

The Information Technology Strategy Plan dated July 1999[24] describes the MC information technology mission:
Montgomery County uses information technology where it adds the most value:
• To enable our employees to be the best at serving their customers;
• To deliver information and services to citizens at work, at home, and in the community;
• To increase the productivity of government.

•   The strategy plan provides the following:
• An overview of the current status of information technology initiatives;
• An overview of the used planning model, identifying stakeholders for various types of initiatives;
• A table summing up strategic objectives (including priority, costs and scope) and an action plan for accomplishing these objectives;
• Requirements in the light of which goal-directness can be judged.

The Department of Information Systems & Telecommunications (DIST) plays a central role in the execution of e-government initiatives in MC. An important task of the department is the Information Technology Review Process (ITRP). ITRP has been established, because many heads of departments indicated a need for coordination of information technology budgets within the administrative branch of government. Another need existed for guiding and assistance in preparing and defending budget requests. ITRP satisfies these needs by demanding from all departments that they first discuss their budget requests with DIST and the Office for Management and Budget (OMB) within MC, before submitting them. DIST offers the departments technical and strategic knowledge in developing their budget requests and makes suggestions about the relative priority of requests (determined by the strategy plan). The ITRP objective is to improve coordination of information technology projects. DIST therefore does not have the authority to forbid initiatives or on the contrary force implementation of an application.

Obstacles need to be overcome before and during the implementation of an e-government application. Many of these problems stem from the organization of the MC government, comparable to the federal government. There is a difference between the administrative and legislative branch. Both parties must be convinced of the use of establishing an e-government application. The government is used to "brick-and-mortar" provision of services. DIST spends much time to convince and educate politicians. Most staff in the government insists on the present way of doing business and refuses to learn a

---

24 IT Strategic Plan. Available at: http://www.co.mo.md.us/services/dist/stratplan.html

new way of thinking. This is in direct conflict with the strategic plans of DIST. These plans include technologically advanced applications that can prove their use only after several years. The emphasis on the way in which these applications improve the mission of business, is therefore one of the most important tasks of DIST. This demands a review of the whole organization, which is an enormous and difficult task in a large county like Montgomery County.

Another problem that stems from the organization of the governments is the distribution of the information technology budget. This is a mixture of centrally and departmentally related funds. Each department draws up its own IT-plan. Inter-organizational initiatives therefore will not be off to a good start. The objective however is to create a citizen-centric portal. For this a workgroup has been created with representatives from every department. DIST leads this workgroup and stimulates interdepartmental cooperation when implementing similar initiatives. This leads to improved efficiency and interoperability.

The role of the Central Information Officer within MC is described as follows: "Think far enough ahead to design, sell an implement big enough and quick enough to not get left behind in the fast pace of technology change." To get an overview of the technological possibilities of e-government, a study into the added value of possible initiatives has been conducted. The projects with the highest scores were:

1　Online requests for permits;
2　Online student admission and registration;
3　Online bookstores with direct payment options;
4　Real estate taxes;
5　Parking tickets.

These projects have already been or will soon be implemented.

The MC web site was set up at the beginning December 1995. In the beginning of 2000 the infrastructure was completely renovated for the first time. A first renovation after this long a period was made possible because in the first set-up much attention had already been given to important aspects like security and data indexation on the servers. The information on the web site currently still reflects a mainly organization-oriented approach. In the near future this will change. MC wants to, as said earlier, implement a "citizen-centric" portal. The web site of Indianapolis and Marion County, Indiana (http://www.indygov.com/) will be used as a model. Further standardization is also an objective. As an example, the layout of government web sites will be standardized.

Figure 2. The Montgomery County web site

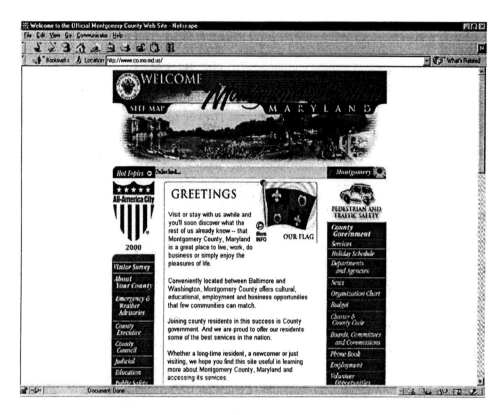

Several possibilities that are currently available on the web site:
*   Requests for permits;
*   Payment of parking tickets;
*   Searching and applying for jobs;
*   Search for recreation and bookings;
*   Reservation of services (rental cars, hotels, etc.);
*   Payment of water board taxes.

The central web site is shown in Figure 2.

A slowing factor for the implementation of e-government applications is that government agencies are charged for electronic payment processing when credit cards are used. In general, the charges are two to three percent of the transaction amount. These costs rise, when transaction values are high, above the advantages, with the danger of slowing the development of new applications. MC charges the customer for these transaction costs. Also an amount of about two dollars is charged for the request of specific information, like legal documents of a court case.

Case Study Boston City web site – http://www.ci.boston.ma.us Boston, Massachusetts has a population of almost 600.000. On the web site of the city all online services are grouped on a "Transaction" page. A special function on the site is the "Mayor's 24-Hour Service", enabling civilians to report problems online. The site offers access to over 50 departments and agencies sites, all with the same format as the central pages. The most important services the city offers are directly accessible, removing the need to search a long list of departments. These are the only question-oriented structured services. Figure 3 shows the web site of the City of Boston.

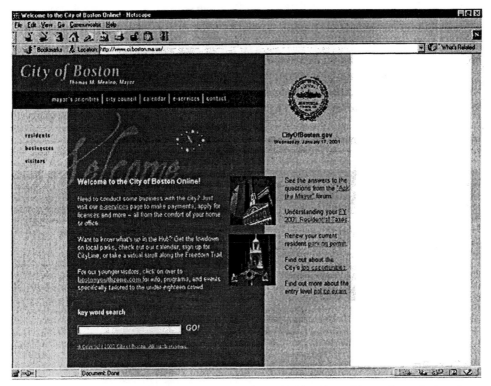

On the web site only public information is made available. The subject privacy is therefore not as important as it is on web sites where private records are accessible. Safety when performing online transactions with credit card payments is guaranteed by means of Secure Sockets Layer technology. To avoid security problems of SSL, credit card numbers are not saved on servers.

Boston wants to make available all kinds of government information online, not only serving the local population and businesses, but also visitors of the city and other governments. The web site rests under the responsibility of the department Management and Information Services (MIS). Various other departments, on the basis of a standardized makeup, provide the contents. Here lies the greatest challenge for MIS: Keeping the information on the web site up to date. This is a difficult task, because it creates extra work for the providing departments, of which the purpose is not always clear. To make it easier to keep the web site up to date, MIS has made sure that each department has a so-called 'champion', who is knowledgeable on the subject, works together with MIS and has convincing powers. The champions have also eliminated the resistance to implementation of e-government initiatives (which was very low to begin with) by keeping the involved people informed, thus convincing them of the purpose to do extra work.

Vertical integration is not used in Boston. Horizontal integration, on the other hand, much more. The organization of the departments has not changed because of new e-government initiatives. More cooperation is nevertheless needed because of integration of information on the web site. This cooperation sometimes leads to problems, because responsibilities are unclear. At present, giving MIS the final responsibility is solving this. Within MIS however it is acknowledged that this responsibility is too much for one department. In the near future this will therefore be a subject for discussion.

An example of horizontal integration is an initiative to make data exchangeable. A 'Parcel ID' uniquely identifies all data. It simplifies looking up data in databases and can be used by different departments and agencies.

Case Study Massachusetts State web site – http://www.state.ma.us

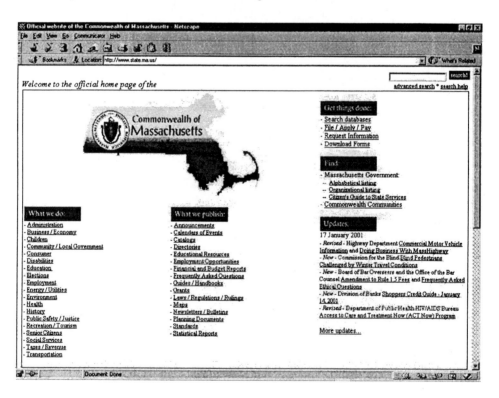

In a comparison study the web site of Massachusetts stood out as one of the best (Table 1). In the past years accessibility of government information and services in Massachusetts increased sharply with the help of web technology. Agencies such as the Registry of Motor Vehicles and the Department of Revenue have won awards for applications of web based transactions.

An interview with staff of the Information Technology Division Strategic Planning Group showed that the implementation of e-government brings carries with it a lot of problems. The state of Massachusetts has a decentralized character: there are 175 state government agencies. The implementation of e-government has always been aimed at innovation. Innovation requires a high degree of freedom. A disadvantage emanating from this decentralized character is 'island automation': different agencies do their own thing, reinvent the wheel several times, and do not share information. In some cases it has also lead to incompatible systems. Not using 'best practices' is not good for efficiency. A recurring problem is the design, development and implementation of e-government from a government or agency perspective, resulting in applications that do not serve citizens or business to the full extent.

In the past, savings from e-government in Massachusetts were not substantial. Conventional services do not become obsolete with the emergence of electronic services and information. An additional service, although offering higher productivity, leads to extra work caused by an increase in the number of 'access points'.

Resistance to the implementation of e-government applications has been minimal. This can be explained by the bottom-up way of development: the law was imposed from the top. Implementations that require cooperation and sharing of information between agencies encounter more resistance.

Privacy and security have not been big problems so far, because critical transactions have not yet been implemented. Public Key technology is not yet used, because tests have shown that it still lacks user friendliness. Another problem of this technology is that not all certified authorities use the same standard. Public Key technology is still seen as immature. Access control with a username and password is sufficient for the current applications. Research has been done into a central authentication mechanism, a so-called 'Common Business identifier'. This mechanism simplifies electronic interaction between companies and government. Companies that do business with the government on a regular basis are automatically identified based on a one-time registration at the first transaction.

Massachusetts wants to prevent by all means that the charge for credit card transactions is charged to its citizens (as is the case with filing federal taxes online: an amount of ten dollars is charged for doing so, which for many people is a reason to file their taxes in the 'old fashioned' way). Charging citizens has a double negative effect: apart from the supply the demand for electronic transaction possibilities will decrease too.

The state recognizes that it is important to offer the customer an integrated and consistent service. That is why the state wants to stop agency-specific approaches and come to an integrated approach. This is a difficult process involving 175 agencies. It also is questionable if the portal-based solution functions, mainly because the larger agencies have already taken far-reaching initiatives. The government aims at developing systems with the perspective of the customer in mind. Hereto four objectives are set:

1 The establishment of leadership and coordination: a mandate of the governor is needed to emphasize the central interest and increase pressure for change. A central steering committee will be established to provide leadership and coordination. This group will consist of administrators, people with the required technological knowledge, business people and citizens;

2 Establishment of a legal and policy framework: in order to increase the number of available types of electronic transactions, legislation and policy is required. Electronic transactions should have the same legal value as paper-based transactions. Privacy, security and tax legislation issues are also considered within this scope;

3 Establishment of a government fund: a fund subsidized with money from profitable e-government applications to support inter-organizational initiatives and central services that have been developed to support e-government applications. The fund will also be used to finance credit card transactions;

4 Make sure e-government reaches everyone: to bridge the digital divide in Massachusetts, the number of public places with Internet access will be increased and subsidies will be given to establish "Community Technology Centers" that also offer training and support for Internet users.

The present web site is divided in five parts:

1 What we do: in this category a review is given of agency web sites and publications, according to subjects;

2 What we publish: publications of agencies according to the kind of publications;

3 Get things done: an overview of information and financial transactions that can be performed online: "online instead of in line";

4 Find: the possibility to search within all government agencies, in an agency-based or alphabetical way;

5 Updates: new and revised information on agency web sites.

These five categories have been organized, keeping the thinking process of citizens in mind. It is not just an enumeration of departments, which only shows what information lies beneath after several mouse clicks. The site has been structured horizontally. This means that a large number of underlying sites is directly accessible from the central web site. The contents of the site are immediately visible. This simplifies navigating the site and finding the desired information. This is important, because the average Internet user does not feel like searching extensively unless there is enough reason to believe the information can be found on the site.

The third category is the most interesting one. A large number of transaction possibilities can be found here. Citizens can search databases (for example a database of available jobs or of hazardous materials), issue complaints, pay fines, request information and download forms. Downloading of forms is not only limited to tax forms, but permit requests and job registration forms can also be found. Most forms are in Adobe Acrobat format, a program often used for documents with a standard layout, which prevents Internet users to make changes in the downloaded forms.

Case Study Alaska State web site – Webmart en VoIP project – http://www.state.ak.us

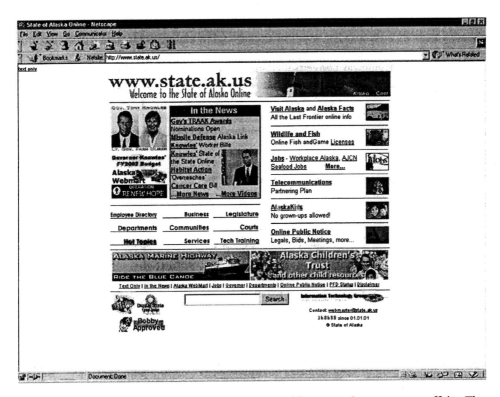

E-government means for Alaska means involving civilians more in government affairs. The large size of the state and the small population of 630,000 makes the Internet, more than anywhere else, an important means of communication.

The online services in Alaska are systematically presented in *Alaska's Webmart*, set up as a portal. Each available service is accompanied by a question-oriented explanation, so that the user quickly knows where to find the information he is looking for. Offered services include for instance license plate registration; information about sex offenders; a list of available government jobs and options to request permits and grants.

The state of Alaska has set the goal to implement a new IP-based voice and data network that connects the central administration building in Anchorage with the 38 satellite offices elsewhere in the state. This project is to be completed in September 2001. Instead of separate LAN-networks for each department, there will be a common Intranet, with double glass fiber as basic connections. This network is suitable for Voice over IP.

Voice over IP (VoIP)
VoIP is the sound of human voice, carried over by using the Internet protocol. This is the transmittal of audio material in a digital form in separate data packages, instead of via circuit based protocols over conventional telephone lines. An advantage of VoIP is that there is no charge for the use of the telephone.

The VoIP forum has developed VoIP. This is an initiative of large hardware suppliers, such as Cisco Systems, VocalTec, 3Com and Netspeak, to encourage the use of a common standard for transmitting sound and video through IP over the Internet and within intranets. In addition to IP VoIP uses the real-time protocol (RTP), to ensure that data packages will be delivered on time. VoIP works as follows:
- The local VoIP gateway converts incoming analog data (sound of voice) to digital data;
- The local gateway finds the desired gateway and sends data packages over the Internet by using IP;
- The receiving gateway converts the digital data to analog sound of voice, finds the dialed telephone number and finishes the local call via the regular telephone network or via a local private telephone line.

Despite technological improvements, the quality of the connection is not as good as regular telephone quality. This is caused by the double conversion together with Internet delays[25].

Two obstacles for the use of VoIP in Alaska are:
1 Justification of the investments for the purchase of IP-telephones, software and servers for the staff of 13,000 people;
2 Technology: at present bandwidth is still the bottleneck, so conventional telephone lines are still preferable over Internet telephony. By performing tests the state government wants to assess to what extent voice can be transferred via the existing infrastructure. The climate also sets high standards to the technology.

Contrary to these obstacles there are three reasons to encourage use of VoIP:
1 The transmission of voice and data communication over the same lines cuts in half the number of telephone connections needed for remote offices;
2 Most offices are located in remote areas, so long distance savings alone already offer a high return on investment;
3 According to the IP-telephony manager of Cisco Systems, the company is capable of delivering a completely scaled VoIP system before September 2001. Scalability is a necessary prerequisite for use in Alaska, since it concerns a government agency with 13.000 employees.

---

25 What is VoIP? Available at http://www.gtswashington.org/telegblobe/teleglobe.htm

7   Private Sector E-government Applications

Microsoft has developed a framework to increase the use of XML in the public sector. The emphasis is on adapting existing data models to increase the efficiency of e-government applications[26].

The IBM Integrated Tax Application offers governments an all-in integrated payment system. It contains (among other things) a standardized, but flexible processing mechanism for tax forms, which can be changed according to the needs of the user[27]. Besides the big players in the public sector a number of "portal providers" emerged, which may play a prominent role on the state and local government levels in the near future, according to a recent Gartner group investigation[28].

8   Internet Usage

Taking into account the developments in the field of e-government, it is of importance to know to what extent the public has Internet access. Statistics and figures covering this subject are inconsistent. Predictions done in the past often turned out to be too low. The emphasis in this paragraph will therefore be on figures concerning the past. An overview of the US situation will be given.

Internet access in the United States
A Gartner group investigation in 1999 yielded that more than 50 percent of the American population had Internet access as of June 1999. In March 2000 this percentage has risen to 63 percent and in November 2000 this percentage is expected to be over 70 percent.

A side note should nevertheless be made: there are substantial demographic differences in Internet usage. The already treated term digital divide is used to define these differences: inequalities in access to technology, caused by income, education level, geographic location, and ethnic origin.

The section of the population with the highest percentage of Internet access mainly consists of white or Asian households with a high average income, of average age and with higher education. Most households in this category are married couples with children. The highest concentration of these households lives in the west and in the urban areas. An investigation of the National Telecommunications and Information Administration[29] showed

---

26 Industry Solutions. Available at http://www.microsoft.com/europe/industry
27 The IBM Integrated Tax Application. Available at:
   http://houns54.clearlake.ibm.com/solutions/government/govpub.nsf/detailcontacts/The_IBM_
   Integrated_Tax_Application?OpenDocument
28 More information about some of these companies can be found at:
   http://www.ezgov.com/, http://www.freebalance.com/, http://www.govworks.com/,
   http://www.nicusa.com/ and http://www.sdr.com/.
29 Falling Through the Net: Defining the Digital Divide. Available at
   http://www.ntia.doc.gov/ntiahome/fttn99/contents.html

that the section of the population with the lowest percentage of Internet access can be defined as households with a low income, of African-American, Hispanic or Native-American descent, of higher age, unemployed and with a low education. An important group of digital have-nots are one-parent families. The highest concentration of households with a low degree of Internet access is found in the centers of big cities and in rural areas, mainly in the Midwest and South of the US.

Figure 7 gives an overview of the mutual dependability of income and the extent of Internet access, showing the percentage of households with Internet access. Striking in this figure is the fact that only in the in percentage points smallest group with an income higher than $ 75.000, more than 50 percent of the population had Internet access.

Figure 7. Percentage of households with Internet access, divided by income (1998), Source: (Price, 1999).
It is now obvious that Gartner group uses a broad definition of Internet access, to come up

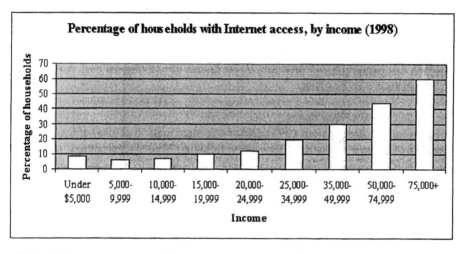

with their figure of more than 50 percent Internet access in June 1999. Gartner group also counts the connections at the workplace and Internet access in public agencies. Internet access in one's residence is nevertheless preferred for many e-government applications. Not including Internet access in other places also gives a more accurate estimate of the digital divide.

The foregoing shows that the Internet population in the United States is a non-representative part of the population. This is an important fact to take into account for a government, which has far-going plans for electronic services.

9   Conclusion

E-government has been given a central place within the US government policy. A question-oriented approach is seen as the means to provide better services at all government levels. Aspects such as privacy and security are getting a lot of attention. Case studies showed that implementation problems of e-government applications mainly concerned cooperation between organizations, or within organizations. Another problem of e-government is that it cannot fully replace conventional government services, because not everybody has access to the Internet. Research turned out that there is a growing divide between people with and without Internet access. Bridging this divide has therefore been given a high priority.

References

Balutis, A.P., Digital Government – When All is Said and Done, *Electronic Government Journal,* Vol. 2, No. 6, November 1999.

Price, T., *Creating a Digital Democracy, the impact of the Internet on Public Policy-Making,* Foundation for Public Affairs, Washington DC, 1999.

Zweers, K.T.W.A., Checklist of a number of American state web sites, February 2000, Washington DC.

Chapter 8

E-Government: A European Priority

Frans de Bruïne

1 Introduction

Experts often claim that we are heading towards a new economy. Whether this is indeed the case is unclear but we can no longer ignore the fact that the Internet has made an enormous impact on our world. In many respects this specific application of our information society has changed our day-to-day life as well as our economy and society. E-commerce is expanding enormously and e-commerce sales are expected to increase by more than 40% by 2003. Where e-commerce was restricted to new start-ups a few years ago, we now see enterprises in all sectors becoming e-businesses: from airlines to banks. A brief look at recent developments also learns that e-commerce applications not only create many new enterprises, but also a huge number of new jobs. In 1999, the US-market created 2,3 million Internet-related jobs. Not only has this resulted in an economic impact, but these new technologies have also made an important social impact, from skills to healthcare.

These changes and developments have provided the European Union with enough reasons to agree on some landmark commitments at their so-called "dot.com summit", held in Lisbon from 23-24 March 2000. At their summit, government leaders of the various Member States agreed on the following targets:

- access for all European citizens in the e-economy;
- all schools in the European Union should be connected to the Internet;
- a clear framework for e-commerce should be established;
- the Union should become an innovative and entrepreneurial Europe;
- the Union should work on the concept of e-Government: generalised electronic access to main basic public services.

This package of targets has been called the e-Europe initiative. The concept of an electronic government and the European ambitions for such a government are part of this e-Europe initiative. In this chapter, I would like to briefly sketch the setting behind this initiative, the ambitions of the European e-Government plans as well as the future of the European government in an online era.

.

J. E. J. Prins (ed.), Designing E-Government, 121–126.

2   The E-Europe Initiative

Why an e-Europe initiative? Well, the European Commission has noted that, in comparison to the United States, the European Member States lag behind when it comes to joining the Information Society. There are different reasons why. First, Internet penetration in the Member States is relatively low. This has partly to do with the access costs which remain high. Citizens are less inclined to go online because of the costs involved. We also note that today the websites originating from the United States dominate the spectrum. By early 2000, 94 of 100 most visited websites were located in the US. What is more, in comparison to the US, we have relatively few European start-ups. Limited access to the required investment capital appears a key factor which discourages people from starting an Internet business.

Internet penetration vs. Access Cost

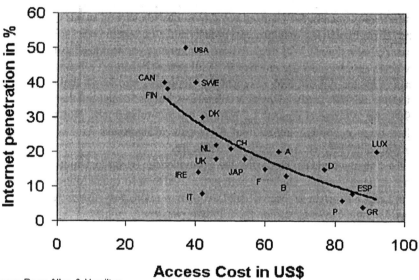

Source: Booz Allen & Hamilton

It is clear that this situation has a considerable impact on the potential for and success of e-Government initiatives in Europe. The access to public sector information as well as opportunities for electronic transactions with government services greatly depend on the 'wiredness' of the European society. In short, action is needed to strenghten the European position.

In developing the e-Europe initiative, Europe should build on its strengths and great potential. Firstly, the degree of mobile phone penetration should be mentioned. The diagram on the following page shows that today in Europe there are more subscribers to mobile telephony than there are in the US. Furthermore, the European standard for mobile communications, GSM, has become the leading world standard. Another European advantage is the development of digital television. Here we note a rapid expansion of this technology in several EU-countries. And again, it appears that the

European standards prevail. Finally, it should be mentioned that the European content basis is very diverse. Both the amount of available public sector information and Europe's cultural heritage contribute to this strong content position.

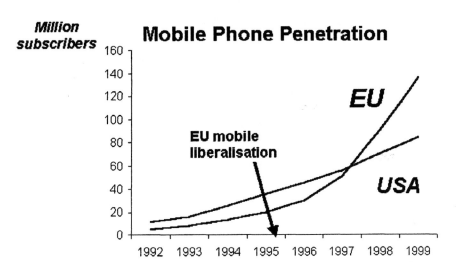

source: FT Mobile Communications
USA: Cellular Telecoms Industry Association

3   E-Government

What is at stake?

As mentioned, the concept of an electronic government is part of the ambitious e-Europe initiative. European leaders consider this issue of great importance. Essentially, for various reasons we cannot afford not to act. One of the first reasons is of course democracy: information and communication technologies offer many possibilities to enhance the participation of the European citizens in the various democratic processes. The Internet could bring governments closer to the citizen. A second reason is competitiveness. As developments in the United States have shown, e-government applications create room for entrepreneurship. Furthermore, this will reduce the administrative burden. For the European Union, a healthy climate for entrepreneurship is of crucial importance and today we note that the US is moving ahead in this respect. In short, working on the e-Government concept is a necessity, not a matter of choice.

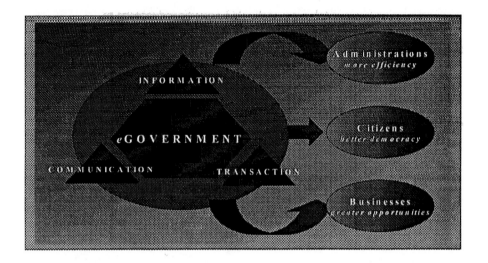

A key issue for the US

As Miriam Lips describes in more detail in this book, the US government has taken several initiatives during the last decade of the 20th century to work on its electronic government. The Electronic Government directive was issued in December 1999. The key targets of this directive were:

- by December 2000, forms for top 500 Government services online;
- by October 2003, transactions with the Federal Government should all be available online for online processing.

Earlier, the Electronic Freedom of Information Act 1996 was adopted. The Act grants access to government information and enhances the dissemination of this information. In addition, it facilitates the commercial exploitation of government information. Looking at these and other US developments, the question arises as to whether Europe is missing out on something?

Where does Europe stand?

So, where does Europe stand in light of the US developments and to what extent can we turn our ambitions into reality? Looking at the situation in the various Member States, it becomes clear that progress is being made, but not at a matched level. Several reasons account for this. First, Internet penetration varies largely within the EU. Second, actions on e-Government are taken in all Member States, but progress is not as fast in all countries. Governments (both the front offices as well as the back offices) have been modernised, targets for electronic public services (such as improving access, portals and one stop shopping) have been set and rules for access and exploitation are being rethought. However, the ambitions and success of the Member States in establishing these targets greatly depends on the political setting, the stage of technology, etc. It is becoming clear that the European Union may play a role in creating an optimum climate in Member States for e-Government ambitions.

What is the EU doing?

The past few years several policy actions have been launched. First, we have created what could be called framework conditions for establishing e-Government initiatives. Mention must first be made of the steps in the area of telecommunication costs: by 2001 the review of the telecoms regulatory framework should be adopted. I also refer to the follow-up to Green Paper on Public Sector Information.Secondly, various catalysing developments are underway. I would also like to mention the projects under the IST Programme, such as the Eurovet-project on the electronic surveillance of livestock. The EU jobs database, EURES, established under the IDA-programme is another example. A final, and key action is the reform of the Commission to establish an eCommission. The prime goal here is to increase the transparency of the various European institutions. In the meantime there are some clearly visible results of this reform:

- Dialogue on Europe: http://europa.eu.int/igc2000/;
- Online register of President Prodi's external mail:
  http://europa.eu.int/comm/commissioners/prodi/mail_en.htm
- Unique portal to European Governments:
  http://europa.eu.int/abc/governments/index_en.html

In addition, progress has been made with respect to online transactions for subsidies, procurement etc. At the previously mentioned Lisbon summit, the following target for the European e-Government initiatives was set: "ensure generalised electronic access to main basic public services by 2000" . To realise this target the EU is at present working towards two goals. Firstly, to make a large number of public data available online. The EU's goal is to have all legal and administrative, cultural and environmental information, real time data on traffic and congestion available for citizens and businesses by means of the Internet by 2002. Secondly, they are aiming at an online interaction between citizens and Government. Again by 2002, the EU should realise a two-way electronic access to basic administrative interactions and feedback on political initiatives

4   How to Move Forward?

From the foregoing it can be concluded that the EU has set the first important steps towards the introduction of an e-Government concept in Europe. How to move forward from here? First it should be stressed that Europe should build on national initiatives and ideas of the various Member States. Best practices lead the way. In addition, it is important to realise a transparent co-ordination of the various developments through a system of benchmarking. At a European level we are now considering an e-Government Action Plan in which we are formulating a coherent strategy on the future of a European e-Government. The key characteristics of this Action Plan is briefly mentioned here:

1 Inclusive:
- information should be made easily accessible to all, thereby giving special attention to disabled people;
- public access points are to be established
2 Interactive:
- online interaction between citizens and Government is a key issue.
3 Multilingual:

- cross-border use of the information is of crucial importance in the European Union, which means that multilingual information should be made available.
4　Entrepreneurial:
  ·electronic transactions between government and businesses should be facilitated;
  ·methods for electronic public procurement should be introduced.

These four characteristics will become crucial in developing a European e-Government concept. All four characteristics are rooted in the essence of both the European Union and the Member States and are part of democracy and competitiveness. As mentioned earlier, both are at stake in Europe's move towards an information society. Therefore, it is of vital importance that Europe does not miss out in the online era because it is the cradle of democracy.

Chapter 9

Dutch Perspective and Initiatives[1]

Roger van Boxtel

Ladies and gentlemen,

The Center for Law, Public Administration and Informatization of Tilburg University displayed a great deal of foresight when it decided last year to select the theme "Electronic Government" for its annual conference. This topic now attracts a great deal of interest, as also became apparent during the European Summit which was held in Lisbon in March of this year. ICT and the knowledge society were prominent items on the agenda at the Summit, and a new strategic objective was formulated for the European Union: the EU must become the most competitive and dynamic knowledge economy in the world, characterised by sustainable growth, rising employment and social cohesion. There will be a commitment to economic growth averaging 3% a year for the whole Union, and to achieving a labour market participation rate of 70% in 2010, compared with 61% now.

"The most competitive and dynamic knowledge economy in the world." The phrase has an impressive ring to it. It expresses courage and a new elan. Europe intends to actively set about overtaking the United States and the countries of Asia, particularly Singapore. This applies for the whole European Union, but obviously has consequences for Dutch policy. Fortunately, we in the Netherlands aren't doing too badly at all: according to a recent survey we are currently in sixth place in Europe in terms of Internet use; 48% of Dutch people currently have access to the Internet.

But our lead also carries an obligation. If everyone starts advancing more quickly, we will have to do the same. We must work towards the European objective of improving the competitive position of Europe, but we must also do all we can to raise the participation rate of the public. The information society is there for everyone. If someone doesn't take part, that must be because they choose not to do so, rather than because they do not have the opportunity. As President Roosevelt said: "No country in the world, however rich, can afford to waste human capital." That was true in the 1930s, but it is a statement which we can still use as a guide today.

---

[1] This text was delivered as a speech by Roger van Boxtel, Minister for Urban Policy and Integration of Ethnic Minorities, The Netherlands, Tilburg University, on the 18 May 2000 conference.

J. E. J. Prins (ed.), Designing E-Government, 127-131.
© 2001 *Kluwer Law International. Printed in the Netherlands.*

The amount of human capital in the Netherlands is greater than ever. The average Dutch citizen is well educated and assertive. We have gone a long way to becoming a genuine knowledge society. There is a small consultancy in Canada, Nuala Beck Consultancy, which publishes a new indicator each month on the Internet. In April this was a list showing the most knowledge-intensive countries in the world. And sure enough, the Netherlands was at the top, followed by Switzerland, Sweden and Singapore. You can check it out on www.newconomy.com. Unfortunately, the site does not explain how this indicator was arrived at, and I would therefore suggest that it be regarded more as an encouragement than as a gold medal.

A knowledge society thrives on information. Because many Dutch people have a reasonable command of the English language, a great deal of English-language information is accessible to us. The problem, however, is that we are in danger of being overwhelmed by all that information. As yet we are not very adept at processing large quantities of information properly and judging its worth. I see that as a deficiency in our present education system, which is still insufficiently geared towards processing and structuring large amounts of information. We shall have to devote a great deal of attention to this in the years ahead.

Knowledge and information are by definition public assets. They are not competitive and they do not exclude. This makes them the perfect raw materials for a society in which there is a place for everyone. But for a government, this brings the obligation to ensure that that place is *guaranteed* for everyone.

In a democratic society the government exists by the good grace of the members of that society. We must be fully aware of the obligations this brings. As a government we are confronted with a more assertive citizenry which makes heavier demands than every before. And rightly so: the ability to improve the provision of services, for example, has increased greatly. This applies for the business community, but there can be no doubt that it also applies for the government.

We are on the threshold of a new era. A new century has begun, and we are entering it better equipped than every before. There are all manner of technological possibilities which can greatly improve the functioning of an information processing organisation such as the government.

We are also confronted with a society which is in a strong state of flux. It is a society in which, accordingly to Castells, networks are shaping our society and in which our production processes, our experiences, power and culture are largely determined by the logic of those networks. People participate in a variety of networks which, in contrast to the past, are no longer determined as a matter of course by a person's background or ideology. Moreover, these networks are not static, but undergo constant changes in their make-up.

The government, too, is increasingly functioning as one of the actors in a network. In doing so, the government works with and for other actors. This can sometimes lead to a somewhat dualistic position, because the government also has its own responsibilities, such as protecting the public interest. The government therefore continuously has to weigh up the interests of individual citizens against those of the community in general.

Because of this, there is a greater need than ever before for a vision of the present and future role of the government. Based on that vision, answers can be formulated to questions such as:

- How will the information relationship between the public and a government - which is increasingly functioning in an electronic environment - be developed in the years ahead?
- What freedom of choice can be offered to members of the public, and what are the responsibilities and tasks of the government?
- What demands will be placed on the government in the virtual world as regards the exercise of its public tasks?

And finally:
- How can new tasks and responsibilities be fulfilled?

I have set out my view of this new role for the government in a policy document which will be published shortly. However, I can let you have a glimpse of some of the ideas today. Something of a scoop, you might say. And I must say that I am delighted to be able to talk about my view in the present company. Together, you represent a very great deal of scientific and international experience with precise relevance for the topic "Electronic Government". That makes you exactly the right people to be the first to hear about the contents of my policy document.

The policy document consists of three parts. The first part sketches the social and technological developments that have made it necessary to reflect on the new role of the government in the network society. This reflection leads to the *leitmotif* of my vision: "freedom with ties". For I am firmly convinced that every citizen should have freedom of choice regarding the way in which he or she wishes to be "tied", wishes to make contact with the government. The many new technological assets mean there are more options, and I believe that every member of the public has a right to those options.

The notion of being "tied" is also an oblique reference to the virtual networks in which government organisations are linked to each other, but also to businesses, community organisations and members of the public. But the notion also refers to the arrangements, the contract, between government and citizens on the form of the information relationship. There is a degree of tension between the expectations society places on the government and the ability of the government to meet those expectations. In the arrangements, the contract, between government and citizens, a balance has to be struck between the setting of norms by the government and the influence of the public on the policy process.

The second part of the policy document deals with "The Accessible Government". I believe that the government must be accessible and approachable, must deliver quality, but must also offer freedom of choice and possibilities for participation. These are new roles which ensue from my vision. How all this will change has not yet become entirely clear. I am therefore having exploratory studies carried out in a number of fields. I won't list them all, but I do for example want to set up a user panel to find out what people's experiences and wishes are with respect to the functioning of the electronic government on the Internet. Once we know that, we can investigate which elements are important for the quality of a government website.

I also wish to examine, together with the various government sectors, where the opportunities lie for optimum use of ICT in those sectors. I am convinced that this will help us create a much more effective and efficient government organisation.

I would like to give members of the public control over their own personal details. That means that individuals will own that information and that the electronic government only records personal information if and in so far as this is necessary. I believe this to be a point of principle and I would also like to see members of the public receiving periodic updates advising them of the information stored about them by the government.

It also seems to me to be a good idea to establish parameters for digital debates which the government initiates or in which it takes part. It must be clear what will happen to the contributions made by members of the public. This is the only way to encourage involvement.

The third part of the policy document is called "Government on the move". A great many initiatives have already been taken. I tabled the "Electronic Government" action programme in Parliament as long ago as 1998. But we all know that today's society is changing very rapidly and that the opportunities are constantly increasing. The action programme is therefore in need of expansion and updating. There is no time to lose if we are concerned about the role of the government. Things are going well in the economy. The time is ripe and the people are ready for change. We must invest now in order to benefit from today's measures in the future, even when things are perhaps going less well.

We do not know much about the future. What we do know is that the government organisation as we know it today is by no means a blueprint for the government organisation in the years ahead. We must remain alert, invest in the future and in the changes which confront us. Only a flexible government can survive. Because let us make no mistake: even if we do nothing we are investing; the only difference is that we are then investing in future organisational problems.

The third part of the policy document therefore deals with actions which cannot wait. I shall mention a few. Government organisations must begin working closely together and must release resources for the major renewal of policy and operational processes. Together we are strong and can reflect on how we as a government should define our exemplary role and encourage new developments. That is good not only for the government, but also for Dutch business and research institutes.

I wish to encourage every local authority in the Netherlands to have its own Internet site by 2002. I am also keen to create a financing facility which encourages government sectors to invest in ICT with a view to providing a better service.

A centre of expertise will be set up for innovative decision-making, which collects "best practices" and advises public authorities on how to involve members of the public in interactive decision-making. A great deal of effort is going into the Electronic Voting project. The aim of this project is to develop a system in which voters can cast their vote in any poling booth anywhere in the Netherlands. Research is also being carried out into whether voting could be made possible from a person's home or workplace.

Finally, I should like to mention a project of which I am very proud. "Digital Playgrounds" are currently being set up in 30 major cities. These are meeting places where everyone can drop in for help in learning the skills needed in the information society. I hope that many unemployed young people will also receive training there which can serve as a stepping stone towards a mainstream job in the ICT sector.

There is a great deal to be done in the years ahead. We must continue making headway to prevent ourselves sliding backwards. We have been given the present in order to make something of it, and under the best possible conditions. I have every confidence that we shall succeed.

The past is history, the future a mystery, But today is a gift. That' s why it's called the present.

Chapter 10

The Italian Approach to e-Government

Silvio Salza and Massimo Mecella

1   Introduction

Introducing Information and Communication Technology (ICT) in the public administration has been for a long time a clear priority both for the Italian Government and for the Italian Parliament. This has actually been part of a more complex and long reform process of the Italian administration, meant to improve the efficiency, cut down the cost, and finally achieve a full attainment of the Republican Constitution of 1948, which clearly referred to a decentralised administration model.

The organisational structure of the Italian Government consists now of the following entities:

*   *Central PA* (Central Government), which consists of government *Departments* and Agencies (about 1,900, with 44,000 employees) located in Rome.
*   *Peripheral PA*, which consists of branch offices (about 4,000 with 430,000 employees) of the Central PA that are spread in the whole country.
*   *Local PA* (Local Government) which consists of entities (20,000 with 1,000,000 employees) such as *Regions*, *Districts* and *Municipalities (City Councils)* characterised by a high degree of autonomy from to the central government, which is continuously increasing as a consequence of the decentralisation process.

In the following we will refer to all these organisations as the 'Public Administration' (PA). Like in any other country, the purpose of the PA is essentially to provide services to citizens and in order to achieve this goal all the organisations that are part of the Italian Government are typically involved in the execution of joint administrative activities.

In the last decade, the Italian Parliament has taken important legislative actions concerning the modernisation of the PA, these concern (law n. 241 of 1990) some fundamental rights of the citizens, such as the right to be informed and to freely access any administrative documentation concerning them, as well as the structure of local administrations (Regions, Districts and Municipalities), the organisation of local governments, and their relationship with the citizens (law n. 142 of 1990).

These laws have just been the starting point for a number of subsequent reforms that concerned both the co-operation among different levels of PA, and the interaction between the administration and the citizens. For instance, to guarantee the citizens' right to be correctly informed, and to effectively communicate with the administration, new offices for the interaction with citizens have been created,

J. E. J. Prins (ed.), Designing E-Government, 133–152.
© 2001 *Kluwer Law International. Printed in the Netherlands.*

called *Uffici Relazioni col Pubblico (URP)*. Citizen were also granted the right to know at any time (and in a reasonable time) exactly which information the PA detains about them, and the current status of every administrative procedure concerning them. Further actions were taken to simplify the interaction with the administration (One-Stop-Government), by introducing the so called *Sportelli Polifunzionali* (polyfunctional windows).

Moreover a thorough reorganisation process was started in all public structures, beginning from the Central Government (*Presidenza del Consiglio dei Ministri*). The main goal of these actions is to abandon the traditional highly hierarchical organisation, and to move instead towards a more flexible organisation, closer to that of private companies. This includes giving high level public officials more responsibilities as well as salaries and regulations more similar to those of private company executives. Finally a new system of internal control has been introduced in the administration to strengthen management controls, evaluation of the results, and quality control of the service delivered to the final user.

All these legislative actions had a great impact on administrative procedures, that were already obsolete and inadequate, and left politicians and bureaucrats with few alternatives to choose from. Moving towards e-government, i.e. heavily relying on ICTwas actually the only way out. This was in some way a very positive element, since it gave a way through the traditional reluctance of bureaucrats to changing their procedures. In most cases they had no alternative: the old procedures just had to be dismissed, and new ones had to be designed, almost from scratch, thus incorporating the new ideas in administrative sciences and in ICT.

The final goal was clear, but achieving it proved (and still proves) to be a very complex and challenging task. A major problem, as was clear from the beginning, was that several administrations had already undertaken individual actions in this direction, and there was a total lack of co-ordination, leading rapidly towards incompatibility. This could have finally prevented any further successful effort of integration. On the other hand, the decentralisation process granted the local administration a good deal of autonomy, and therefore both Government and Parliament could only take indirect actions. The most important one was without doubt establishing a central authority (AIPA) for ICT in the PA, as we will discuss in more detail in next section.

In this chapter we shall analyse the problem in detail, and we shall discuss the main decisions and the related regulatory actions taken by the Government to ensure a correct and ordinate evolution toward a more modern efficient administration based on a widespread use of ICT. Moreover, although the innovation process is far from its end, we also discuss some interesting preliminary results of this policy of co-ordination and indirect action that has set Italy, at least in some important fields like for instance the digital signature, as one of the leading countries in the European Union in the move towards e-government.

2   The Authority for Information Technology in the Public Administration

The Authority for IT in the Public Administration (*AIPA, Autorità per l'informatica nella Pubblica Amministrazione*) was established according to Labour Decree n. 39/93. AIPA's tasks are promoting, co-ordinating, planning and controlling the development of information systems within the government central organisations and agencies, through their standardisation, interconnection and integration. The main objectives are better services, less cost, better communication and a wider support to the decision process within the Government. AIPA's assignments may be schematised as follows:

- *Strategic tasks*, including preparation of strategic actions, co-ordination of all projects concerning the management and development of the administrations information, and setting criteria for the monitoring of contracts related to their projects.
- *Regulatory tasks*, including setting standards and criteria on planning, design-ing, developing, managing and maintaining the administrations' information systems and their interconnections, quality, organisation and security.
- *Promotion tasks*, to supervise inter-sectorial projects that include the Public Administration's Unified Network and other IT infrastructures.
- *Financial control tasks*, including auditing and evaluation of costs and benefits of the administrations' projects, and activities related to IS/IT procurement.
- *Education tasks*, to improve IT competence in the public sector, and to control the activities developed by the administrations in this area.
- *Advisory tasks* on issues related to Information Technology for the President of the Council of Ministers during the law-making process.

Due to its role, both of promotion of new technology and of control of auditing and evaluation of the administrations' projects, AIPA has played and is playing a crucial role in setting up the right premises for all actions aiming at integrating procedures of different administrations.

The approach that AIPA has adopted in planning its activities in the past years is inspired by the classical innovation life cycle:

- *assessment phase:* understand the state of evolution of ICT in the organisation, by performing a diagnosis that guides in the definition of priorities in the interventions;
- *planning and implementation phase*: issue regulations and standards, plan and implement projects;
- *checking phase:* measure the results and check the effectiveness of the action.

The first step of a general assessment on the use of IT in the Italian Administration was carried out by AIPA during 1994-1995. In order to precisely perform such an assessment, AIPA has developed its own original methodology, tailoring existing approaches and methodologies for information system planning (U.S. Department of Commerce, 1988) and inventory organisation (Thompson, 1993) to the particular characteristics and rules of the Italian Government. The main project decisions characterising the investigation have been the following:

- To focus the investigation not only on technological issues (i.e., applications, computers and networks on which applications operate), but also on the organisational aspects, to identify the structure and the characteristics of the organisational units, the human resources involved and the work processes performed within organisational units.

- To perform the investigation not only on the organisational units responsible for the computer-based information systems, but also on the other organisational units participating in administrative processes, which are important for the information flows in which they participate.
- To perform the investigation by means of questionnaires, filled in by the users of the organisational units, with the assistance of a team of experts trained for the purpose.

These guidelines have made the AIPA investigation peculiar with respect to previous investigations on the Italian Government, which had concentrated mainly on technological aspects and on EDP manager organisational units.

The investigation has been performed with a bottom up strategy, leading to the identification of groups of activities in specific organisation units (executed either manually or by IT applications) performed to provide services to internal and/or external users. Such activities (processes), can be modelled in terms of causal relationships as *macro-processes*. Macro-processes correspond to sequences or aggregations of processes that are to be executed jointly in order to serve a request of service (from a citizen). Organisational units can be both clients or suppliers of processes, while the clients of macro-processes can be only external users (i.e. citizens or non administrative organisations such as private enterprises).

Figure 1 shows an example of macro-process, i.e. the whole procedure needed to grant a subsidy to a disabled person. It consists of four different processes located at the Department of Internal Affairs (DoIA) and its peripheral units, at the Local Medical Unit, and at the Department of Treasury. The picture makes clear that altogether as many as 16 interactions are required. The citizen requesting the service has to perform 4 interactions with 3 different administrations. The remaining interactions represent internal document exchange between the administrations. Here is where the problem lies, and most of the time and resources are consumed.

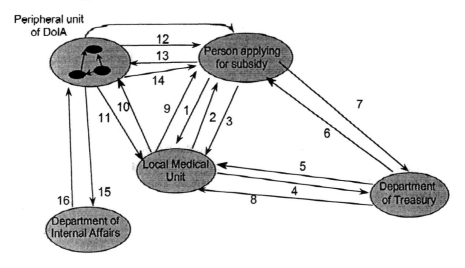

Figure 1. Schema of the macro-process *assigning subsidy to a disabled person*. Arrows represent the interactions with administrations and between administrations, numbers represent order of execution

The inefficiency in the execution of macro-process is mainly due to both the high level of fragmentation of responsibilities, and to the numerous *interruptions* of processes, even inside a single administration. Such interruptions are often a direct consequence of laws which assign to some administration the responsibility of actions to be performed for the completion of processes carried on by other administrations. A typical process starts in a public administration A, then the work stalls waiting for the completion of a task to be performed by a sub-unit B_1 of administration B, which in turn at a certain moment interrupts its sequence of activity to involve another sub-unit B_2 of the same administration, and so on.

Currently most information exchange among administrations is through paper documents and often through ordinary mail. It was found that in 38% of cases the operator has not direct access to all the information he/she needs in order to complete the process, therefore he/she needs to issue an official request to some other administration. Often this information has to be provided directly by the citizen (the only one seriously interested in the completion of the process), who consequently plays the role of 'messenger' among administrations, by requesting 'certificates' from one administration and delivering them to another. But recently a bill was passed that acknowledges the citizen's right to present an 'autocertification' instead of a certificate (i.e. to directly declare under his/her own responsibility whatever information is detained by the PA). If the administration likes to check it, it can do so since it must have that information somewhere in some file. This brings in some justice but threatens to make the execution of macro-processes even slower.

The general assessment has allowed to draw a picture of the status of technology penetration, the investments, and the organisation in the Italian PA. The following figures give an idea of the size of the problem to be tackled:
- 1,800 structures in Central PA;
- 500,000 employees;

- 2 Billion Euro of IT budget per year;
- 12.000 processes;
- 500 major data repositories;
- 12,000 Gigabytes of data storage
- 5 billion of instances (records) in the repositories
- 300,000 millions of lines of computer application code;
- 120 main legacy systems.

To monitor the penetration of IT technologies in the PA, AIPA has also introduced a small set of aggregate indicators, which have been measured every year since 1994. Value of the indicators for the last five years are shown in Table 1, and clearly show that the situation has only partially improved.

Table 1. IT penetration in Italian public administration

	1994	1995	1996	1997	1998
Percentage of processes supported by EDP applications			15		
% of CPU time spent per type of administrative mission			Social security 55% Resource management 20% Public revenues 16% Customs 3% Justice 2% Labor 1% Other (cultural heritage, etc.) 3%		
Number of employees per PC	3,5	2,8	2,9	2,7	2,5
Number of employees per PC in central and peripheral administrations			1,56 vs 3.22	1,43 vs 3.12	1,33 vs 3.03
% of dumb terminals	31	24	22	19	16
% of PCs connected in LANs			44	47	53
% of PCs connected in WANs			40	34	40
Languages used in applications development	Cobol 75% New gen. Languages 13% Other high level lang. 12%		Trend in 1995-1998 developments: Cobol 45% New gen. Languages 17% Other high level lang. 37%		
Number of connected PCs per type of hardware platform in EDP centers		Mainframe 93% Mainframe + servers 3% Mainframe + PCs 2% Server 2%			Mainframe 89% Server 16%

On the whole, the assessment performed through the investigation led to the following conclusions:
- Workstation penetration is still very low.
- The number of internal administration processes is still very high.
- 95% of the workload is carried out by 12% of the employees.

- Lack of co-ordination in developing information systems. In the past years, applications pertaining to different departments have been implemented separately, pursuing local objectives, without a global vision of the organisation. As a consequence, different departments are often characterised by similar applications. In one case (applications concerning personnel), at least 30 independently developed versions of the same application were found.
- Information systems are isolated. Most information systems are hierarchical, strictly tailored to the organisational systems they serve, with scarce or zero horizontal communication with other information systems, thus resulting in fairly efficient processes inside the single administrations, but in high inefficiency in moving products of processes in the chain of macro-processes.
- Processes are frequently interrupted, both for lack of useful information inside administrations, and for the jungle of authorisations, controls, etc. imposed by the huge amount of laws and regulations existing in Italy.
- Information not available through mainframe applications cannot be searched or requested through the net.
- Messages exchanged between administrations are considered valid only in case they are signed in paper letters or documents.
- IT is generally used more as a means of automating existing processes; in such a way often the improvement in performance is much more limited than in case of complete/partial BPR (Davemport 1993, Hammer 1990, Hammer and Champy 1993). Experiences of real reengineering frequently fail, due to the resistance that is opposed to change.

According to the results of the assessment AIPA has started several important actions that range from planning the architecture of the network infrastructure, to setting up the standards and the framework for the digital signature and personal identification, to promoting education and training activities. Especially interesting have been *integration* actions. These have concerned the ICT infrastructures (e.g. computer and communication networks), the data repositories and the document interchange procedures. All these matters will be discussed in more detail in the next sections.

3   The Public Administration's Unified Network

One of the main points focused during the assessment phase was the urgent need for computer network communication and interconnection standards. At the time the study was started, information systems of different administrations were largely evolving in an independent way, thus leading to incompatibilities that prevented integration efforts, if any were attempted. The analysis of macro-processes discussed in the previous section had clearly pointed out that a crucial problem was inefficiency of information interchange between different administrations. This very often involved going back to paper and manual handling. Shipping was done in many cases by ordinary mail. A primary goal was then to make actually possible a direct exchange of information by efficiently exploiting the new technology.

Setting up a common standard would be therefore a necessary preliminary step to the integration of the procedures and the improvement of the digital information interchange between different administrations. Moreover, in a broader perspective, an efficient network infrastructure would have also allowed citizens to remotely interact with the administration without the need to physically access the PA offices.

AIPA then identified the creation of a Public Administration's Unified Network (*RUPA, Rete Unitaria della Pubblica Amministrazione*) as the main inter-sectorial project, in accordance with the directives of Labour Decree n. 39/93. Preliminary activities in this direction were carried out by the during 1994 and the first half of 1995, and companies also invited to make proposals with their contributions and suggestions. A feasibility study on the Public Administration's Unified Network was arranged by AIPA with the co-operation of the technical bodies of the Department of Postal and Telecommunication Services. The study mainly concerns those aspects regarding the interconnection and interoperability of the networks that will form the Unified Network. It provides a general architectural solution for the aspects regarding the co-operation among the administration's information systems. A directive issued in September 1995 by the Prime Minister subsequently established the aims of the system, the areas and the modes of action along with the phases of the execution. With reference to this last point, the feasibility study represents the first real step towards the setting up of the Network.

The target of the unified network is "to guarantee to any authorised user the access to data and procedures residing within the automated information systems of his/her own or other administrations regardless of the networks they cross and of the technologies adopted by the single information systems. In summary, the intent is to produce an integrated information system that enables the various public administrations to be connected by the network and their information systems to inter-operate and co-operate". The basic qualities provided by the unified network are:

- *Connectivity*, i.e. the possibility to transmit reliably information and messages;
- *Interoperability*, i.e. the availability of conversion and adapter functions that will allow the exchange of information between systems, networks and non-homogeneous applications;
- *Co-operation*, i.e. the capacity of the applications of an administration to use the application services available from other administrative offices.

Initially the possibility of having a completely uniform architecture was considered, but later this hypothesis was ruled out since it violates the autonomy of each single administration. Therefore the final choice was rather to give a way to integrate the heterogeneous existing networks, by setting up interconnection standards and functions that would guarantee the interoperability.

The Unified Network project will act as a reference point for all the actions that will be taken over the next years to reorganise the Italian public administration. The Network in fact, because of its structure, represents a significant occasion for supporting reform processes able to combine efficiency gains with increase in quality and performance.

As for the integration of the procedures and the efficient implementation of macro-processes, the Unified Network provides a fundamental framework for the interoperability of the existing proprietary networks. This greatly simplifies the implementation as far as the exchange of information and the access to remote resources are concerned. Moreover the layered structure of the network, providing transparency at different levels, allows for the decomposition of complex applications and a largely independent development of their modules.

4   Digital Signature and Personal Identification

The second main point AIPA had to face has been setting up regulations and standards to ensure *integrity* and *authentication* of electronic documents, in one word digital signature. To unveil the mystery that often surrounds this word, and to understand what digital signature is, and how it is regulated in Italy, we cannot avoid going through a few theoretical elements, but we shall try to do that avoiding any unnecessary technicality.

Digital signature is based on a cryptographic process, i.e. a process originally meant to provide secure communication between two people (that we shall call *source* and *destination*) exchanging a message (or document) that we shall denote by *m*. This involves using two procedures or functions, *encryption* and *decryption*, and two *keys* (i.e. strings of characters), to be used during the encryption and decryption process, and on whose secrecy relies the secrecy of the communication.

Figure 2. a-c Integrity and authentication cryptographic schemes

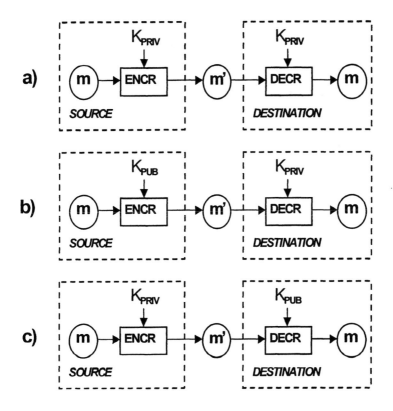

Fig. 2 a) shows the simplest scheme, called *symmetric*, in which both correspondents use the same key K_{PRIV} , which is called a *private key* since it must stay so to ensure secrecy: nobody without knowing K_{PRIV} may decrypt the encrypted message *m'* into the original message *m*. Fig. 2 b) shows instead an *asymmetric* (or *public key*) encryption scheme, based on a couple of keys: a public key K_{PUB} and a private key K_{PRIV}, the former is used by the *source* to encrypt *m* into *m'* and the latter by the *destination* to decrypt *m'* into *m*. This couple of keys is selected in such a way that K_{PUB} can only be used to encrypt and is of no help in decrypting. The destination, can then freely distribute the public key K_{PUB}: only he/she as the owner of the private key K_{PRIV} may still decrypt the encrypted message *m'*. The scheme of Fig. 2 b) is today largely used over the network, to ensure secure communication, since it doesn't require any previous key exchange between the correspondents. The *destination* may send the *source* its public key even over on insecure channel since it is indeed 'public' (or could be without any harm). It also plays a fundamental role in most e-commerce payment schemes.

But the same couple of keys K_{PUB} and K_{PRIV} can also be used in the reverse order, as shown in Fig. 2 c). Here the private key K_{PRIV} is used by the *source* for encryption, and the public key K_{PUB} by the *destination* for decryption. The communication is obviously not secure, since any holder of the public key K_{PUB} may decrypt the message. But *authenticity* and *integrity* of the message are guaranteed, since the *source*, being the only one to detain the private key is the only one that could have generated the encrypted message *m'*, and then must be the author of the message, and the message could not be later manipulated by anyone else. Moreover the message cannot be repudiated by the *source*, unless he/she admits his/hers private key K_{PRIV} is no more private.

Figure 3. The digital signature encryption scheme

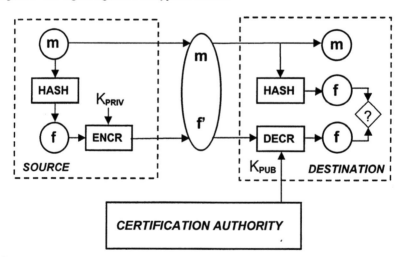

The digital signature is actually based on the scheme of Fig. 2 c), and is meant to guarantee the *authenticity* and *integrity* of an electronic document (computer file). There are anyway two main addition to the basic scheme:

- The encryption is not performed on the whole document or message m, but on a short résumé of it f called *fingerprint* or *digest*, computed from m through a complex *hash* procedure. The reason of the term *fingerprint* is because it sums up all the peculiarities of the message and, if even a minor change is made to it, then the hash procedure would produce a different fingerprint, say f'.
- There is a third party, a *trusted authority*, called a *Certification Authority (CA)*, that keeps in a register all the public keys of all the individuals and organisations that want to utilise the digital signature to guarantee the authenticity of their documents.

The complete scheme of the digital signature is represented in Fig.3. The *source* produces from the document m with a *known hash procedure* the fingerprint f, then it encrypts it to f' using its private key K_{PRIV}. The *signed document* is composed by the couple (m,f'), i.e. by the original document m (not encrypted) and by its encrypted signature f'. To check the *authenticity* and the *integrity* of the document m, the *destination* requests and obtains from the *Certification Authority* the public key K_{PUB} of the *source*, which must be deposited there, uses it to decrypt f' and obtain f. Then the *destination* computes again the fingerprint of m, using the same *known hash procedure*, which should produce the same value f, if m has not undergone any change from its original version.

As one can easily guess this schema can be used for several purposes:

- transmitting documents over an insecure channel, notably the Internet;
- storing large authenticated documents in electronic format, e.g. on magnetic or optical support;
- produce an unlimited number of *authenticated copies* of these documents;
- remotely checking the identity of a person who is initiating a transaction anywhere on a computer network.

The latter case is a very interesting one since it shows the connection between the problem of personal identification, a crucial issue in e-government, and the digital signature, making even more clear that providing the legislation for the digital signature, and all the complex technical regulations, is a fundamental pillar for the implementation of e-government. This was indeed clearly understood by Italy, that was the first country in the European Union (almost together with Germany) to give full implementation to the digital signature, even before EU legislation was issued.

- Law n. 59 of March 1997 states that: "All acts, data and documents produced by the public administration and private subjects by using computer and communication technology, contracts stipulated in the same form, and their filing using computer technology, are valid and relevant under all respects of the law...".
- Presidential Decree n. 513 of November 1997 and Government Decree of February 1999 give the criteria and regulations for the application of Law n. 59/97. Among others they introduce the term *digital signature*, define the main details concerning the encryption and hashing algorithms, the size of the keys to be used, the criteria to guarantee the secrecy of private keys, the requirements and the duties for the CA, and finally the criteria that a new company must

follow to be included in the National Register of Certification Authorities (i.e. they carefully specify every detail for the application of the schema of Fig. 3) .
- At the end of 1999 eight companies were included in the Register of Certification Authorities and could start issuing certificates. The whole process of the digital signature was finally on the move.

From a legal point of view the Italian legislation refers to what is usually called *strong* or *advanced* digital signature. That means that the only kind of digital signature which is 'explicitly' acknowledged by law is the one that strictly follows all the regulations stated by law. A similar approach was used in Germany, but not in all *Länder*. Other EU countries are currently experimenting, especially in the private sector. In most of them the process has started, but in none it is yet concluded.

The EU finally adopted its Directive on electronic signatures in December 1999, that is actually more meant for business applications than for public administrations[1]. It makes a distinction between *advanced* and *normal electronic* signatures, the latter being 'not so strictly' linked to all the complex regulations of the stronger version, which may in some cases become a significant source of cost, and therefore may slow down e-business.

The strong signature, as in the Italian legislation, is actually well suited for the public administration, for whose purposes it was mostly designed, but it is too rigid and demanding for private business. On the other hand the Italian law explicitly acknowledges the *advanced signature*, but does not prevent a single Court or Judge to acknowledge, in specific cases (e.g. business applications) some weaker scheme as a valid one in that context. Nevertheless issuing further legislation on these matters, by specifying regulations for one or more kinds of *normal electronic signature* would possibly speed up things and give further momentum to e-commerce.

From a technical point of view the Italian digital signature system heavily relies on smart cards, i.e. credit card sized plastic support with a microprocessor and permanent storage inside. These can be used to generate couple of keys and to securely store them. Unlike ordinary magnetic-band cards, these are virtually impossible to forge, and it is also impossible to read their content, at least without destroying them. Moreover their processing capabilities allow them to implement sophisticated encryption procedures and to perform cryptographic challenges as part of secure remote identification procedures. According to these characteristics a smart card issued by a CA physically represents the ability to put a given digital signature, and its legal holder becomes responsible for its use, and must of course immediately inform the CA in case of loss or theft.

Smart cards are used in many applications as secure personal identification tokens. After several experimental projects in this direction, independently carried

---

1   The Directive however, does not exclude application in the public sector. Consideration 19 particularly stipulates: "Whereas electronic signatures will be used in the public sector within national and community administrations and in communications between such administrations and with citizens and economic operators, for example in the public procurement, taxation, social security, health and justice systems".

out by local administrations, the Italian Government has finally issued regulations for a national *Citizen Electronic ID Card*. This consists of a smart card that will be distributed to every Italian citizen and will be used not only as an ID piece, but also as a multifunctional card to gain access to all automated services of the Italian PA, both from ad hoc windows and from a remote connection through the Internet. The ID card provides for the digital signature, and will therefore guarantee the validity of documents transmitted and of transactions performed through the network. Its use will not be limited to the PA, but it will be possible to use the ID card also for business and financial transactions requiring secure identification procedures.

5   Access Portals

Another important action concerns provisions given to citizens for remote access to the PA services information repositories. These are in agreement with the EU e-Europe initiative and strongly rely on digital signature and secure personal identification tokens and procedures discussed in the previous section. This action is based on *Network Access Portals*, i.e. Internet sites to whom the citizen may directly connect, since it is assumed that in a quite short time most of the Italian population will have direct or indirect access to the Internet. This would bring a dramatic improvement to the quality of service, since citizens would not have to move from their home and to stick to limited timetables.

Some projects are already operational and some of them are based on electronic ID card systems set up by local administrations (Salza and Marsocci, 1999). As a matter of fact a large number of projects has been started by individual administrations because the Internet technology is very attractive and it may provide a good image improvement at a very reasonable cost. Almost all projects were started and run independently from each other, with a lot of duplication of efforts, and, what is even worse, setting up the premises for a future incompatibility, that could finally prevent any integration effort. In some way, the same situation we have discussed in Sect. 2, where single administrations have been designing and building their information independently and without any co-ordination, is rising again.

Fortunately in this case the central Government could react in quicker and in a more effective way, setting up as a final goal to have only a single portal, or at most a few portals, providing integrated access to all services supplied by the PA. This target is planned to be at least partially achieved by the second or third quarter of 2001. Therefore the Government is taking some important initiatives in this direction to set up a series of regulations. These leave the individual local and central administrations the freedom they deserve in starting and implementing immediately their own projects, but on the other hand they guarantee that their efforts will not be wasted.

There are substantially two kinds of portals: *information portals* and *service portals*. The main difference is that portals of the first kind only support *inquiry accesses*, i.e. allow citizens only to get information from the PA, either generic data or specific data from some repository, but without stating any administrative procedure and/or modifying the content of any repository. A service portal would allow instead to support a *transaction*, i.e. to start an administrative procedure that could finally result in some change in the repositories. Referring to the more familiar banking environment, an inquiry access would be looking for stock prices or even checking the balance of his/her own account, and a transaction would be requesting to move some money to another account. Service portals are considerably harder to implement, because of obvious security and reliability requirements, and because of problems connected to supporting secure transactions that update several different data repositories, possibly managed by different administrations.

An effective example of integrated information portal is *Norme in Rete* (literally 'Law on the Net'), that gives access to all Italian laws and regulations. The portal was implemented by integrating the access to many data repositories (currently more than one hundred), most of which already had a network interface, but each one according to its own interaction formats and standards. The integrated portal, does not require from the user any knowledge about which sites exist, what data they contain, where can they be found on the Internet, and how each one of them can be searched. The access is instead *fully transparent*, to use the IT jargon, and all the end user has to do is to submit a single query through a single user-friendly interface, and get all the results the system has collected by searching in the appropriate sites.

The main idea behind this approach is not trying to collect all the information from all the different organisations and storing it in a single central database, but instead to grant each participating partner its full autonomy in managing its own repository, and just asking for some right of access, and some minor co-operation to set up and maintain a central index. This approach has indeed proved very powerful, since it avoids both complex negotiations connected to 'borrowing' proprietary data from 'jealous' organisations, and the burden of keeping up to date the central database while the other change.

Several service portals are already operational as well, for the time being mostly at the local level, based on electronic ID cards. The two most interesting projects are the *Siena Card* and *City of Milano Citizen's Electronic card*, both born from the co-operation between Town Administrations, the Central Government, the Internal Revenue Service, the Department of Internal Affairs, and other private and public organisations. Both projects are based on a electronic ID piece (smart card) and allow citizens to access, from special kiosks with a smart card interface, a large variety of services as:

- accessing the data stored in the smart card, with the only restrictions set by the laws about the privacy of individuals;
- getting and printing formal acts and documents of the public administration;
- getting access to several databases managed by various public administrations, both to query them and update them through fill-in forms;
- sending to various administrations formal legal certificates that have been requested to carry on administrative procedures;
- performing autocertification, and to get access to electronic signature services;
- paying taxes and fees for services provided by the public administration.

6   Database Integration

The Italian Public Administration owns a great amount of information, notably data concerning citizens and enterprises (together referred to as *subjects*), which are spread over a lot of different repositories owned by different central and local administrations. Some data are in the repositories of the City Councils (CC) where the subject was born, lives and carries out its activities; additional data are kept in the repositories of several central administrations, such as Italian Social Security Service (ISSS), the Department of Finance (DoF), the Department of Internal Affairs (DoIA), the Department of Justice (DoJ), etc. All these repositories were designed independently, and are managed according to rather different policies and criteria. Replicated information then naturally leads to inconsistency, i.e. having different, incompatible values for the same information item.

Such a situation is no more acceptable, since it substantially prevents, or makes extremely difficult, the implementation of automatic procedures that need to get information from more that a single repository. Moreover most of these repositories are not even databases, i.e. do not have a clear and visible structure, but are part of so called *legacy systems*, a sort of IT mammoth that defies any attempt of change and improvement. Even just getting the raw data out of it may become an unfeasible task. The integration of data repositories was therefore seen by AIPA as a strict priority and a necessary precondition to the implementation of e-government. Several actions were then started in this direction, with the co-operation of research Institutions, in the field of *reverse engineering*, to select effective policies for the design of new systems and the integration of the existing ones.

When heterogeneous systems must co-operate, it is necessary to set up an architecture that allows the updates in a system to correctly propagate to others. To understand the problem let us consider the case of such an *event*: a citizen goes to its CC and notifies a change of address. This first triggers an update of the CC information system. The CC should notify other central administrations the event with the new information, so that they can update their databases as well. Right now it is the citizen who has to carry the burden, by going to the other administrations (and/or send them a legal document assessing the event).

The real cause of these notifications lies in duplicated information present in the co-operating and duplicated systems; if they were organised as unique systems with a common database, any update will be immediately available to all the systems; instead the systems were designed in different times and very often these duplicated data were imposed by legal and organisational constraints. The aim of co-operation is having zero latency in the notification of updates without requiring a re-engineering to a common database, which would in fact be impossible since most of the participating systems are legacy systems.

The solution currently proposed is to use the idea of *Data Steward* and the architectural pattern of *Publish & Subscribe* (Mecella and Batini,2000) The concept of Data Steward is used in the context of the Data Quality studies, as the entity responsible for the quality of a particular data, from when it is created and made available to the system for the first time. For each data maintained by the system and for each data defined by input and output processes (and therefore also for the data indirectly feeding the system) a data steward must be defined. The definition of a data steward is generally based on law; a particular entity is responsible for the data. This is true not only in public administrations, but also in private business organisations: for example the production department is responsible for the product data, and the marketing department for the client data; in private organisations, law means the rules managing the organisational system. This idea is extended to events, by defining *Data Steward* (of an event) as the organisation/system originating the event, responsible for the definition of the information contained in it. Therefore the Data Steward exports the definition of all the events it generates.

The Publish & Subscribe architectural pattern consists in having two types of entities: *publishers*, which produce information (as events), and *subscribers*, which are interested in being notified of these events (thus receiving information). Among the publishers and the subscribers there is a *decoupling* element (*Event Manager*) in charge of routing the events. In this way subscribers do not tie themselves directly to the publishers, but to the Event Manager that typically offers subscription lists from which to choose; the publishers notify events without knowing the subscribers.

According to this schema, the co-operation consists in each organisation defining the events it is data steward for, and the others, independently, subscribe to some events. The co-operative architecture, i.e. the Co-operative Service layer in the Italian Unitary Network, is actually implementing, among others, the functions of the Event Manager. Currently some projects are experimenting these solutions. When these projects will be ended off, the subjects will be able to notify all the administrations with a single action, simply dealing with the Data Steward for that particular type of information. This one will propagate the event to the others. Moreover, if an additional administration wants to have this particular information maintained up to date, all it has to do is to contact the Data Steward and to subscribe.

Nevertheless not all problems can be solved through a Notification Service. It is also necessary to create an index which, for each instance of a particular event, gives a pointer to the particular database where the data about it reside. As an example the reader can consider the citizen again, and the situation in which a client wants to access the information without knowing where the particular citizen resides. Therefore additional projects have been started to set up these indexes for some interesting types of entities, such as for instance cadastral data (Arcieri et alii, 1999).

7   Document Management

Document management, i.e. all activities connected with the transfer of official documentation between different administrations, or even different offices of the same administration, and the management of the inward/outward registers, are a prime target for the e-government action. In the Italian PA these activities are currently carried out in a semi-automatic way, involve about 20,000 offices, draining resources for 100,000 man/year at a yearly cost of about 7,500 millions Euro.

The first step in this direction is the automation of the register of documents, because this functionality has a central role in any administration for all management activities. It is in fact being connected on one hand to the workflow systems supporting the service processes (often carried out through document exchange), and on the other hand to the document management and storing systems (see Fig. 4).

Some important recent laws (the DPR 513/97 on the 'Electronic Document', and the DPR 428/98 on the 'Automatic Register') recognize this and trigger a sequence of actions meant to complete this innovation process. A first step is the definition of *hOmogeneous Organizational Area (OOA)* as a collection of offices and sub-units inside a main administration, which, for their nature (functionality, services supplied to citizens, etc.), can be considered as a whole and thus need to have a single *Automatic Register System (ARS)*. Each OOA represents a sub-domain inside the main administration, with its own ARS, co-operating with other OOAs, both internal and external to the administration. The introduction of the OOAs is going to greatly reduce the fragmentation of different offices dealing with separate document registers, and will allow a co-ordinated development of the new automatic systems.

Each OOA is given a good deal of freedom in developing its own Document Management and Automatic Register Systems, but a set of *core functionalities* must be guaranteed, to provide a set of *standard certification services*. As a matter of fact each inward/outward document, according to the Italian law, must be registered and some minimal identifying information must be permanently linked to it (e.g. date, OOA sender and the register number of the OOA sender system, the newly created number in the OOA, subject, etc.): these data are called *register signature*. The act of registering these data implies a responsibility assumption by the OOA:

- The existence of the document, since the registered date, is certified.
- In the case of received documents, the certification of the fact that the document has entered the OOA, and that consequently some procedure has been started.

Figure 4. The automatic register of documents as the center of the document and workflow systems of an administration

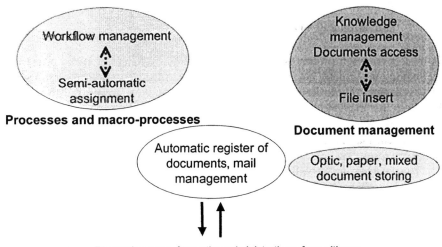

Electronic, paper, from other administrations, from citizens, unstructured, semi-structured (forms)

According to the Law all the inward/outward documents into/from an OOA must be registered through the ARS. In the current practice, this operation is carried out by hand, by updating paper registers, a slow and expensive procedure. With the new procedures, this operation will be carried out in a quite more efficient way:

- for electronic documents transmitted on the net (e.g. through e-mail) and with an attached document containing structured tag data, a software application will automatically create the signature (as an XML document) and will attach this electronic signature to the original document through classical digital signature algorithms;
- in the case of paper documents, an operator will inspect the document, insert the needed information in a software application and will print and put on it an adhesive label with optical codes that will be directly read in further steps.

In both situations, register information is also inserted into a database, so allowing immediate tracking of all the events tied to the exchange of documents.

As, hopefully, more and more electronic documents will be used in the Public Administration, the former case will become the standard one, thus leading to a considerable speedup and cost cut. To achieve this goal, it is crucial to set up common network and application protocols and a standard format for tag data attached to the documents. To set up these regulations AIPA is currently (summer 2000) carrying on, with a dedicated task force the *Collaborative Register project*. Two main decisions have been to use XML (a sophisticated evolution of the HTML for network based applications) for the exchange of the information needed to automatically derive the register signature of the documents, and to rely on standard Internet technologies, as opposed to proprietary protocols, for the documents exchange. It is worth noting that according to these directions, from now on every official document will be uniquely identifiable and it will become straightforward to trace all its moves through the sequence of register signatures.

8   Education and Training

In most innovation processes the hardest and more delicate part is not setting the technology up to date, but setting the people up to the new technology. Bringing ICT technology in the Italian PA and setting it on the move towards e-government has been no exception.   This has been clearly focused by AIPA during the assessment phase, and the priority has been correctly understood by the Italian Government that has started an Education and Training Plan, and devoted to it the necessary resources.

The problem is actually twofold. On one hand it concerns managers and employees who have to interact with new automatic procedures, on the other hand the technical staff that has to design the procedures, to provide for their implementation and keep them running. These are quite independent targets and should not be confused. As for the first face of the problem, clerks mostly need specific training connected with their duties but also what some call *computer alphabetisation*, i.e. to understand the basic concepts behind the technology. Managers are in a somewhat different situation (and are typically the worst 'customers' for the education system) since they do not need to know about the details, but are involved in strategic decisions about introducing ICT technology in their offices, and so they need a deeper understanding of it, to get convinced that it is really useful, and finally to give up their conservative attitude.

As for the technical staff, the main idea is that applications should not be implemented, and not even designed by them, because of evident efficiency reasons. These people should instead be able to integrate with teams from the outside during all phases of the application development process: analysis, design, implementation and testing. So they really need more than specific technical training. They need also education, possibly at university level.

Such a delicate action, could not be simply devolved to the initiative of individual administrations. This would have brought to an enormous duplication of efforts, to a considerable budget fragmentation, and finally to a loss of efficiency and quality. Therefore, even in a general policy that was mostly aiming at co-ordinating and regulating, as seen in the previous sections, education is managed in a centralised way. AIPA has invested a large amount of resources in designing a set of courses and in preparing, with the help of academic institutions and private consultants and companies, a good deal of ad hoc student reference material both printed and on multimedia support.

A set of courses has been designed according to reference *professional profiles* that have been defined to cover all technical and administrative functions in the PA, and in compliance with the regulations issued by the EU. Each course consists of a set of modules, each module consists of five days of intensive residential lectures and labs. Altogether a single course is roughly equivalent to four or five credits (referring to standard values in the European university system), and includes a final abilitation exam. Each course is replicated several times and in several locations around Italy every year, and local and central administrations may apply, with some limitation in the number of people, but without any charge to send their employees.

References

Arcieri F., Cappadozzi E., Naggar P., Nardelli E., Talamo M. (1999*)*, 'Access Keys Warehouse: a new approach to the development of cooperative information systems.' Proceedings of *the 4th IFCIS International Conference on Cooperative Information Systems (CoopIS'99)*, Edinburgh, Scotland.

Mecella M., Batini B. (2000*)*, 'Cooperation of Heterogeneous Legacy Information Systems: a Methodological Framework.' Proceedings of *the 4th International Enterprise Distributed Object Computing Conference (EDOC 2000)*, Makuhari, Japan.

Davenport T.H. (1993), *Process Innovation: Reengineering Work Through Information Technology*. Harvard Business Press.

Hammer M (1990), 'Reengineering Work: Don't Automate, Obliterate.' *Harvard Business Review*, July-August 1990.

Hammer M., Champy J. (1993), *Reengineering the Corporation*. Harper Business.

Salza S., Marsocci P. (2000), 'One-Stop-Government in Italy', in M. Hagen and H. Kubicek eds*., One-Stop-Government in Europe, results from 11 national Surveys*, Bremen University Press.

Thompson C. (1993), *Living an enterprise model. Database Programming and Design*, March 1993.

U.S. Department of Commerce, National Bureau of Standards (1988), *Guide to Information Resource Dictionary System Applications: General Concepts and Strategic Systems Planning*. NBS Special Publication 500-152, U.S. Government Printing Office.

Chapter 11

E-Movements or Emotions?
ICTs and Social Movements: Some Preliminary Observations[1]

Wim van de Donk and Bram Foederer

The smoothest road to control over political conduct is by control of opinion. (...) those who have actual instrumentalities at their disposal have the advantage. [John Dewey, The Public and its Problems, London, 1927, p. 182/184].

1   Introduction: New Media and New Social Movements

After being very successful in using duplicating machines, fax machines and other traditional media, (new) Social Movements are now increasingly using the Internet and other applications of new Information and Communication Technologies (ICTs) (e.g. Ayres, 1999). Contrary to the activities displayed on the Electronic Highway, however, the academic research into the ways these new media are used and what kind of impact they have on social movement organizations (SMOs) is lagging behind. In our contribution to this conference book on electronic government, we want to explore some of the theories and questions that could guide future research into the ways social movements are using ICTs to strengthen their role in (global) democratic governance. In two recent anthologies on ICTs and democracy (Hoff *et al.*, 2000; Hague and Loader, 1999) one will look in vain for questions, let alone research results on how these more and more important players in the democratic game are using ICTs. When we compare the attention that is devoted to the meaning of ICTs for the more formal players in that game (e.g. governmental agencies, political parties, parliaments, campaigning politicians) to the research that explicitly concerns (new) social movements and interest groups, one cannot but conclude that the

---

1   An earlier draft of this chapter was presented at the XIVth meeting of the permanent study group on informatisation in public administration, Glasgow, September 2000. Wim van de Donk is currently involved in a research group, funded by the COST (Action A14) that will launch a comparative research project into the use of ICTs by Social Movement Organizations.

J. E. J. Prins (ed.), Designing E-Government, 153–171.

research community seems to neglect the role of ICTs in the extra-institutional sphere of 'politics'. This is even more remarkable given the much-debated 'extra-institutional' characteristics and capacities of these new technologies (especially the Internet). According to some authors in the field of informatisation, ICTs and more specifically the Internet are a challenge to traditional forms of organisation in general and to traditional democratic practices in particular (e.g. Bekkers, 1998, 2000; Frissen, 1999). The more flexible and less-organised nature that characterises especially the new and newest types of social movements seems to have a kind of *wahlverwandschaft* with the (networking) nature of the Internet, that enables for a variety of organizational patterns that contradict the principles that reign the more formal part of the political system (e.g. clear jurisdictions and hierarchical power relations).

Most social movements have always been operating mainly in the fringe of the democratic system. Moreover, the more or less 'disorganised' and even 'anarchistic' and 'virtual' way in which at least some (especially the youngest ones) of them are working, seems to fit the network-character of especially the latter generations and applications of ICTs very well. As much as private firms do, they see the radically decreasing 'transaction costs' for communicating and participation which enable all kinds of tele-engagement. Like in E-Commerce, in E-Movements, we see processes of deterritorialisation, hori-zontalisation, and virtualisation. Territoriality and distance do not always count anymore: The municipality in Leyden (Holland) is now confronted with a virtual interest group formed by far off descendants of the so called Pilgrim Fathers in the United States of America. The descendants of the people who left Leyden to take up residence in the U.S.A. more than three centuries ago are now calling upon their wired brothers and sisters in New England to boycott the supermarket chain that is trying to convince the Leyden municipal administrators to pursue the demolition of some of the houses their ancestors lived in, in order to be able to expand their surface. Both the supermarket and the municipality are confronted with E-mails that 'suggest' them to change the projects so that the supermarket can be enlarged without demolishing the controversial houses.[2]

It is, furthermore, very interesting to see how social movements (such as the environmental movements) are using the Internet for their presence at the global level. This increasingly important level of decision making is to a large extent characterised by an unsettled mix of institutional indolence and emptiness as far as the formal institutions are concerned. It is very interesting to see how social movements like *Greenpeace, Justitia et Pax, Amnesty International* and *Friends of the Earth* are frequently and successfully using the Internet and related applications to be effective in this institutional vacuum (e.g. in mobilising their 'electorate'). They sometimes almost seem to be more effective than regular political parties in the management of public opinion and the management of policy formulation and agenda setting (e.g. the example of Doherty we mention below).

But also at the national and regional level, social movements appear to be successful in using the Internet As far as the membership of the younger generation of citizens is concerned, they are more successful without any doubt than most political parties are. Of

---

2   NRC Handelsblad, 26 October 2000, p. 13.

course, political parties also have discovered ICTs and the Internet (e.g. Frantzich, 1989; Bogumil & Lange, 1991; Van de Donk & Tops, 1992; Depla & Tops, 1995; Smith, 2000; Löfgren, 2000). It is, in this respect, interesting to see how parties that are using the Internet seem to rediscover some of the movement-like qualities and characteristics they have often lost since they have transformed themselves from the social movements they once all were to a certain extent, into the tightly organised, centralised and professional political organisations they –most of the time- have become now. In the machine age, they were much more decentralised at the level of constituencies, wrote petitions and mobilised masses. Now, they are smoothly managed political enterprises that more often suppress than encourage dialogue and public debates because such publicity might endanger their power in the political arena.

Whether such a defensive attitude will last or not remains to be seen, but it is interesting that political parties of the Information Age are in many cases using digital means to democratise their party-organisations, creating discussion groups, using the Internet to involve 'ordinary' or 'ad-hoc' members in the drafting of political agenda's, voting on selected issues and so (e.g. van de Donk & Tops, 1995; Depla & Tops, 1995; Nixon and Johansson, 1999; Löffgren, 2000; Smith, 2000). Much is still unclear, and it is especially difficult to predict how the use of ICTs is related to other factors that transform the political parties as we know them. But is it unthinkable that political parties will be using ICTs to redesign themselves into a more 'social movement' like type of organisation, or that social movements are using them to compete with political parties? ICTs might perhaps not change the 'logic' (but we are not sure) of collective action, but they seem to change, in any case, the means that are used for it.

For the moment, however, one can still clearly discriminate between political parties and social movements, the old (like the unions) as well as the new ones (the environmental movement, the feminist movements). Their somewhat 'disorganised', unconventional but still purposive character is recognised in the following definition: "Social movements are a strategically and/or thematically connected series of events, produced in interaction with adversaries and carried out by a coherent network of organisations and participants who use largely unconventional means in attaining political goals." (Duyvendak, 1995). Although quite differently than most other actors in the political arena, social movement organizations are, of course, organizations, but quite complex ones, and difficult to observe. Those who wanted to formulate typologies of this political phenomenon were, not surprisingly, confronted with a '(...) a bewildering variety of organisations with differing degrees of visibility, power and activeness.' But: 'Although they vary greatly in scope and specific purposes, their general purposes are broadly similar -to do things business and governments are either not doing, not doing well or not doing often enough' (Levitt, 1973:49).

In our contribution to this conference-book, we want to focus on social movements, that very particular kind of political actor. It is very much more a starting point of research than a systematic presentation of results. Our aim is to get a first impression of how SMOs are using these technologies, and how that is influencing the way social movements function, internally as well as externally. Some interesting evidence that they are doing quite well, thanks to the Internet, can be found at the international level: the 'battle of Seattle' was –at least for the time being- won by a multicoloured and virtually organised coalition of social movements, some of them already of a predominant virtual character themselves. According to Doherty, the RAND corporation pointed already in 1993 at the potentialities of the Internet for international networking in the global political arena: 'Open to everyone, the Internet offers new possibilities to those trying to challenge the established order. "The revolutionary forces of the future may consist increasingly of widespread multi-organisational networks that have no particular national identity, claim to arise from civil society and include aggressive groups and individuals who are keenly adept at using advanced technology for communications." So spoke the Rand Corporation in 1993. But did they mean multinational corporations or the social movements opposing them? Both sides could fit the description, and that tells us something about the most important political battle of our time, one in which the Internet is playing an increasingly important role' (Doherty, 1996).

Our purpose is to generate some conceptual tools that can help to design a more systematic comparative research into the hypothesis that ICT's are changing social movements. Before we will be able to do so in a more or less systematic and fruitful manner, we think we need a kind of conceptualisation that will help us to guide and focus such an empirical endeavour. In this contribution, we want to see if we can find some more or less explicit dimensions in the scholarly literature on SMOs. Dimensions, that can help us to formulate more specific questions and expectations. As we know from earlier research in the field of public administration, we know we cannot start with the well-described characteristics of ICTs alone (apart from the question whether it might not be wise to restrict such a more empirical study to some more or less well-defined applications of these technologies, like E-mail communication or Web-sites, see in Van de Donk & Snellen, 1998). A study into the implications of ICTs demands knowledge of the field in which these implications are studied, merely because of the fact that the use and impacts of these technologies are, to a large extent, 'socially constructed'. ICTs are changing the 'logic of the situation', and fostering new optima that challenge existing practices. When we want to generate some questions about the meaning of ICTs in this part of the polity, we thus need some idea of the main dimensions that are used to describe and explain the role SMO's play in the democratic and political arena in a more general way. This will also help us to avoid an all too exclusive (or even 'deterministic) focus on technology in studying its 'impacts' on social and political practices. It is very important to underline that these 'impacts' generally must be considered as *'outcomes'* that emerge from a complex interplay between new technologies and existing institutions and practices (Van de Donk, 1997; Van de Donk& Snellen, 1998; Brown & Duguid, 2000).

In this chapter, we will try to analyse some of the most authoritative knowledge in this fields from an information- and communication perspective. The modest but nonetheless not unimportant goal we have set ourselves for this contribution is to see to what kind of hypotheses about the 'impacts' of the use of the Internet we can derive from our reading of the scholarly literature on (new) social movements (e.g. Della Porta, Kriesi & Rucht, 1999; Kriesi, Koopmans, Duyvendak & Giugni, 1995; Meyer & Tarrow, 1998).

As far as this literature is concerned, it immediately becomes clear that it is much more adequate to speak of literatures: we came across a number of quite different models and approaches. We think that it is –at least for our purposes- possible to discern five generations or approaches of social movement theory (SMT). Each of these approaches uses a rather specific, more or less developed conceptualisation about the way social movements emerge and about the way they are finding their way into the democratic and political arena. We will see that information- and communication dimensions, up til now, are given attention only in a very implicit manner.

In section 2 we will briefly present the main characteristics of these approaches in the study of (new) social movements. We will try to re-examine these theories and approaches in light of the information- and communication technologies that are now more and more finding their way into these organisations and into the 'interaction' contexts in which they are functioning. We will try to single out some key-dimensions that might be interesting for the conceptualisation of the way ICTs change social movement organisations. These dimensions will be used to formulate some questions and expectations, and some 'educated guesses'. These' guesses' will also be informed by another part of SMO-theories, the part that regards typologies of the different kinds of SMOs we find. In section 3, we will discuss some typologies that have been constructed as an analytical tool for discerning and distinguishing different types of social movements (e.g. different goal orientations, different repertoires, different kinds of organisation). We will see that the frequently used distinction between 'old' and 'new' social movements is an important (but just one) dimension that is used to construct these typologies. Other dimensions, too, seem to be interesting when looking at the complex interplay between ICTs and these social movements. It might very well be that some types of movements are much more 'receptive' to specific applications of ICTs than others.

Before we try to use the theoretical work on social movements to elaborate some more questions and explorative guesses regarding on the possible ways the Internet might affect the internal and external functioning of social movements (in the final section, 5), we also present a quick scan of some (in section 4) examples of how the Internet is used by some of the well-known social movements in the ecological field.

2   Social Movements: Five Theoretical Approaches

Looking into the world of social movements, one is quickly aware of the fact that the term encompasses a multitude of organisations, differing in size, object and work methods. "I'll know one, when I see one", is a phrase that best seems to fit the description. The dimensions of the functioning of social movements cannot, it seems, be derived from one or more authoritative definitions. Looking into the field of social movement theory did learn us two lessons. The first is that there is a multitude of approaches and theories, that all reflect and represent a certain 'generation' of research into the phenomenon. The second lesson is that no -or hardly no- explicit attention is paid to the information- and communication aspects and dimensions that underlie the functioning of social movements. Here again, it is clear that looking into the meaning of ICTs, functions as a kind of X-ray that demands a re-examination of the knowledge in the field (e.g. Taylor, 1998).

The empirical research into the phenomenon of the new social movement has mainly been developed in the eighties and nineties, following earlier research in the United States in the fifties and sixties. Although it is possible to speak of a development in generations, this development is certainly not cumulative. Therefore, it seems more appropriate to speak of them as 'approaches' (let alone paradigms), that can be discerned by the method with which the phenomenon of the social movement has been observed. Reading some of the most seminal works in the field of social movement theory, we think we can discern the following approaches:

*   the classic (collective behaviour) approach;
*   the resource-mobilisation approach;
*   the political opportunity approach;
*   the approach on ideologically structured action, and;
*   the discourse, 'framing' or social construction approach.

In the following, we will first give a short outline of the main characteristics of each of these approaches. After that, we will try to extract some key dimensions that may be used to generate some ideas about how the Internet might effect the functioning of social movements.

1 Classical approach (collective behaviour)
Leading authors within the so-called collective behaviour approach of social movement are Kornhauser (1959), Smelser (1962) and sociologists (e.g. Talcott Parsons) originating in the well-known Chicago School. Most of them conceptualised the emergence and the functioning of these movements from a macro-perspective on 'structural strain'. Most authors using this approach used social-psychological models to study fascist and communist mass-movements. They considered the emergence of social movement as a sign of 'system strain' and a certain level of societal stress. Social movements were considered to be societal alarm bells, and both the consequence and the cause of disturbances within the regular political or administrative mechanisms. These extra-institutional political phenomena are indeed considered as a kind of 'writing on the wall'. Social movements were seen as toxins: their establishment and growth an indication of the fact that the regular institutions were not able to resolve political problems in a normal way. They are indicators of an institutional deficit. They were considered as an anomaly. Social movements were, moreover, depicted as a both irrational and temporal type of political behaviour. In most cases, it concerned people that were alienated, most of the time not very well educated, and violent. Social movements were considered to be anti-establishment forces. '(…) The threats these movements represent are most likely of a transitory nature:, that could be successfully countered by further modernisation strategies of the political elites '(…)' if modernizing elites are not overwhelmed by the resistance, and institutions are successfully defined, the resistance is bound to fail. Modernisation will eventually provide the blessings of progress to all. [3]

---

3   From: Mayer, M. (1991) Social Movement Research in the United States: A European Perspective. In International Journal of Politics, Culture and Society, vol. 4, no 4, pp. 459-480

Social movements were seen as '(…) mindless eruptions, lacking either coherence or continuity in social life.'[4] The more sociological approaches (e.g. Blumer, 1951) were less disparaging towards social movements: 'Social movements can be viewed as collective enterprises to establish a new order of life. They have their inception in a condition of unrest, and derive their motive power on one hand from dissatisfaction with the current form of life, and on the other hand, from wishes and hopes for a new scheme of living. (Blumer, 1951). Blumer (despite the fact that he was also a psychologist that tended to explain collective behaviour on the basis of characteristics on an individual level) was the first to pay attention to the organisational dimensions of social movements (see also in McAdam, 1982; Buechler, 2000).

Key Dimensions
This approach might very well be the least interesting one for our aim, but still not completely irrelevant. The principal idea is that social movements are an extra-institutional source of renewal and change, located in the margins of the formal political system, as an alternative form of collective behaviour. This idea can withstand the criticisms that have been brought in against this perspective, and does not need some of the much debated presumptions (the presumptions that collective behaviour is psychological, to be found at the level of the individual, and dangerous and irrational) that dominated the sixties. This was mainly due to the work of scientists who observed that social movements were not always founded in back allies. Actually they were found(ed) in their own garages, and even by their own children. Moreover, these 'irrational' movements were capable of rapidly transforming themselves into highly effective organisations, proving to be a threat to the elite powers, and placing their own ideas onto the political agenda.

II Resource Mobilisation – Rational Choice
It may well have been this observation that has tempted Schwarz to claim that 'participants in social movements are at least as rational as those who study them'.[5] From the criticism that social movements were mainly organisations in which individuals joined from the rationale of costs and benefits, developed an alternative approach. Some important authors are McCarty, Zald, Tilly and Kitchelt, whose work can be situated in the seventies. Their work is inspired by the study of the civil rights movement and other social movements that were developing during those years (McCarty en Zald, 1977). Not deprivations (because these do not always result in social movements), but the access to and the availability of relevant resources and support appear as the critical factors. Others are as the ability to organise and gather these resources for direct action. Supply and demand and a rational approach to deployment become notions that earn themselves a place in the theory of social movements (see, for example, the work of Zald en McCarty). Tilly adds the dimension of

---

4   From: F. Fox Piven and R.A. Cloward (1991) Collective Protest: A Critique of Resource Mobilization Theory. In: International Journal of Politics, Culture and Society, vol. 4, no 4, pp. 435-58.
5   Schwarz, cited in Buechler, 2000:34.

political struggle, which will take an even more important place in following approaches (see below and McAdam, 1982).

Key Dimensions
The resource mobilisation approach is especially focussed on the organisational aspects of the functioning of social movements like structure, culture, and the problems and opportunities associated with growth, democratic leadership, and the relationship between leaders and followers. Processes of institutionalisation and professionalisation are studied in light of Michels' Iron Law of Oligarchy. This famous law seems to be challenged by the newer type of social movements: their grassroots character, as Dalton -among others- points out in his study of the European environmental movement, perseveres. One of the criticisms of this approach is that it is a mainly technical organisational approach, which devotes (too) little attention to the ideological and sub-cultural aspects of the functioning of social movements (Buechler, 1983; 2000). It is focussed on the micro- and meso-levels, largely ignoring the connection with the macro-level. Additionally, it is seen as rather a-historical and instrumental (see Buechler, 2000).

III Political Opportunity Structure/Political Process
Important authors connected to this approach are Tilly (1978), McAdam (1982), Tarrow (1994), Kriesi, Duyvendak en Rucht. They focus mainly on the instrumental and organisational dimensions of the functioning of social movements, by pointing out relevant differences in success and operational methods that can be explained by the inclusion and exclusion of political processes. The political opportunity structure is the main notion of this approach, and consists of a large number of variables and dimensions that proved to be of critical importance to the functioning of social movements. This is especially apparent in the international comparative research that was partly responsible for the development of this approach. Why is the peace movement successful in Germany and The Netherlands, but not in France? The explanations could not be found in the capability to organise the available resources, but rather in the structure of possibilities that were connected to the political system. Resources and action repertoire are explicitly studied in connection to the political opportunity structure. Within this approach, the focus is on the most important political divisions/contradictions (can a social movement break free of the dominant divisions between left and right, and how does an electoral system contribute to that?); the formal institutions (e.g. the level of vertical centralisation, horizontal concentration, the representativeness of the electoral system and the role of direct democracy), and the dominant strategy towards social movements that is employed by the formal political institutions (facilitating, assimilative, co-operative, or repressive, confrontational, and polarising).

Key Dimensions
This approach is focussed on the political-administrative environment as a structure of opportunities. We prefer to see these environments as a series of interaction contexts that also include the relationships with other social movements and society at large (and, we would like to add, corporations and the media). Also, the attitude of government towards

social movements (oppressive, assimilating) and some other variables regarding political cultures and structures are important (e.g. degree of centralization, election systems). The use of referenda, for instance, is, in a perspective that seeks to explain the functioning of social movements, an important characteristic of an opportunity structure. What could be interesting here is that referenda can now be organised by movements themselves. This perspective also makes clear that in order to study the meaning of ICTs for social movements, the use of ICTs in relevant interaction contexts (media, politics, administration, citizens, enterprises, infrastructure) has to be taken into account.

IV Ideologically Structured Action /Identity Action Approach
Dalton (1994) criticises the approach mentioned above based on extensive empirical research of the structure and recent history of European environmental movements. At the end of his argument, he concludes that 'Any systemic differences between nations are outweighed by the variation across groups within nations.' (Dalton, 1994: 209). He emphasises that the choice of repertoire and goals is mainly the result of core values and ideological principles, rather than an intelligent anticipation of the opportunity structure. He shows that movements that are financially supported by their government are less inclined to use unconventional methods, and are focussed on influencing policy rather than mobilising public opinion. He argues that '(...) the data support Lipsky's dictum that protest is the politics of the powerless, organisations with abundant resources were more likely to work through conventional channels.' (Dalton, 1994:202).

Key Dimensions
The key dimensions of this approach are the analyses of the relationship between core values, goals, instruments/repertoire and the capability to form alliances. The connection between core values and -identities and strategy and tactics is suitable to a time in which a lot of new social movements developed, focussed on identity (gender, sexuality). Furthermore, considerable attention was devoted to the success of small social movements, not striving for maximum size and professionalization, success that could not be explained by the resource mobilisation theory.

V Discursive / Framing / Social Constructive Approach
Yet another approach to the phenomenon of social movements was developed under the name of social constructivism: an approach that studies social movements from the perspective of so-called 'frames': connected constructions of language and images, describing or representing a problem that is seen as a socially constructed problem. The approach is also known as the narrative or discursive approach, and is focussed on the reconstruction of behavioural practices from their contribution in influencing 'frames'. For example: is the problem of congested roads an environmental problem or an economic problem connected to mobility? How are the perceptions of a certain 'problem' managed? Important authors in this tradition are Klandermans, Snow, Benford, Gamson and Haijer (e.g. Snow en Benford, 1992; Klandermans, 1989; Haijer, 1985; Gamson, 1995, 1998). 'Frames' are frameworks of interpretation, which can be in conflict, or can be part of a certain hierarchy. Snow en Benford argue that 'master frames' are the most essential, as they

can provide an entire group of social movements with a sense of direction: 'Master frames refer to the broadest structures of meaning in social movements that define grievances in terms of oppression, injustice, or exploitation, and call for liberation, fairness or equity. Their generality is what allows master frames to be adopted by more than one constituency, multiple groups can find a home under the broad symbolic canopy of a masterframe.' Masterframes are strongly connected to cycles and waves that characterise a social movement as a whole: 'Master frames influence the goals, tactics, strategies, coalitions and resources of entire social movement industries[6]'. For this reason, the concept provides a potential bridge between the largely microlevel focus of the framing (narrative approach, WD/BF) perspective and the macrolevel, ideological questions about public, political and media discourse (Buechler, 2000: 42; see also Pellow, 1993; Capek, 1993; Perrolle, 1993). Activities of social movements aim to influence competing (corporate, political) frames by making connections, changing or expanding interpretations, or by redefining the entire frame.

Key Dimensions
Important in this approach is the analysis of the way in which what Gamson refers to as 'robust collective-action frames' are shaped: by connecting everyday experiences, media discourse and more or less clear core values (equality, injustice). The role of media (who as access, who determines images) and information-ecologies (who owns, produces, controls relevant data?) are likely to be relevant dimensions that might be influenced by new media, or ICT-development. What does it mean that the Internet will facilitate environmental groups to have their own unmediated broad (and narrow) casting channels?

Approach	Some Key Dimensions
Classical approach (Collective behaviour)	• Organisational growth • Relationship with members • Shaping the agenda
Resource mobilisation - Rational Choice	• Organisational structure/culture • Participation/mobilisation of members • Professionalisation/Institutionalisation
Political Opportunity Structure	• Connection to opportunity structure • Relevant actors in societal/political environment • Action repertoire
Ideologically Structured Action	• Core values • Identity
Discursive/Social Constructive Approach	• Language/Images • Frame-management • Management of perceptions

Table 1: Some Key Dimensions we inferred from the Theoretical Approaches to Social Movements

---

6   The notion is formulated by Zald, who discerns Social Movements (SM's), Social Movement Organizations (SMO's), that are clustered in Social Movement Industries (SMI's) who together form the Social Movement Sector (SMS) (see Mcarthy en Zald, 1977; Buechler, 2000).

3   Social Movements: Mapping a Heterogeneous Phenomenon

The variation that is so characteristic of the theoretical approaches towards social movements is mirrored by the diversity of social movements active in the public domain. In his research into the environmental movement, Dalton states that the movement as a whole is characterised by a variety, which seems to be a kind of requisite variety, a variety that enables the environmental movement 'industry' to establish and maintain connections with different groups in society: 'This diversity in methods and goals enables environmental groups to mobilise a variety of supporters and to attract resources from various sectors of society; diversity enables different elements of the movement to develop alliances with other interest groups and political institutions, and diversity enables the movement to utilise a variety of tactics in influencing the policy process: all in the name of environmental action.' (Dalton, 1994:112). When that variety is replaced with specialisation and concentration based on a more radical and exclusive ecologism, the possibilities to get connected to other actors in society and politics decrease. Dalton's comparative study shows that ecological movements have a relatively weak connection to the political-administrative system, and rely on media attention and media-based public support: 'Our findings also carry several implications for the strategies and tactics of environmental groups that follow from their negative perceptions of most polity members. If we accept the classification of the overall movement as political outsiders, environmentalists (and especially ecologists) will frequently find themselves dependent on unconventional tactics to upset the prevailing political balance. This might entail dramatic actions meant to pressure public agencies or spectacular events designed to capture media attention and to mobilise political support for their cause. Indeed, the one important ally that was missing from these analyses is the broad popular support that environmental reform receives from the European public. The populist base of environmentalism makes the relationship between these groups and the mass media especially important, because media coverage is vital to developing and mobilising public support in order to tilt the political balance.' (Dalton, 1994:175).

Dalton distinguishes conservationists and ecologists, a division to which Rucht (1997) adds the environmentalists. The latter tries to improve nature from a pragmatic perspective, the former is focussed on the conservation and repair of nature. The ecologists are the most radical group, operating from a fundamental critique of economy and society, and arguing that the root of the environmental problem lies in the structure and functioning of economy and society. Ideological radicalism is more important to them than pragmatic results.

Another well-known distinction is that made by van der Heijden (1997). He discerns instrumental movements (focussed outward, trying to realise goals by influencing politics and, more and more, corporations), subcultural movements (focussed inward, establishing projects, education and training based on collective identity), and countercultural movements (focussed outward, characterised by the development and deployment of a fundamental critique of society).

It is very likely that an investigation into the use of ICTs by social movements explicitly has to take into account that great differences between movements in this sense do exists, and can make a difference in the acceptance, moment and type of use, type of outcomes that are related to ICT-applications. Some of these differences are already coming to the fore in the next section, where some cases are presented that report on the use of the Internet by environmental movements.

4   A Quick Scan of some Websites in the Domain of Ecological and Environmental Movements

In this section, we present a limited and highly inductive and still impressionistic 'quick-scan' of some environmental movement websites. Websites are of course just one way to look into the way these movements are using new media. It is like saying something about a house and a family by only studying the front door at a given moment in time. Still, websites are interesting as a starting point, for at least some of them do reflect some of the essential (new) functions these organisations wish to fulfil. A more complete research would also demand an approach that combines website-analysis with on-site analysis. On the other hand, it is clear that some of the more or less completely virtual movements (like virtual communities) will demand both a research strategy and –methodology that adequately reflects the characteristics of the new phenomenon it wants to study. In this stage of our research, we only are able to present a set of 'interesting practices' we have found on the net. It seeks to explore the ways in which they take advantage of the possibilities offered to them by being present on the World Wide Web. We visited five websites[7]: Greenpeace, Friends of the Earth, the World Wildlife Fund, the Sierraclub, and the Institute for Global Communication's EcoNet.

Stop Japanese Whaling: www.greenpeace.org
The Greenpeace website offers a wealth of information concerning different environmental issues: toxics, forests, even the Olympics. Visitors can interact by Emailing Greenpeace offices, join or leave a mailinglist, and even become cyberactivists (although it is not clear what that entails). Visitors can also join Greenpeace by making a donation (a site which conveniently keeps popping back to the screen) In addition, Greenpeace offers the visitors to its website the possibility to 'Let the Japanese Prime Minister, Yoshiro Mori, know of your personal opposition to the hunt by e-mailing a letter to him via the Japanese Embassy in your country'. The action alert is set to automatically choose the correct embassy for each country. Greenpeace does realise that some countries are more powerful than others: if the visitor is a US citizen, he or she can also send a letter to President Clinton. The visitor is asked to fill in his or her mailing address, which is then automatically added to the letter. A possibility is built in to review the letter suggested by Greenpeace and modify the letter before sending it.

Gifts Among Friends: www.foe.org
The American site of Friends of the Earth establishes its radical character by devoting its website to 'Fighting Environmental Destruction where it Begins'. The visitor is presented

---

7   All the sites mentioned were studied in the second half of August, 2000.

with a load of information concerning its international program, its community, health and environment program, and the upcoming presidential elections, including profiles on both the Republican and Democratic candidates. Visitors can join Friends of the Earth by making donations, and the visitor is given the possibility to 'let all your Friends and loved ones know that you are a Friend of the Earth by ordering our great environmentally friendly products! Perfect for any occasion, your Friends of the Earth gift purchase allows us to continue to fight environmental destruction where it begins'. All these products, including publications, t-shirts, tote bags, mugs and labels, can be ordered electronically and paid by credit card.

Cyber Voices Against Climate Change: www.panda.org
A visitor trying to find the World Wildlife Fund on the WorldWideWeb is confronted with a site mainly consisting of links to WWF's National Organisations, Program Offices, and Associate Offices (www.wwf.org). The visitor is then directed to www.panda.org, displaying WWF's major campaigns, photo and art galleries, as well as an educational site dedicated to kids. The website reports on a coalition of leading environmental Organizations that recently launched an international web-based initiative 'to give citizens around the world a voice in demanding a halt to global warming. The website www.climatevoice.org has been launched by 16 Organizations, including WWF, Greenpeace and Friends of the Earth. The site aims 'to send 10 million messages from the public to world political leaders demanding that they use the November summit to reduce the pollution that causes global warming'.

Congressional VoteWatch: www.sierraclub.org
The Sierraclub is one of the more traditional environmental movements in the United States. Its website offers environmental news, daily electronic updates, press releases (including Sierra Club's endorsement of Al Gore for President), as well as a possibility to 'join or give'. One of the more interesting aspects of the site is the typically American VoteWatch, where the American voter can check how Congress voted on issues related to the environment. It features a mission statement, bookstore, and can be contacted by ways of three different electronic addresses.

Connecting People who are Changing the World: www.igc.org
The Institute for Global Communications (IGC) is a non-profit organisation introducing social movements to email, online discussions, mailing lists and the Internet in general. IGC offers individuals and groups 'a place on the Internet to learn, meet and organise'. Activists and non-profit are introduced to technologically based instruments as information sharing and collaborative tools. IGC's EcoNet features a calendar of upcoming events, discussion forums on a wide range of issues, a news service, as well as the possibility to make a donation.

This quick-scan into the activities of environmental movements on the web seems at first sight to confirm the wide-held belief that technology is currently a facilitator of a certain type of repertoire social movements use. Letter writing, mobilisation and donations are of course very well possible in the physical world, but have been made easier and more accessible by means of technology. The scale that can be reached with web-petitions and cyber-activism cannot, however, be compared with that of paper ones. Still, we do not have yet the evidence that this will make a difference for those receiving them, although the mentioned example of the angry Pilgrim Fathers does show a kind of distance danger. With the activities of many of these movements largely comparable, the diversity in movements is expressed in mission statements and site layout, accentuating different aspects of social movement activity. Notable is the absence of the use of the Internet's interactive possibilities. Although all of the sites mentioned here have Email-addresses, only a few provide online discussion forums, and communication is still largely a one-way street, the movement providing the visitor with information. However, E-mail communication and hyperlinks are used to communicate with supporters. The absence of links to other, likeminded movements, is also remarkable. Although movements like Greenpeace and the World Wildlife Fund refer to their numerable national sites, none of the movements mentioned above refers the visitor to one of the other. However, as the initiative mentioned at WWF's site proves, collaborative initiatives do exist, but not as part of the individual websites. Instead, a separate website is created, devoted to a single issue or event, a trend started by the already legendary site devoted to the WTO Summit in Seattle.

5   ICTs and Social Movements: A Double Pattern of Institutionalisation?

In the former sections we have explored some of the major theoretical work that has been done on social movements. Each of the approaches has suggested one ore more specific dimensions that might be of interest when studying the way the Internet is changing existing ways of organizing, mobilizing, action and institutionalisation. We concluded that in most of this work there is no explicit reflection on dimensions of information and communication, dimensions that nevertheless seem so obviously important for both organization and action in this field. We also have seen that the 'social movement industry', as Zald once called it, is in fact a quite heterogeneous ensemble of quite different kinds of organisations. It is very likely that some of these movements are much more inclined to introduce and use some applications of ICTs than others. Some of them have a 'cultural' attitude that is very eager to integrate these new technologies, others are much more reluctant towards processes of virtualisation. New combinations and patterns of institutionalisation are expected to arise. Already, a quite limited look at some websites of globally oriented environmental movements mirrors a series of different aims that are pursued by this type of use of the Internet. Some of these sites are used to organise or mobilize, some others notably serve specific campaigns and actions. The dimensions mentioned in the earlier sections (like organizational growth, the relationships with members and supporters and the organization of participation and mobilization) are very likely to be affected by the use of websites, although we still do not now very much about how and to what extent this is the case. A more elaborate examination will demand a much more extensive look behind the screens that are so colourfully presented on the web. Our contribution to this conference book must be limited to an effort to prepare the start of such a more elaborate examination. Both theory and methodology of such research will have to be developed much further in the years to come. Still, we think that it is possible to formulate some questions, guesses and expectations on the basis of the earlier sections.

Virtual movements: new patterns of organization?
As the availability and accessibility of information is greatly improved with new technology, many of the social movements look at the Internet as a cost-effective way to reach a large number of people (both supporters, volunteers as well as those who they are trying to influence). How this will affect future patterns of mobilization, organization and even institutionalisation of SMOs seems to be an important question. Most of these movements will most likely remain on a double course of institutionalisation: they will probably combine a virtual and a real institutionalisation. Others seem to be much more on the virtual side: which probably means that a whole array of new types have to be added to the typologies that have been developed so far. The political opportunity structure approach, developed by Kriesi and his colleagues, suggests that the ways that governments will be opening up their information and communications infrastructures will very much determine the extent to which social movements will be successful in using the Internet in pursuing their political and social goals.

The resource mobilization approach leads us to questions about the way ICTs are changing the internal organizations of social movements. Following Bekkers' typology of virtual organisations, we might expect the emergence of federal, concentric, platform, portal and web-based kind of patterns of virtual movements (Bekkers, 2000). These virtual patterns can both challenge and reinforce existing patterns that are found in the social movement industry. Especially in the field of the more ideologically oriented, grass-roots movements, a radical virtualisation might be a viable scenario (which probably means that decision makers will have to cope with 'surprise-movements': we might expect a great future for virtual movements that will appear as quickly and surprisingly as they disappear). Membership (mobilization and participation patterns) will most likely develop in many more ways than we now know. deterritorialisation and virtualisation do will most probably challenge some of the important 'organizational dimensions' (traditional mobilization potential, participation patterns and radius of action).

On the streets, or on-line?
Moreover, these characteristics of virtual politics might also add substantial and powerful instruments to the action-repertoire of these movements (why not block the information highways?). Especially in the field of agenda-setting and policy-formulation, these radically enhanced information- and communication powers are already used very successfully on both the regional, national and transnational levels. Organizations like Greenpeace and Friends of the Earth do not only provide information on their own activities, but also on governmental, non-governmental and corporate policies. These changing information powers largely contributed to the success of some NGO's in blocking OECD policies in the field of multinational corporations. Doherty describes how new weapons are used by non-governmental organisations and social movements to block OECD-policies: '(...) in the campaign against the Multilateral Agreement on Investment (MAI) - an agreement between the OECD nations that would have placed major restrictions on the ability of states to

regulate the activities of multinational corporations - there were no significant street protests but a lot of online activity. In fact, it was the Internet that gave campaigning groups the power to derail the agreement. Once the main discussion document was leaked and posted on the Web, then unions, environmental groups, consumer groups and others promised so much opposition from such diverse sources that it became politically untenable for the OECD to proceed. The authority of civil servants and their private briefings was undermined by the fact that non-governmental organisations often knew more about what was going on than they did. (Doherty, 1999).

Technology has also increased the mobilising capability of social movements by enabling them to reach out to a large number of people at the same time. Social movements are traditionally associated with mass rallies and demonstrations, thus putting pressure on governments and businesses to adjust policy. This mobilisation function of social movements is facilitated by information and communication technology as those involved can post information on upcoming events on the Internet. Activists from all over the world can be invited to participate in demonstrations, rallies, etc. (see, for example, the homepage devoted to the 'Mobilization for Global Justice' at www.a16.org). Afterwards, reports and photographs can be placed on the Web in order to let people share in the excitement and gain support. However, there is great uncertainty about the question whether a lack of physical meetings and rallies will diminish this capability: can virtual demonstrators do without the emotions that for many activists are the motivation behind their engagement? This issue is even more important, now that the forming of horizontal and vertical coalitions between different organisations is for a large part a result of the activities of facilitating organisations like the Institute for Global Communication (IGC). Many of the collaborative efforts of social movements are focussed on a certain theme or event. In this respect, the position of the 'supra-movements' or 'umbrella-websites' is of particular interest. The increased focus on events, facilitated by multi-media technological developments, raises the issue of the rise of so-called virtual members, as social movements are already faced with an increased level of checkbook-participation, as well as an aging support group. The costs of participation in social movement activity however, have shifted from travel expenses to the cost of an Internet connection. Not clear is, however, how this shift will affect actual participation patterns, which perhaps cannot be completely reduced to a kind of tele-engagement. Will digital demonstrations really be able to replace the thrill of participating in a mass rally in Seattle?

References

Ayres, Jeffrey M. (1999) 'From the Streets to the Internet - The Cyber-Diffusion of Contention. (The Social Diffusion of Ideas and Things)', *The Annals of the American Academy of Political and Social Science*, 566, 132(12)

Bekkers, V.J.J.M. (1998) *Grenzeloze overheid - over informatisering en grensveranderingen in het openbaar bestuur*, Alphen aan den Rijn: Samsom

Blumer. H. (1951) 'Social Movement', in A.M. Lee (ed.) (1951) *New Outlines of the Principles of Sociology*, New York: Barnes & Noble

Bogumil, J. and H.J. Lange (1991) *Computer in Parteien und Verbänden*, Opladen: Westdeutscher Verlag

Brown, J.S. and P. Duguid: (2000) *The Social Life of Information*, Boston: Harvard Business School Press

Buechler, S.M. (2000) *Social movements in advanced capitalism - the political economy and cultural construction of social activism*, New York: Oxford University Press

Capek, S.M. (1993) 'The "Environmental Justice" Frame - A Conceptual Discussion and an Application', *Social Problems - Official Journal of the Society for the Study of Social Problems*, 40, 1, pp. 5-24

Dalton, R.J. (1994) *The Green Rainbow - Enviromental Groups in Western Europe*, New Haven & London: Yale University Press

Della Porta, D., H. Kriesi and D. Rucht (eds) (1999) *Social Movements in a Globalizing World*, Houndmills: MacMillan

Depla, P.F.G. & P.W. Tops (1995) 'Political Parties in the Digital Era - The Technological Challenge?', in W.B.H.J. van de Donk, I.Th.M. Snellen and P.W. Tops (eds) (1995) *Orwell in Athens - A Perspective on Informatization and Democracy*, Amsterdam: IOS Press

Doherty, B. (1999) 'Change the world via e-mail - the Internet offers new possibilities for challenging the established order', *New Statesman*, Nov. 1 1999, pp. xviii-xix

Donk, W.B.H.J. van de (1997) *De arena in schema - Een verkenning van de betekenis van informatisering voor beleid en politiek inzake de verdeling van middelen onder verzorgingshuizen*, Lelystad: Koninklijke Vermande

Donk, W.B.H.J. van de and P.W. Tops (1992) 'Informatization and Democracy: Orwell or Athens? - A Review of the Literature', *Informatization and the Public Sector*, 2, pp.169-196

Donk, W.B.H.J. van de and P.W. Tops (1995) 'Orwell or Athens? - Informatization and the Future of Democracy' in W.B.H.J. van de Donk, I.Th.M. Snellen and P.W. Tops (eds.) (1995) *Orwell in Athens - A Perspective on Informatization and the Future of Democracy*, Amsterdam, Oxford, Tokyo, Washington, D.C.: IOS Press, pp.13-32

Duyvendak, J.W. (1995) *The Power of Politics - New Social Movements in France*, Boulder, CO: Westview Press

Frantzich, S.E. (1989) *Political Parties in the Technological Age*, New York: Longman Inc

Frissen, P.H.A. (1999) *Politics, Governance and Technology - A Postmodern Narrative on the Virtual State*, Cheltenham: Edward Elgar

Hague, B.N. and B.D. Loader (eds.) (1999), *Digital democracy - discourse and decision making in the information age*, London: Routledge

Heijden, H. van der (1997) 'Political opportunity structure and the institutionalisation of the environmental movement', *Environmental Politics*, 6, 4

Hoff, J. et al (eds.) (2000) *Democratic governance and new technology - technologically mediated innovations in political practice in Western Europe*, London: Routledge

Klandermans, P.G. (ed.) (1989) *Organizing for change - social movement to organizations in Europe and the United States*, Greenwich, Conn.: JAI

Kornhauser, W. (1962) *The politics of mass society*, Glencoe, Ill: Free Press

Kriesi, H., R. Koopmans, J.W. Duyvendak and M. Giugni (1995) *New Social Movements in Western Europe - A Comparative Analysis*, London: UCL Press

Kutner, L.A. (2000) 'Environmental Activism and the Internet', *Electronic Green Journal*, 12

Levitt, T. (1973) *The Third Sector - New Tactics for a Responsive Society*, New York: AMACOM

Löfgren, K. (2000) 'Danish Political Parties and New Technology: Interactive Parties or New Shop Windows?', in: Hoff, J. et al (eds.) (2000) *Democratic governance and new technology - technologically mediated innovations in political practice in Western Europe*, London: Routledge

Mayer, M. (1991) 'Social Movement Research in the United States: A European Perspective', *International Journal of Politics, Culture and Society*, 4, 4, pp. 459-480

McAdam, J.D., D. McCarthy and M. N. Zald (1996) *Comparative Perspectives on Social Movements - Political Opportunities, Mobilizing Structures and Cultural Framings*, Cambridge, England: Cambridge University Press

Meyer, D.S. and S. Tarrow (1998) *The Social Movement Society - Contentious Politics for a new Century*, Lanham, Maryland: Rowman & Littlefield

Nixon, P. and H. Johansson (1999) 'Transparency through Technology - The Internet and Political Parties', in B.N. Hague and B.D. Loader (eds.) (1999) *Digital democracy - discourse and decision making in the information age*, London: Routledge, pp.135-153

Pellow, D.N. (1999) 'Framing Emerging Environmental Movement Tactics - Mobilizing Consensus, Demobilizing Conflict', *Sociological Forum*, 14, 4, pp. 659-683

Perrolle, J.A. (1993) 'Comments from the Special Issue Editor - The Emerging Dialogue on Environmental Justice', *Social Problems - Official Journal of the Society or the Study of Social Problems*, 40, 1, pp.1-4

Piven, F.F. and R.A. Cloward (1991) 'Collective Protest - A Critique of Resource Mobilization Theory', *International Journal of Politics, Culture and Society*, 4, 4, pp. 435-58

Rink, D. (2000) ' Soziale Bewegungen im 21. Jahrhundert'. *Forschungsjournal Neue Soziale Bewegungen*, 13, 1, pp. 26-31

Rucht, D., B. Blattert and D. Rink (1997) *Soziale Bewegungen auf dem Weg nach Institutionaliserung*, New York: Campus

Smelser, N.J. (1962) *Theory of collective behavior*, London: Routledge & Kegan Paul

Smith, C. (2000) 'British Political Parties - Continuity and Change in the Information Age', in: Hoff, J. et al (eds.) (2000) *Democratic governance and new technology - technologically mediated innovations in political practice in Western Europe*, London: Routledge

Taylor, J. (1998) 'Information X-ray - What is Public Administration for the Information Age?', in I.Th.M. Snellen, I.Th.M. and W.B.H.J. van de Donk (eds.) (1998) *Public Administration in an Information Age - A Handbook*, Amsterdam/Berlin/Oxford/Tokyo: IOS Press, pp. 21-46

Tarrow, S. (1998) *Power in Movement - Social movements and contentious politics,* Cambridge: Cambridge University Press

Tilly, C. (1978) *From mobilization to revolution,* Reading, Mass.: Addison-Wesley

Zald, M. and J. McCarthy (1990) *Social Movements in an Organizational Society - Collected Essays*, New Brunswick, NJ: Transaction Books

Zelwietro, J. (1998) 'The Politicization of Environmental Organizations through the Internet', *The Information Society*, 14, pp. 45-56

Chapter 12

Citizen Centred Government. The Dutch Approach

Matt Poelmans

1   Reinventing Dutch Government

In 1996 the Netherlands government started a program to improve public service delivery by introducing the concept of a single window to government under the name *Overheidsloket 2000* (Public Counter 2000). Its two main elements are: integration of services from the perspective of the citizen instead of the logic of the organization; and the use of the Internet as the new way of communication between government and its citizens. In organizational terms it means the separation between the front- and back office and necessitates a major change in internal procedures. In order to respond to citizens needs, separate branches of one organization or different administrative bodies in different tiers of government have to work together. The focus of cooperation is what is called citizen's demand patterns: life events that should be dealt with as a whole. Examples are: moving to a new town, starting a business, building a house, finding a old-age home for senior citizens and so on.

In order to promote this concept amongst the 537 independent municipalities in Holland (and approximately the same number of other public bodies such as regional councils, chambers of commerce, tax offices, land registry bureaux and so on), the government instituted a special task force and bureau (www.ol2000.nl) . With a budget of about 50 million Dutch guilders a three year program was executed of which the main action lines were: a pilot-project scheme; a research program; a nationwide promotion campaign. This first phase was quite successful and last year it was decided to continue the program for another three years.

2   Customer Orientation

The idea of responsive customer-oriented government is in itself not new. But people are getting used to low prices, high quality and quick service in the market sector. They are in a way spoilt by the business sector and will demand the same kind of service from the public sector. This means a major change in attitude. Civil servants are still raised in the Weberian tradition which values risk-avoiding cumbersome decision-making, but will have to cope with a more demanding, rapidly changing and client-driven environment. Internet as a metaphor of the network society we are heading into, enables this transfer. One of the fundamental differences of the new

J. E. J. Prins (ed.), Designing E-Government, 173–175.

information technology is that is facilitates cooperation whereas in former days automation in many cases was a reason for growing divisions.

Although we are moving into the virtual age, we remain physical beings living in a concrete world. On the other hand we easily forget that many contacts in a way are already virtual. Approximately 80% of contacts between citizen and government go by phone. People will be visiting physical counters in the future, but will do so less and less and instead use e-mail, Internet, phone or fax. Organizations should prepare for multichannel consumer relations management which is required. Also the boundaries between internal and external personnel will gradually vanish. A citizen who electronically fills in a form which is fed into your database has become, at least temporarily, a civil servant!

The results of integrated service delivery are first of all customer satisfaction; secondly improvement in efficiency (less costs and quicker services); and thirdly and probably most important: more effective policy because of a better reach of target groups.

The first three-year pilot phase of the OL-program was expressly designed to find out in practice wether the idea of a single counter was feasible. On an experimental basis physical and virtual counters were introduced in 15 municipalities (large and small) in the domains of real estate, services for handicapped and elderly, moving to a new town, etc. After evaluation the main obstacles proved to be legislation and cooperation, whereas resistance from change remained relatively small. From this is was concluded that one could go further by developing portal sites for certain complexes of integrated services.

In the meantime it became apparent that many governments and organizations already had undertaken al kinds initiatives of their own to change their citizen relations. Therefore is was decided to try to standardise developments by defining a reference-model for the architecture of a virtual counter. A toolkit for an integrated service counter is being developed which consists of ten components. Some of these are: a standardised description of demand patterns, a catalogue of matching products and services, an interactive electronic form, a model integrated web site, and so on.

3   Implementation Phase

On the basis of the pilot projects the Dutch cabinet decided in 1999 that the program was be continued for another 3 years. During the period 2000-2002 three types of single counters will be developed on an operational basis: a Business counter; a Building and Housing counter; and a Health and Welfare counter. This will be done in 30 test projects all over the country. With the help of the OL program bureau they will develop a toolkit composed of 10 instruments, such as a demand pattern inventory, a products and services database, a virtual prototype counter, a model cooperation contract, and so on.

At the same time a fourth counter is under construction: the Work and Income counter, which moreover is done on a compulsory (legal) basis. This will result in 200 physical one-stop-shops for job-mediation, vocational training and unemploy-ment benefits .

The idea behind each single counter is that the most relevant organizations work together. The first stage is for them to pool their information: make it available in digital form and also be cross-referenced. This is not al all easy and if realised is a great service to the public and to other government partners as well. The second stage is to provide for questions to be answered: what does the general information mean for a certain individual or what is he entitled to. This consultation should be available in both physical and virtual form alike. The final stage is that a transaction is effected: either an intake is done on line, a registration filed electronically, or a permit is being delivered electronically. A roll-out is scheduled in the year 2003

Finally, as is the case in the private sector where B2B-commerce is at present more important than B2C-commerce, in the public sector too the use of the internet is not restricted to the relation citizen – government. One should not forget that E-Government has a major role to play in business to government or inter-government relations, such as procurement.

4   Demanding Citizens

The new possibilities of ICT have until now become manifest in the field of service delivery, both commercial and public. The banking and insurance branch has demonstrated the necessity and nicety of electronic orders and transactions. In the Netherlands about 40% of annual income tax forms are filled in electronically and vehicle-tax registration can also be done on line.

When people get more and more used to this type of·dealings, they might want to have the same level of service in other sectors. However, one should keep in mind that the citizen is not only a client or customer, in which capacity (voter) he is the master of government. Access to information is a prerequisite for optimal democratic behaviour. That's why in 1999 a portal web site was opened (www.overheid.nl) which offers access to public authorities on all levels of government.

Because of the complexities of modern society we apply the system of representative democracy. Modern media however offer possibilities for direct democracy, ranging form electronic voting once every four years to permanent digital referenda and all levels of participation in between.

The Dutch liberal-democrat minister Van Boxtel who is responsible for E-Government has a well visited web site on which he discusses his policies during regular chat sessions (www.rogervanboxtel.nl). My own experience as former alderman with email is that Internet does indeed lower barriers. But in order to make this a normal way of working, fundamental changes have to be introduced. In Holland we have had several examples of public digital debates about major policy issues. Whether these are successful or not depends on the attention people are willing to pay to it . Because of their non-verbal character, modern media appeal to many people. So why not use them in politics? But when the barrier to political participation is effectively lowered, it does not automatically enhance the number people taking part. The real test for government and political parties is to make public policy choices as interesting as other choices which people are willing to vote (and also pay!) for, such as a European Song Contest.

Chapter 13

Integrating E-Commerce and E-Government
The Case of Bremen Online Services

Herbert Kubicek and Martin Hagen

1   Introduction

Electronic Government and Electronic Commerce are often viewed as two very different spheres. The first one is launched by governments and is to deliver governmental services online which have to do with forms, signatures and adherence to formal bureaucratic rules. The latter is run by private companies for delivering goods and services and has to do with marketing, credit card payments, and in the end with profit.

But in both areas we find reference to the same set of technologies, the Internet, Electronic Data Interchange, databases, distributed systems.

In this chapter, we want to argue that there are real-life needs to integrate E-Government and E-Commerce to Electronic Services because that is what the customers will claim and the only way to achieve economically sustainable solutions. Citizens want to solve a problem and do not care whether the contributions for solving this problem come from a governmental unit or a commercial business. And as they want all the different partial contributions which are to solve their problem from one stop, in a single window, providers of E-Government and E-Commerce have to put together their offerings.

This is not an easy task as different cultures have to cooperate and different legal requirements have to be implemented in the same technological platform. However, this is the challenge sociotechnical design and development have to solve.

We will illustrate this integration with an ongoing project in the city-state of Bremen, Germany, which started in autumn 1999 to implement One-Stop Government organized according to certain life events such as moving, change of employer, birth of a child, or wedding. And soon it turned out that consequently, following the customers' requirements, a complete service provision had to include services by private businesses as well.

2   Background

The Free Hanseatic City of Bremen (550,000 inhabitants) together with the city of Bremerhaven (100,000 Inhabitants) forms the smallest federal state of Germany. In recent

J. E. J. Prins (ed.), Designing E-Government, 177–196.

years, it has undertaken major efforts for modernising its public administration. Serious financial deficits put the implementation of new public management tools on the top of the internal reform agenda. Recognizing the importance of customer-orientation, an elaborated public administration information system was developed as part of Bremen's online presentation, "bremen.online" (www.bremen.de), and new, decentralized citizen's offices bundling some of the most sought-after public services were established. When the German federal government launched a competition challenging local authorities to develop concepts for implementing digital signatures and online services, the city's administration evaluated these and other projects. It specifically analyzed them in regard to how these projects could be improved or expanded by electronic service delivery.

As many states and cities in Germany and around the world, Bremen is actively promoting electronic commerce with various initiatives. The federal competition, called "MEDIA@Komm", has helped to coordinate these initiatives in a better way and linked them with the public electronic service delivery projects, leading into the plan to create a common platform for electronic services of all kinds.

In Bremen's unique position as a city-state, which combines the function of local and state government on one administrative level, it was possible to include public services offered by state governments in Germany. As these are tax-, law- and higher education-oriented, these services are very attractive for prospective customer groups, for example lawyers, tax preparers, and students, who are likely to adopt and use electronic services most easily. In addition, it is easier to adopt and change the necessary laws, as these can only be drafted by state legislations at many times.

This project is not a pilot for a limited time period, but it is aimed to develop and run a platform for authentic, legally binding and secure electronic transactions which shall be economically self sustaining, at least in the middle run. Therefore a Developing and Operating Company, Bremen Online Services (BOS), has been formed in Public Private Partnership. Private business partners include the Deutsche Telekom and the Sparkasse Bremen (local savings bank), as well as BreKom, a local telephone carrier and operator of the public administration's telephone network, Brokat Infosystems AG, an online banking software developer, VSS and Signum, two local software development companies, the Bremer Straßenbahn AG, the local public transport authority, and Multimedia Centrum Bremerhaven, who represents the City of Bremerhaven in the project. The project is consulted by the Center for Computer Technology (TZI) of the University of Bremen (who also authors this report) and Eutelis Consult, a consulting firm specialized in telecommunications and value-added services. The partners have invested approximately 10 million EUR in the project, matched for the most part by the federal government.

A tentative business case showed that providing online services for the city state of Bremen would never reach a break even point. Therefore a second set of partners had to be won who were ready to share development efforts and /or buy services offered by BOS. The city of Bremerhaven, the city of Oldenburg and the county of Soltau-Fallingbostel, both in the neighboring state of Niedersachsen, the Free and Hanseatic City of Hamburg, the second city-state in the north of Germany, as well as several regional computing centers for public administration throughout Niedersachsen and in another German state, Hessen, have signed letters of intent for a cooperation with BOS.

The main conceptualization and most of the work in the concept phase was done by the project leadership made up of the Technologiezentrum Informatik of the University of Bremen, the consulting firm Eutelis Consult and the Senatskommission für das Personalwesen (SKP), the main agency responsible for IT planning in Bremen government. The main decisions were made by a steering committee, made up of the project leadership, the Senator für Wirtschaft, Mittelstand, Technologie und Europaangelegenheiten (= the State Ministry of Commerce), the Sparkasse Bremen, the Deutsche Telekom AG, the Brekom, the Handelskammer Bremen (= Chamber of Commerce), the Wirtschafts-örderungsgesellschaft Bremen and the Bremer Innovations Agentur (two economic development agencies). Today, the BOS company is running the project (see http://www.bos-bremen.de).

3 Basic Principles of the Bremen Concept

Statements from industry, surveys of citizens and reports from local governments culminate in an impression that everybody wants to offer or receive public services online and that solely some security problems are to blame that this has not become a wide-spread reality yet. The technical instruments for providing secure, trustworthy and legally binding transactions have been in place for quite some time now. The necessary judicial framework was set up by the German Digital Signature law and its accompanying ordinances, as well as by the EU Commissions Directive on Electronic Signatures, which is currently implemented in Germany. However, the diffusion of digital signatures is all but self-propelling. Rather, this goal cannot be accomplished easily because of a series of mostly economic problems.

Digital signatures solve a security problem. But this problem does not exist for most citizens at first. And in addition, to solve it, they have additional expenses. Instead of sending or bringing an application to an office, they have to go first to a certification authority, apply for a digital signature, pay for the certificate and have to mail in the application from home, paying for telecommunications costs all by themselves. Citizens will only do so if the additional value from choosing this procedure outweighs the extra expenses. Extra expenses depend mostly on the configuration of the central electronic service platform, and the extra benefits largely rely on how the services made available on this platform are designed.

More generally spoken, with electronic services the problem emerges that a mediator or secondary service provider steps in between the customer and the primary service provider, who offers additional services - depending on the form of transaction – like electronic transmission, encryption or certification and who wants to earn money with them (see Fig. 1). For these services the customer has to acquire additional technical equipment and competence and change his communication habits; moreover, the primary provider has to adapt his technology and the organization of his business processes, and he has to train his personnel.

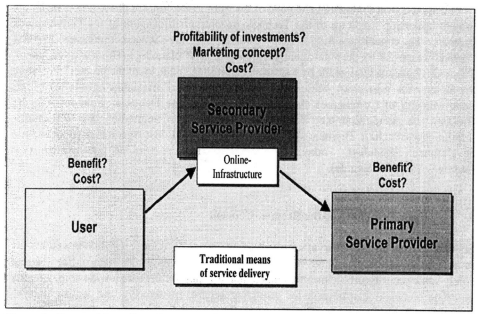

Figure 1: Cost and benefits of secure online services for users and providers

In order to become profitable and sustainable, an online-platform has to comply with three principles which sound self-evident at first sight, but which can only be put in practice by innovative approaches:

1. Electronic transactions must be more useful or less laborious than the present method of personal appearance, phoning or writing a letter. It must be possible to save time and ways and to decrease the telecommunication costs.

    a) The public discussion focusses on the enhancement of citizen-orientation. "Public services at home for 24 hours" is an attractive guiding principle. But most of the citizens are rarely in contact with the administration. For these few contacts, the citizens will not take upon themselves additional efforts and detours like the acquisition of a digital signature and pay monthly fees, like some trust centers expect. This can be achieved by bundling several services required for a certain life event which normally are claimed from different authorities up to now. An example could be moving, where a variety of agencies have to be informed of the same data. According to the principle "services out of one hand", called "one stop government" in the U.S., the change of address can be communicated via one interface and a single platform and be sent to the appropriate agencies (Figure 2).

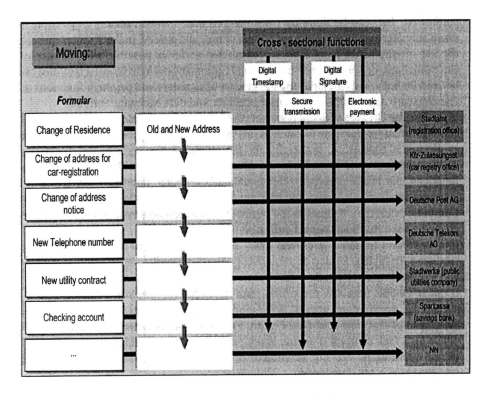

Figure. 2: One-Stop Government for the life event "moving"

There is no doubt that this is a great advantage for a citizen in this situation. But within a city this situation does not occur so often - normally the individual citizen changes address at long intervals – so that the costs for the required online infrastructure cannot be covered at marketable prices for this application. But it can become an attractive additional service if the infrastructure is financed by other high-volume applications.

b) In many cases, professional intermediaries handle the administrative matters for the citizens. For them an electronic transaction is already attractive with a small amount of time saved because of the number of transactions. In the long run, the citizens may handle certain electronic services directly, without contacting the intermediaries. An example of this is booking flights without travel agencies. But it seems to be promising to promote the electronic transaction between intermediaries and administration in the first phase. Not only the intermediaries and the administration will benefit, but indirectly also the citizens, because the intermediaries can offer their services faster and/or cheaper.

2 Additional burdens like special technical equipment, new skills, costs, and changes of habits have to be minimized and made usable for as many transaction areas as possible Electronic transactions cannot be realized without any burden, though. But it must be

minimized. This can be done by combining as many service sectors as possible to drastically decrease the overall expenditure of time and money. In the Bremen concept, the use of administrative services is combined as far as possible with the use of electronic banking services, so that technical equipment and individual capabilities can be used for both. This includes the integration of signature and payment functions on one chip card as well as a similar user interface and data exchange formats.

Therefore the Bremen concept does not provide for a special platform for electronic administration services, but a common platform for public and private services as well as electronic commerce, especially for the so called b2c section, the interaction between business and consumers. As data exchange format with high-value safety functions, the HBCI standard (Homebanking Computer Interface) developed for financial services is adopted and enhanced to the OSCI standard (Online Services Computer Interface). At least in the beginning, products approved in online banking are being used for the universal online platform.

3   It is important to gather a critical mass of users in a limited period of time. This requires a strategic selection of attractive application bundles, an effective marketing and a professional moderation of the varied cooperation processes.

Bremen Online Services recognizes that in order for electronic services to be successful, appropriate access, infrastructures and applications all have to be developed *at the same time* (see Figure. 3). Otherwise, electronic services will fail, either for a lack of users if access is not promoted, or for a lack of attractiveness if useful applications are not promoted, or for a lack of feasibility, if a useable infrastructure is not developed.

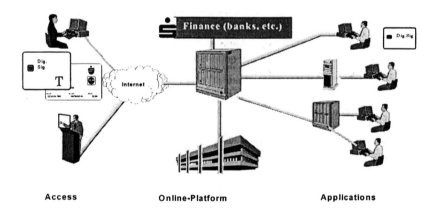

Figure. 3: Three pillars of Bremen Online Services all developed at the same time

This is where the great importance of the federal subsidy lies. Often the infrastructure providers are waiting for others to invest in attractive applications, and the potential providers of applications want to invest only after an efficient, area-wide and easily accessible infrastructure has been developed. Such a blockade can be overcome by means of the federal subsidy. By doubling the funds it is possible to invest earlier and to develop the platform and the application bundles at the same time, so that already after one to two years an attractive offer will emerge, and a critical mass of users will be reached after three years. Therefore, the Bremen concept aims at equal and balanced investments in the online platform and services bundles which will be described in the following sections.

4   Selected Application Bundles

The application bundles were selected in three steps:

1   An original first list of life-situations was completed by further suggestions for possible online applications bundles. On this basis, interviews were held with the administration agencies and private providers in this field concerning the size of the customer group, the frequency of use and the necessity of a legally binding signature. Further, it was discussed how useful the electronic transactions are for customers and administrations, how large the expenditure for the modification of the existing electronic procedures would be and which legal restrictions apply as well as how they might be overcome.

2   In a second round, the positively assessed application bundles were examined again more thoroughly. Each business transaction within the application bundles had to be examined separately, because the registration of one's address, car or phone differ very much. These questions could be clarified only because the administrative bodies as well as the private providers were very much willing to cooperate. The critical factors for each transaction were collected by means of a detailed and modified questionnaire. With a catalog of criteria determined by the steering group, the transactions were assessed; those with the highest number of points were selected for implementation within the application bundles. In this phase, additional application bundles were included which do not necessarily require a digital signature but make the overall online offer more attractive and are an example for the e-commerce applications aimed at, such as electronic ticketing.

3   On the basis of this assessment, at first 12, later only 10, application bundles were selected to be carried out in the implementation phase applied for (see table 1).

The application bundles include 2 to 26 transaction processes each, with more than 70 processes in all. They were examined as to what will be required for their implementation. Requirements range from a complete re-engineering of a computer-based administrative process (e.g. registration and building permit) to the development of new interfaces for existing procedures or data bases and simple client software for the encryption and de-encryption of signed e-mails. Accordingly, the development costs vary between thousand and several millions DM per application bundle.

Citizen	Intermediary/Professionals	Business
(1) moving	(4) building a house	(8) public procurement
(2) studying at university	(5) car purchase	
	(6) correspondence between lawyers/notaries and district court	
(3) leisure time (ticketing and reservations)	(7) communication tax consultant – tax office / taxes and tax report	
all users		
(9) electronic payment to the administration		

Table 1: Selected Application Bundles

In several application bundles, moving, building a house, correspondence between lawyers and court, between tax consultants and tax offices, electronic payment and public procurement, the Bremen administration and BOS optimized business processes integrating electronic transactions. In addition, legal requirements which unnecessarily impede conversion of electronic processes have been identified. The first rules have been changed, while on others joint actions have been taken together with federal legislators, who are in charge of some requirements. Software development for these applications has started in most cases. Therefore processes can be implemented once the platform will be running in full operation mode, which turned out to be more time consuming than had been planned originally.

In the following, the 10 application bundles are described. It is also pointed out which long-term perspective these projects open up beyond implementation in Bremen.

1 Moving / Change of Address

This application bundle is the perfect example for the idea of integrating services by life events. It includes 26 transactions with 18 different agencies with whom the form of data exchange has been firmly agreed and who have submitted cooperation promises. Participants include not only the administration of Bremen and the public utilities, but also national agencies such as the GEZ (central office collecting public broadcasting fees), the Deutsche Telekom and the Deutsche Post AG. For these providers the interfaces and exchange formats have been defined with their national headquarters, so that the solutions implemented in Bremen can be integrated by other local governments into their concepts.

Five of them, the public registrar's office, the Deutsche Post AG, the local savings bank, the public utilities company and the public transport company served as pilot partners. Together, 15 applications were implemented, which range from the change of address to the order of birth, death and marriage certificates (which are being developed even though they do not belong to the life event). On Sept. 5th, at the occasion of the first yearly conference of the Media@Komm project, these online-transactions involving both digital signature and payment were successfully presented in an online-version. During time of printing of these proceedings, the full operational roll-out is planned.

But this example shows also that the economic benefit will be very limited in the beginning. There are only a total of 30,000 moves within Bremen per year and not more than a share of 10-20 per cent of these can be expected to be submitted electronically within the next year. Therefore efforts are made to offer these services to the neighbouring cities and counties, so that moving from and to Bremen and its suburbs can be included. Besides transactions from home, there should be access possibilities with a help service, especially in the registration offices. There, the citizens could fill in the simple notice of a change of address themselves at a PC in the waiting hall. For more complicated transactions, an officer could help them or enter their data for them, so that it is not necessary to go to other offices or to send postcards and letters for a change of address to many agencies separately.

2 Studying at University
The University of Bremen, the Hochschule Bremen and the Hochschule Bremerhaven and the International University Bremen jointly introduce cards with signature and payment functions for the student administration (reregistration, registration of holiday terms, change of name or address, printing of study confirmations, exmatriculation) and for the examination offices (registration for tests and examinations, printing of test records etc.) as well as library passes, application for an e-mail account, student maintenance, application for a room in the dormitory as well as the term ticket for public transport. In many respects, the students are an interesting target group (technical competence, internet access, but also in regard to their critical attitude against potential "big brother"-technologies).

In contrast to existing projects which are introducing a special campus or student card in this case a card is employed which is applicable on all spheres of student lives including governmental services as well as cinema tickets.

3 Leisure Time Activities
This application bundle includes transactions like booking or purchasing of tickets for sport events, theatre, cinema and continuing education as well as an electronic bus ticket as an additional application on the chip card. Cooperation has been agreed with one or two institutions of each category: with the famous socker club Werder Bremen, with a tennis club, a theatre and a cinema. Even if a signature is not required for buying a cinema ticket via Internet, but only the payment function is deployed, this application increases the value of the chip card because its holder is not required to be at the cinema half an hour before the movie starts if an electronic ticket is loaded on the card. It is assumed that this kind of additional value finally will decide how many citizens will acquire the card or personalize the functions on their bank card.

4 Building a House
This application bundle aims at architects as intermediaries. It includes building permits, planning inquiries, partition permits as well as the administrative transactions after the initial building permit is issued. The added value in this case lies in the option for the architects to inform themselves online on the progress of the application handling. This requires a comprehensive reengineering of the procedures in two offices. This application is revolutionary because it will give complete transparency of the agency's workflow and the status of the application to the citizen. In technical respect, the handling of the large

annexes (construction plans, maps, etc.) will be an interesting challenge.

5 Buying a Car

Not the purchase itself but associated services are the subject of this application bundle. First, the car dealers are enabled to do the registration electronically. Therefore the Gelsenkirchen Procedure, a software-package developed by and implemented in the city of Gelsenkirchen, is extended by a signature function according to the signature act in cooperation with the agency which has developed this package. One of the first users will be the Daimler-Chrysler factory in Bremen where up to now two employees are occupied with having the cars registered which are picked up by customers at the factory.

6 Correspondence between Lawyers/Notaries and Courts

The correspondence between lawyers and courts offers many applications for legally binding electronic communication. For the electronic correspondence during a complete trial, all parties must have the necessary equipment. In Bremen the local court will first accept simple electronic notices from lawyers as legally binding. A further transaction will be changeover from the software-based access protection to a chip card with digital signature concerning the notaries' access to the electronic real estate register. On the basis of these first steps, further transactions will be selected and implemented in cooperation with the courts and the Lawyer and Notary Associations. This application bundle offers the opportunity to make experiences with attribute certification in connection with digital signatures.

7 Communication between Tax Consultant and Tax Office / Tax Declaration

This application bundle includes electronic tax estimation and tax declarations as well as the correspondence between tax consultants and tax office in general. The Minister of Finance supports – in the framework of his possibilities – the testing of these transactions with signatures corresponding to the signature act in one of the tax offices; he will further support a corresponding opening clause in the working group "Electronic Tax Declaration" (ELSTER) on a national level. Due to a cooperation with DATEV, it will be possible to test two currently competing procedures of attribute certification

8 Procurement

Already today, the specifications and offers are submitted on discs. A complete electronic handling using digital signatures will reduce costs on both sides as copying will no longer be required. This procedure is planned for the placing of construction orders and for the electronic procurement list for electronic data processing.

9 Electronic Funds Transfer to and from the Administration

Many administration services include payment transfers, e.g., fines for wrong parking, taxes and remunerations for register information. This is not an application bundle like the others, but provides core functionality for many applications. It is aimed at implementing three forms of payment via Internet besides the cash payment at the municipal payments offices. Besides remittance and direct debit, payment by charge cards has to be emphasized which is not yet widely in use with communal and regional administrations. With the demonstration of the pilot in September 2000, the use of the charge-card via Internet was demonstrated as well.

On the basis of today's figures and estimations on the diffusion and use of signature cards, the BOS partners made a business case testing the economic viability of offering all of these services. Table 2 shows those ten transactions which will presumably be carried out most frequently in the year 2002. The pilot phase has shown, however, that the development of the platform will take more time than expected, so delays in reaching these numbers have to be expected.

	Service Provider	Transaction	Cases per year today	Estimated online transactions in 2002
1.	Cinema	Ticket	1.2 Mio.	58332
2.	Tax Office	Sales Tax Advance Return	152000	25297
3.	Landeshaupt-kasse	Fines and Fees	1 Mio.	24305
4.	University Administration	Student's Pass and Reregistration	36000	17577
5.	Lawyers / Court	Remindering	50000	14986
6.	University Administration	Printing of Study Documents	68.800	14620
7.	Zentrum für Netze	E-Mail-Account	18000	12648
8.	Einwohner-meldeamt	Inquiry at Registration Office	70000	11650
9.	Tax Office	Communication with Tax Consultant	57000	9487
10.	Tax Office	Tax Declaration	180000	7742

Table 2: The ten most frequent transactions

The transactions within the ten application bundles form the core of offered services. They will be extended during the course of the project and afterwards. For many of these transactions there are several service providers (e.g., insurance companies, transport firms, cinemas, DIY superstores). Normally, only the link to one firm as a testing and demonstration case will be supported by project funds. But any other service provider can connect at his own expense, because the interface standard will be open to all. As it is aimed to use only commercial-off-the-shelf products, they can be purchased freely. The development and operation company will arrange such business transactions on a commission basis, if the producers are no members of the consortium.

Furthermore, the company will offer other communities to carry out electronic transactions for them. That means another local government can make its forms available on the Bremen Online service platform without having to invest in a corresponding infrastructure; they would only require an interface to its own procedures.

5   Technical Infrastructure

5.1   Basic Considerations and Procedures

In order to serve the great variety of applications, the technical infrastructure has to be modular and scaleable. If possible, already existing products and standards are to be used. These must, however, meet the requirements of the applications.

In the framework of a public contest, companies have been invited to participate in the conception of an online platform for legally binding and trustworthy transactions. More than 50 firms, partly from Bremen, partly from other parts of Germany, worked out requirements in six working groups during a period of several months. On this basis, the consulting firm Eutelis Consult defined functional procedures as a basis for a limited invitation of tenders in the framework of the contest. The result was 24 bidders offering 140 work parts. An evaluation group of the SKP (procurement), the State Ministry of Economy, TZI, Chamber of Commerce and Bremer Innovations-Agentur (technology promotion) assessed the offers.

When doing so, a conflict of aims emerged. Some offered the supply of systems which have already been tested for Internet banking and shopping. They could be put into service within half a year and are relatively inexpensive. But it is not sure if these systems will come up to the more complex administrative procedures. Therefore these bidders were invited for a presentation which showed that they were very much interested in opening an additional market of administrative services, but that they had neither experience nor a comprehensive knowledge of administrative procedures, legal requirements, data protection regulations etc.

On the other hand, new developments were offered strictly following the functional requirements defined which would take one and a half to two years and cost up to the tenfold. Considering a project duration of three years, there would not be enough time to win the critical mass of users in the last year. Moreover, the costs would be so high that even within a period of ten years no amortization could be expected.

In order to deal with this conflict, the steering group agreed on a double-tracked action in two steps. On one hand, Twister, the product of the company Brokat, developed for Internet banking, was chosen because it makes it possible to offer simple transactions within three to six months. Simultaneously, a firm with experiences in the back-office sector (Atos) will work out a specification. After the first more complex transactions are being offered, it will be possible to judge how Twister can handle them. Then it will have to be decided if the product will be extended by the additional specifications or if a new product will be developed instead. Taking two steps – at first simple transactions, then more complex ones – ensures that the target group will gradually get used to the signature card and procedure. Double-tracked action ensures that there will be no unnecessary delay, at the same time minimizing the risk to depend on one bidder only who might not be able to manage the transition from financial to administrative services.

At the moment, BOS has gathered its first experience with the Twister platform, when developing the above mentioned pilots. This showed indeed that concerns regarding the applicability of the banking platform to public services applications were in order. At the moment, the BOS team and its contractors are finishing work on the pilot and are in the process of evaluation. Then, the decision on which technical platform to move on will be made.

5.2   Components of the Online Infrastructure

Figure. 4 shows the components of the planned online infrastructure. In the following, the several components will be explained in more detail.

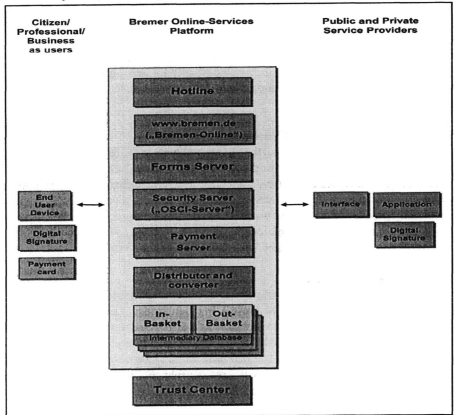

Figure. 4: Components of the Online platform

(1) Terminals
Terminals for citizens, companies and intermediaries are normally commercially available personal computers complemented by a chipcard reader. The question if and to what extent unserviced terminals (kiosk systems) are to be implemented was examined by a kiosk system analysis. The result of this survey suggests to focus mainly not on traditional stand-alone kiosks, but on serviced terminals which can be placed in the waiting rooms of citizen centers, branches of the Sparkasse, branches of the city library, a transport company and at the public utility company's Internet cafe.

(2) User Interface / Client
The following Java applets can be downloaded from a form server:
- Form applets representing the individual business transactions
- Integration applets for the intermediate storage of certain generally required data
- OSCI applets following the new homebanking standard HBCI which take the data from the form, transfer them into the defined data format and ensure the signing and coding of the data record.

In order to make sure that software of different manufacturers can be used, the same path is followed that the banks took for the HBCI standard. They had a so-called HBCI kernel programmed which carries out all central functions of a HBCI software, but does not have a complete dialog interface with the user including user surface. These kernels are given free of charge to all software producers who program the functions of the business transactions around the kernel.

(3) Telecommunications Network and Services
For the connection of the terminals and the service providers to the Bremen Online Service Platform, all telecommunication networks and services are used. Besides analogous and ISDN accesses, ADSL connection have been made available in Bremen in 1999. Besides a switched connection via the Internet Service Provider a direct connection via the public telecommunications network will be possible. Administration agencies and their serviced terminals are connected via the administration network operated by BreKom which offers ISDN switched connections, dedicated lines and ADSL connections.

(4) Chipcards as Security Media
Only chipcards will be certified as safety media. But a single-function signature card is deployed only in the beginning of the project. In order to ensure an immediate start, the TeleSec card certified according to the signature act is distributed. But the focus will be laid upon the charge card of the Sparkasse Bremen with its signature application. From the year 2002 on, all ec-cards issued by any German bank will include a signature function in its chip. This has been decided by the Zentrale Kreditausschuss of the three German banking branches. This means that at this time more than 35 million people in Germany will posses such a card which only has to be activated via a trust center.
But up to this time, services have to be tested and private customers will certainly not pay 30 to 50 EUR as annual fee for a signature card. Therefore BOS decided to pay the costs

for production and distribution of the charge card with a signature function by project funds and to offer it to the customers for a more or less symbolic fee of 5 EUR per year. Of course the system must allow for the acceptance of charge cards from other banks and all signature cards certified according to the signature act.

(5) Payment Procedures
The platform must offer the usual payment procedures:
- The project focusses on the charge card, account-bound on ec cards or not account-bound, reloadable with cash at automats or – in the near future – via Internet from the checking account. The corresponding HBCI transaction has already been specified by the Sparkassenorganisation and will be implemented soon. This is simultaneously a strong test for the complete HBCI platform and for the OSCI system aimed at. If the system is assessed as being safe enough to load money on a charge card via the Internet, it will also comply with the safety requirements for all the transactions listed above.
- Besides the cash payment, especially the payment by direct debiting is used in the administration. For this procedure, a signed direct debiting authorization is required. The authorization is defined as a transaction which can be handled with a digital signature.
- Payment by credit card via Internet is widely used in e-commerce, and a very secure standard is available, SET (Secure Electronic Transaction; a standard used by Visa, MasterCard and others for a secure handling of credit card payments via Internet). The administration of Bremen will not accept credit card payment in the foreseeable future due to the relatively high provisions payable to the credit card companies and requirements to collect the same fees and fines from every customer. But depending on the demand from the private sector, the credit card payment function will be added to the payment server easily (see below).

(6) Hotline
A hotline will be implemented for the users as well as for the service providers giving information on technical problems and on questions concerning the transactions. This hotline is already working and can be reached in Germany at 0800-BOS BREMEN.

(7) City Information System
Transactions which can be handled electronically must be found by the potential customers first. It seems reasonable to integrate them into the city information system bremen.online under the Internet address www.bremen.de, where the user can either search in an alphabetical list of subjects or institutions or enter his own search term. A public service guide allows a search by requests. A variety of forms of the administration of Bremen in html or pdf format have already been entered into the form server which can be downloaded, filled in, printed and sent by mail or delivered. These forms are also equipped with search terms and can be found via a search machine. The pilot has been put online at http://www.bremer-online-service.de.

As a local completion and for the future broadband access online help features and explaining animations or video clips (guided tours, walkthroughs) will be made available in the city information system. They can relate to individual transactions and the filling in of the forms, but also to the path of an application through the system, to answer frequently asked questions (FAQs) on security and confidentiality, asymmetric coding and so on.

(8) Form Server

The form server will be a file server containing the Java-programmed applets listed under (2), the charge card payment applets and other signature and payment applets. It shall replace the existing form server. The city information system bremen.online (www.bremen.de) will route a user's request to the new form server, as soon as the user has selected a concrete transaction. This applet opens an interface to the online services platform.

(9) Security Server (OSCI-Server)

The security server receives the OSCI messages of the user, decodes the outer (transport) envelope and verifies the signature. As a service, it is possible – and even the normal case with financial services (e.g., Twister) – to have the OSCI server decode the form envelope and to check the user signature. This procedure can only be recommeded if a safe channel between the OSCI server and the workplace of the service provider exists, if there is the necessary confidence, and if it is not impeded by objections concerning data protection due to the strong purpose-tying requirement in the public sector. So, in administrative applications, a double envelope needs to be used: the inner containing the signed and encrypted data for the service provider, and the outer to send it securely to the platform. For checking the signatures in both envelopes the OSCI server is connected to the certifying agency which transmits certificate revocation lists to the interface to the trustcenter of the certifying agency.

The security server keeps status protocols on the OSCI messages. Normally it transfers the data received in the form of a closed form envelope also in OSCI format to the process and interface control.

(10) Payment Server

The payment server handles all card payments via the Internet. Together with the chipcard reader, the keyboard and the monitor, the payment server forms a (virtual) POS cash terminal. The internal cables of this POS cash terminal are extended via Internet, so to speak. It sends a confirmation upon successful completion of the payment process, i.e., when the amount of money has been transferred from the charge card to the terminal of the trade or when the authorization has been confirmed by the credit card company.

(11) Protocol and Interface Control (PSS)

It is the task of the PSS to distribute and convert messages. At first, the PSS function will be taken over by the product Twister of Brokat which will in the end carry out the four separate functions of security server, PSS server, intermediate data base and payment server. By the end of the project period, however, there will be a separate module with the interfaces to be defined for each function.

The PSS administers the temporarily stored messages which could not be transmitted to the service provider or to the user, e.g., because he was not online at the time (which will be the normal case for kiosk users). As soon as a user or a service provider is online, the PSS will deliver the messages – that means that the PSS together with the intermediate data base is a kind of substitute for e-mail accounts.

(12) Intermediate Data Base
The intermediate data base functions as an in and out basket. In these baskets the messages, closed form envelopes with the addresses of the users or service providers, are deposited. PSS and subsequent procedures can access the intermediate data base. Uncompleted transactions – signed for retrieval and coded for keeping confidentiality – are also deposited in the intermediate data base.

(13) Certifying Agency (Trustcenter)
The certifying agency is concerned with two main tasks: registering the users and service providers and producing keys and certificates for the signature cards of the users and service providers.

In the end, the user can choose from a list of certifying agencies where he wants to apply for a chipcard with signature application. During the project period, this will primarily be the certifying agency of the German Telekom AG. The list will be extended by further certifying agencies later. According to the signature act, everybody has to register personally, i.e. the user will have to visit the certifying agency or one of its branches.

(14) Service Provider Interface
The modular organization of the Bremen online services platform enables the service providers to make use of the services of some or all modules. If only a few services are made use of, the service provider himself needs the omitted functionalities. So each service provider can choose between them.

6   Adaptation of Legal Provisions

Legal provisions for administrative procedures often stipulate the written form, a handwritten signature, a certain form or the presentation of documents. These stipulations may be an obstacle to the electronic handling.

In principle, freedom of form is permitted for administrative procedures. The federal administrative procedure law and the mostly identical state law already include regulations which allow electronic transmission. The regulations do not define exactly what is meant by written form. The corresponding regulations of the administrative procedure law of Bremen (§ 37 par. 3 BremVwVfG) only stipulates that a written administrative act has to show the issuing authority and the signature or the name of the head of the authority or his deputy or his representative.

The special regulations for the individual administrative procedures are authoritative for the electronic handling and digital signatures. If an application is required, it must be filed in writing, i.e., a document has to be drawn up which has to be undersigned by the applicant or his representative. Therefore an examination of the individual case is required and each law has to be changed explicitly.

A further field of relevant legal provisions deals with documents to be submitted and pertaining appendices. These often stem from other administrative agencies or third parties, are not in electronic form and are therefore an obstacle for the electronic handling of an administrative procedure, even if the application itself has been drawn up in electronic form and can be signed digitally. A solution could be to check if a submittal is required and to do without, if possible, or to procure the corresponding information from the agency handling the application. A transitional solution could be to scan the documents and to accept the corresponding electronic file, e.g., on account of the digital signature of a certifying administrative official.

If in these individual cases, the sufficiency of electronically transmitted and digitally signed applications and administrative acts is doubtful or if the provisions for papers to be submitted have to be checked, the question arises which appropriate measures can be taken by the legislature. A conceivable idea is to treat electronic transactions and digital signatures as equals for the complete scope of the respective provision. Due to the lack of experience, this is a very far-reaching and risky step for the near future. An alternative are experimental clauses which permit the electronic transmission and the digital signature on trial for a limited time for certain administrative procedures and possibly only for the communication between few administrative agencies with the corresponding equipment.

This is the solution the Senate of the Free Hanseatic City of Bremen chose. In 1999, the Senate and the Parliament ratified a law for the testing of the digital signature in the administration, which went into effect in the same year.

7   Implementation by a Development and Operating Company

The concept is not being implemented within a project organization confined to a certain time period; but rather from the start, a steady and medium-term profitable operation in public-private partnership has been created. For this purpose, BOS in the legal form of a GmbH & Co KG (limited liability company with limited partnership) was founded. The business purpose of this company is to offer safe transactions (administrative transactions as well as e-commerce transactions with and without payment) on open networks based on the digital signature and the charge card of the German banks. The company will eventually provide revenue from the following business lines:

- Revenues from the operation of a security server for the administration of Bremen and regional and supraregional service providers. Technical basis is the protocol OSCI (Online Services Computer Interface) as well as signature chipcards as safety media.
- Revenues from the use of the security server by third parties. Other local governments will be offered to use the platform as an alternative to developing their own systems.
- Revenues from the operation of the payment server for administration agencies and firms from Bremen and the surrounding area.

- Revenues from permitting the use of a decentralized OSCI server. A "small" version of the security or OSCI server can be installed with service providers, which would make sense if the service provider does not work in Bremen or if he has computing capacity of his own.
- Revenues from developing form applets. Each transactions requires a form for the user which has to be programmed as Java applet (small operable programs which are transmitted on the Internet, if required).
- Revenues from advertising. Especially in case of citizen-oriented life events a so-called banner-advertisement could be placed. High prices can be asked for page views, as the life events attract special target groups, e.g. a jeweller could advertise in the life event "marriage" or a cinema in the life event "leisure time".

The quantity of these business transactions to be expected was assessed in detail and further application fields for them were assumed; on this basis, a detailed business plan estimating income and expenditure for the period 1999 until 2008 was drawn up. Together with the managerial staff of the syndicate, these figures were checked thoroughly and verified step by step following technical and commercial criteria. During the project period total costs of 22 million EUR are expected for:

- Online infrastructure 5 million EUR
- Application software and licences 10 million EUR
- General measures (e.g., card and trust centers) 3 million EUR
- Development and Operating Company (esp. staff costs, technical coordination, accompanying research, market research) 4 million EUR.

For the time after the federal funding a yearly expenditure of approx. 3 million EUR is expected, especially for the operation of the components and for replacements. In 2005, the Company will make its first annual surplus of approx. 1 million EUR. Critical will be the first two years after the funding has ended; in 2008, the own equity resources will amount to more than 10 million EUR and the equity return to 37 per cent. But the annual surplusses will not yet suffice to return the capital paid in by the partners.

8   Conclusion

This difficult economic situation is the main reason why this platform may not be restricted to e-government services only. But rather the high investment can only lead to profits in the long run when the platform is used for all kinds of electronic services offered in Bremen as well as for any other customer.

This is why BOS set out to integrate electronic government and electronic commerce. Throughout the course of the project, it has been successful so far because it promises substantial benefits to all relevant project partners. The public administration can double its funds for modernization using new information technology. This means a big push for reform initiatives. It also promises a new customer-friendly orientation and better relationships with its customers. In times of increased competition, this is an important aspect for regional economic development.

It must be noted that in the beginning of the project, there was considerable tension if the state should focus on developing applications for public administration, or if it should fund private business in developing (private) e-commerce. The outcome of this process was that both intentions were followed. While more money is spent on public administration applications, local business benefits from more convenient and easier access to government services. In addition, the development of the online platform is likely to attract future e-business as well.

However, it turned out that most of the platform functions are much more complex than was originally assumed and that there are no standard components available for immediate use. Rather every component has to be adapted and each of these projects takes much longer than expected. The divergence does not start when integrating E-Business and E-Government but when the online-banking sphere is transceded. The usual online-banking transactions are simple synchronous point-to-point transactions which are executed or not. Most of the service bundles described here involve transactions which are dependent on other transactions, take place at different points in time and involve different partners. These requirements can only be specified within a real life trial and error process. The experience made so far proves the assumption that integrating E-Commerce and E-Government is necessary and is feasible.

Chapter 14

Applications and Implications of Cellular (Mobile) Telephone Technologies for Electronic Government and Informatisation. An Overview

Christopher A. Theunissen

1   Introduction

It is not the purpose of this chapter to provide an in depth discourse on the myriad technical issues surrounding the potential use of mobile (cellular) telephone technologies *vis a vis* electronic government and associated issues. Rather, the chapter will strive to provide an overview of present use together with possible scenarios relating to the future potential use of such technologies for electronic government, specifically in developing/partially developed states such as South Africa. The chapter will in many respects be speculative due to the dearth of information currently available on the topic within this context. Nevertheless, the intention is to provide some insights and areas for debate with regard to the potential uses of mobile telephone technologies to facilitate electronic government and informatisation initiatives in those states where there is limited access to traditional forms of connectivity such as the Internet enabled desktop computer/PC. (Please note, in order to eliminate excessive verbiage, the terms mobile and cellular will be used interchangeably in this chapter.)

Also, the chapter will not be examining the initiatives for electronic government and informatisation as they manifest themselves within and between the public administrative instruments and structures of government, but will rather focus on those aspects of electronic government that facilitate the provision of public services offered by government to their primary clients, namely the public and civil society.

Prior to focussing on the role of mobile telephone technology a brief overview is sketched of the so-called 'New World Information Order', the 'Information divide' as well as the importance of Information and Communication Technologies [hereafter referred to as ICTs] for democratic processes within the contemporary state. This will contextualise these issues in relation to the resulting discussion on mobile telephone technology *vis a vis* e-government and informatisation.

2   New World Information Order

It can be argued that as a result of the development and utilisation of knowledge based technologies [essentially ICTs] on a global scale, a new 'world information order' has

J. E. J. Prins (ed.), Designing E-Government, 197–212.

come into being. Television and the Internet are the most central of knowledge based technologies available today, with television in particular playing a pivotal role in shaping on a global scale, a common social and cultural outlook. They have also become one of the main commercial instruments utilised to stimulate consumption and distribution of both goods and services.

Although they [Television and the Internet] are capable of serving a mass audience as in the past and present, they are likely to undergo changes when combined with other technologies and processes which will permit them to cater for the unique circumstances/interests of individuals and small groups. This is likely to facilitate the erosion of the concept of national identity which may be replaced by a more disparate set of identities based upon constituents such as region, location, ethnicity and gender (Moran 1994:41). This view is echoed by Sunter (1996:76) who refers to the birth of global cultures resulting from competing religions, value systems and lifestyles which are made clearly visible by means of global television networks, the Internet and mass travel. The shared sense of global awareness was, and is, provided by mass media and television and is giving way to a situation that according to Halal (1993:1983) '...transcends mass communication to provide electronically mediated relationships that actually form living communities'. Clearly, these mixtures of global lifestyles and competing ideologies are beginning to supplant national lifestyles, a phenomenon which does not, however, necessarily lead to a blander more homogenous world partially because cultures remain distinct even though they are becoming more mixed (Sunter 1996:76).

The abovementioned views of Moran and Sunter differ from that expressed by Elaigwu (in Coutts 1996:19) who stated that '...we have arrived at the 'CNNisation' of the world. American values, politics and business are being powerfully transmitted across nations', requiring a redefinition of the nation-state as the continent of Africa's boundaries are redefined as a result of the flow of information. Schiller (in Giddens 1993:559) concurs with this viewpoint and contends that American television exports contribute to undermining local forms of cultural expression while at the same time propagating a commercialised culture. If one subscribes to these views it can be stated that a form of cultural imperialism is taking place which can have negative ramifications for society, specifically in the developing world where the knowledge required to process mass media information is not necessarily developed in the individual consumer of information.

It is likely, however, that a synthesis will take place based on the two somewhat divergent points of view mentioned above. This will in all likelihood manifest itself in a situation where, at the local level, both individuals and groups will tend to follow [and publicise] their own partisan esoteric interests, both nationally and internationally - while at the same time still being subject to influences from those 'technologies without boundaries' represented by the likes of CNN International and Microsoft.

This will in effect entail a strengthening of the commitment and will of small entities who are likely to try to reinforce their own unique identities in response to the seemingly overwhelming global culture processes which are often perceived as posing a threat to their specific interests. Nevertheless, at the same time, such entities will be influenced by the images and symbols of the 'global village' and will either consciously or subconsciously integrate such influences into their own frame of reference or *weltanschauung*. Coca-Cola is one of the foremost examples of a symbol that is global and has received global acceptance, yet which does not pose a specific threat to the cultural or political interests of any specific group or culture.

According to Halal (1993:83-85) the information age [which is in effect being superceded by an age of knowledge] represents a higher order development stage of human society. It will in all likelihood enable an as yet unknown global information system to come into being which will be capable of managing the new world order based on knowledge. Globalisation can be regarded as the forerunner of this, holding serious implications for the way in which democratic governance [and state power] will manifest itself in the future. We have accordingly entered a phase beyond the industrial era (Giddens 1993:663), which Sunter (1996:70-73) refers to as being one of 'postmodernism' in contrast to the previous 'modernism phase' which stretched from the Industrial Revolution *circa.* 1850's to the 1980's.

Contemporary developments in technology, specifically ICTs, are the cornerstone on which this post-industrial [or postmodern] society is based with production becoming increasingly reliant on information technology and the immediate global disbursement of its information-based products (Louw 1994:87). Vorster and Nel (1995:54) note that the production of knowledge in the contemporary world is primarily resultant from scientific and technological developments. Within this context the assertion by Bell (1973), who regards terms such as pre-industrial, industrial and post industrial society as indicative of sequential progression with regard to production and the types of knowledge used in society, is clearly recognisable.

This information or post-industrial age is essentially managed by social networks, whereas the Industrial Age was managed hierarchically (Halal 1993:82). This can be better understood if looked at in the context of the global village – central to which is the role played by satellites and telecommunications technologies (Kumar 1995:10). As Jones (1986:198) notes, it is the development and growth of ICTs which have resulted in a breaking down of the technical barriers relating to the international exchange of information of an electronic nature.

Contemporary society can to a great extent therefore already be regarded as an information society whose reliance on information has escalated with the increase of sophisticated technology. What is important to note, however, is the unequal distribution and access to information which places into question the very existence of the so-called 'new world information order', and which is often referred to as the 'information divide'.

3   Information Divide

Existing postmodern society can be regarded as an information society that is becoming increasingly reliant on information due to the ubiquitous development and use of sophisticated knowledge based technologies. It should be borne in mind however that the 'global village' and its constituent parts are by no means equal as regards their access, capacity and integration with the information age and its successor, the age of knowledge. This becomes apparent when one takes into account the ratio of human population between the 'developed' and 'underdeveloped/developing' worlds which was 1.2 billion persons to 3.8 billion persons in 1988, with projections showing that the aforesaid ratio should change in 2025 to measure 1.5 billion persons to 6.8 billion persons (Williams 1993:155.)

Moreover, even high technology societies are showing indications that they are beginning to suffer from an 'information divide' which results in the existence of an information underclass whose members lack the higher informational skills required to function and work efficiently in contemporary society (Toffler 1990:366-367). Batty and Barr (1994:711) refer to this as being a new geography of the rich and poor specifically as regards those who are deprived of access to contemporary communication technologies.

Historical precedent has shown that the information divide is not unique to contemporary society and has existed in the past albeit to a lesser extent. Persons who found themselves occupying positions in the 'lower class' in class ridden societies such as found in historical England were often denied access to sufficient education, while for those of the 'upper' or 'ruling' classes it was a given. This practise was also practised in apartheid South Africa where access to adequate education [and subsequently knowledge] was denied to the black majority in order to maintain [without success] the political status quo. Knowledge – the product of education – has accordingly been regarded as a form of power and has been [and is] consequently used to structure political and social relationships within states throughout the contemporary world.

The denial of access to information and subsequently knowledge in order to maintain political power and the status quo are not new. One only has to look at how the monopoly over education and literacy by the Church in Medieval Europe placed it in a position of power over the illiterate 'masses'. This power was only subsequently broken after the first 'modern' ICT in the form of the movable type printing press of Gutenberg (*circa.* 1450) came into being.

Contemporary technologies, specifically ICTs, are nonetheless exacerbating the information divide in the postmodern world even though information is now more freely available and accessible than it has ever been in the past. As Pauw *et al.* (1991:10) point out:

'What is new today is not the fact that a society is based on information, as each society is a society by virtue of information and shared meaning; what actually is new is the economic role of the provision of information.'

It is within the economic and political framework wherein the information 'revolution' is being applied where existing social inequalities are being maintained and magnified, with knowledge and information becoming commodities used for sale and profit (Kumar 1995:32; Hepworth & Robins 1988:327). This is contributing to a situation of the 'haves' and the 'have-nots' where persons in the developing/third world – the traditional 'have-nots' – are exposed to the material wealth and quality of life of the 'haves' by the medium of television and radio [and increasingly the Internet] (Patton 1995:online). The gap between these so-called 'haves' and 'have-nots' can also be found within advanced post-industrial states as well as those states who are at a lesser stage of development. The often unrealistic hopes and expectations of the 'developing' world in their desire to aspire to the level of the 'developed world' are, however, sowing the seeds for potential political conflict and instability in the future (Williams 1993:155).

Although the phenomenon of information divide can give rise to considerable social and political instability and the associated consequences thereof it should, however, be noted that it is in poor countries which are lacking in infrastructure where modern knowledge based technologies often offer unlimited opportunities for development.

The very lack of infrastructure is often the catalyst which leads to a growth in technologies such as cellular telephony as can be witnessed in countries such as Cambodia, Brazil and South Africa. (Poor countries are...1996:21.) Notwithstanding this, it should always be kept in mind that ICTs and related technologies are not evenly distributed on a global scale and are unlikely to be so in the foreseeable future. This has the implication that in 'postmodern'/post-industrial states there will be a greater *per capita* number of ICTs in use relative to those being used in developing and partially developed states. Taking this into account it is clear that issues of access, which are primarily a result of the 'information divide' phenomena, should always be borne in mind and factored into any discussion relating to e-government and informatisation initiatives whether in the 'developed' or 'developing' world.

4   Electronic Government and Issues of Access

There are schools of thought which equate the viability of electronic government initiatives with the level of development of societies and infrastructures within states. Such perceptions are primarily the result of traditional thinking regarding the ways in which individuals connect to, and use, 'techno-infrastructures' such as the WWW or the Internet. Such thinking is dominated by the prevailing scenario where desktop and portable computers are still the most popular methods of choice for connectivity, with Personal Digital Assistants [PDAs] becoming more prevalent amongst business and more wealthy ICT users.

In societies such as South Africa there exist considerable disparities, primarily of a socio-economic nature, with respect to the distribution of resources. Increasingly, there is a gap developing between those who have access to contemporary ICTs such as desktop personal computers and associated resources such as the Internet, and the vast majority of the population whose access to such technologies is limited.

According to NUA Internet Surveys (2000:online) there are approximately 3.11 million Internet users/people online in Africa. Of these 1.8 million users can be found in South Africa which is one of the top 20 Internet usage countries worldwide. South Africa has approximately 75 public dial-up Internet access providers serving 650000 subscribers in addition to 5000 digital lines leased to the corporate, government and academic networks - growth forecasts for Internet growth in SA is estimated at 30% for 2000 (AISI-Connect National ICT Profile South Africa 2000:online). When one considers that South Africa is the most 'connected' country in Africa yet only has 1.8 million of its 45 million population with access to resources such as the Internet, it is patently clear that a considerable 'information divide' is in existence. A divide which is only likely to be overcome with rapid socio-economic development combined with innovative initiatives.

Increasingly, efforts are being made in South Africa by both government and civil society to ameliorate the existing 'information divide' by developing initiatives to promote access to these technologies via multimedia information kiosks, schools and the like. Nevertheless, such initiatives are often overwhelmed by the enormity of the challenge and therefore are limited with regard to their impact on electronic government and associated initiatives. South Africa is not alone with regard to these type of challenges. States with a similar level of development such as Brazil and India are experiencing similar conditions and an increase in the gap between the 'information upperclass (haves)' and the 'information underclass (have nots)'.

One has to ask oneself the question "are electronic government initiatives relevant or even practical within developing/partially developed states or are they merely the domain of the post-industrialised states such as found in Europe, North America and the far-east?" The answer to this question is multifaceted yet can be summarised in the words "yes, electronic government and associated initiatives should be part and parcel of government thinking throughout the globe and in no way should be thought of as being a phenomenon only relevant to post-industrialised societies." The reason for this is manifestly simple insofar all societies, states and other actors and role-players in the contemporary environment are part of the postmodern 'highly technocentric' era whether they desire to be or not. Although access to ICTs and global connectivity are by no means equally distributed the reality is that all actors and role players are subject to the influences of such technologies via phenomena such as globalisation.

Electronic government initiatives in many ways are therefore likely to become increasingly essential for all states and not only those who are at the upper end of the development spectrum. The reason for this is twofold. Firstly, in order to remain efficient and competitive in the contemporary environment governments will have to make use of technological initiatives irrespective of their level of development - this is a normative requirement.

Reality is, however, very different and will result in many contemporary states, particularly those who are not at the post-industrialised level, being essentially 'left behind' on the global stage by those states whose governments understand the value and need for e-government initiatives and the overall role played by ICTs in their socio-economic development. In essence the 'information divide' developing within societies (even in post-industrialises states) will be mirrored by the 'information divide' developing between traditional nation-states with the commensurate implications that this holds for global prosperity and security.

The second reason why electronic government initiatives are essential for contemporary states (who subscribe to, or want to subscribe to, the democratic ideal) is their potential as catalysts and enablers for democratic governance and the promotion of democratic practices, as well as facilitating more efficient contact and relationships between government and their primary clients - the public. It is this particular aspect of electronic government which this chapter relates to within the context of cellular (mobile) telephone technology, ICTs, democratic governance and the promotion of democratic practices.

5   ICTs and Democratic Governance

The flow of information and effective communication can be regarded as crucial to the democratic political process (Mulgan 1991:7). This is especially important for nations such as South Africa who subscribe, or want to subscribe, to the democratic ideal.

A knowledge based society [dependant on effective communication and information flow] allows greater democratic freedoms for people due to a shift in the locus of power in modern societies which is a result of the expansion of electronic relationships facilitated by ICTs (Halal 1993:82). Technological advances are putting more computing and communications power within reach of average citizens, resulting in a situation which is difficult to prevent politically even though it can be done to a limited extent in a physical manner by for example, tampering with communication infrastructures, denying access etc. (Katz 1988:174). The power balance between the individual and the state, however, appears to be shifting in favour of the individual notwithstanding some *caveats* that are cause for concern These include the potential for abuse of technologies by the state or commercial enterprises, either with intention, or through lack of sufficient safeguards and ICT managerial capacity/knowledge.

The spread of information from the West as well as the impact of globalisation is regarded as being one of the factors that contributed to one of the most consequential political occurrences of the twentieth century – the decline of the Soviet bloc in 1989. Not only did the technological advances of telecommunications, mass media and information assist in the demise of communism in the Soviet Union and the Eastern Bloc but they are also facilitating changes in the functioning of representative democracies, including *inter alia* the creation of openness and transparency in developing countries (Sagasti 1995:593).

It is apparent that in contrast to the ever-present potential for increased control, electronically founded technologies can and do also lay the foundation for democracy (Brown 1992:46). Moreover, the participatory citizens of today need and receive more information in order to exercise their democratic rights as the effective functioning of democracy has become reliant on critical thought based on the availability of adequate information, and the independent evaluation thereof by the individual (Jones 1986:197:Ionescu 1993:228). Consequently, information and its accessibility has placed immense power in the hands of the citizenry and individual with respect to their relationship with the state. A new relationship which manifests itself in the changing role and practise of public administration in democracies, which has traditionally had an authoritarian relationship with the public, to a more service oriented approach (Lilic 1990:11).

Naisbitt (in Dejoie, Fowler & Paradice 1991:59) also regards the new source of power as not being money in the hands of the few but rather information in the hands of many, an opinion which is supported by Kotter (1985:39-41). Notwithstanding these opinions, it should be noted, that it is those with financial resources who are most likely to be in a superior position to obtain and utilise information - posing questions for the principles of egalitarianism and democratic practices. The cost factors of accessing information and utilising the potential of ICTs in the contemporary world should not be underestimated, even though they are being reduced at a rapid rate in relative terms. The then director of Siemens public communication networks, Bjorn Christensen, stated in 1997 that the largely unregulated network represented by the Internet would revolutionise the telecommunications industry and force costs down while making much of the then existing technology obsolete. He also stated that there would most likely be a convergence of Internet technology and traditional telecommunications technology and that existing telecommunication companies will only survive if they act swiftly - a forecast which has proved remarkably accurate.

Notwithstanding cost factors, the power of ICTs in facilitating democratic governance and individual rights and freedoms are immeasurable. Contemporary ICTs have given access of information, and subsequently knowledge, to millions of people thereby empowering them to think and make decisions for themselves (Cleveland 1990:36-37). Such decisions will naturally be based on the quality and reliability of information received. Quality and reliability can vary however, and may often be influenced by misinformation and propaganda which has the sole purpose of persuading people to make decisions that are not necessarily in their own best interests. Nevertheless, there is merit in Cleveland's (1990:36-37) opinion that the slogan for the age of knowledge or information age should be 'the word will get around' [ie. an accurate reflection of reality], as information grows as it is utilised and tends to leak by means which are both formal and informal.

Moreover, it is a practical impossibility for a government in the contemporary 'age of knowledge' to cut off information from the outside world without destroying its own economy. One of the primary reasons for this being the fact that the world economy has shifted from being [physical] resource based to being technology and knowledge based (Jones 1986:195). As Batty and Barr (1994:711) point out, the global economy is based on communications technology which facilitates the provision of instant contact and 24 hour trading between financial markets and centres such as those of New York, Zurich, Tokyo and London.

Also, contemporary ICTs are such that it is extremely difficult physically and practically, if not futile, for governments to control the cross-border flow of information. The use of cellular and satellite telephones, modems, satellite trans-missions, faxes, virtual private networks [VPNs] and other forms of communication by civilians and civil society make isolation of this nature practically impossible. Specific to the contemporary environment is the Internet as a distribution (and interactive technology) which is becoming increasingly important). To date the Internet has developed into a global network of networks connecting million of users in an anarchical, self-regulating system where no one specific entity has control. The system was designed in such a manner that data would always find a route through one of the myriad networks within the network. So too can persons using the Internet bypass attempts at control by merely finding another route on the network making attempts at censorship not only futile but a waste of government resources. Coupled with contemporary developments such as the Freenet Project together with easy access to encryption technologies the Internet has become increasingly resistant to any attempts at control. As De Mulder (1998) points out, European authorities are not in a position to shut down even a part of the Internet.

To a great extent therefore the Internet can be regarded as a 'living organism' that is constantly growing and regenerating itself while always following the path of least resistance. As a vehicle for practices such as e-commerce the potential for the Internet is considerable as will most likely be the case with mobile (cell) telephony and its future incarnations (e.g. WAP and subsequent next generation protocols).

6   SA Government Presence on the Internet/WWW

The primary government resource on the web and electronic government initiative *vis a vis* the public can be found at the SA government home page at http://www.gov.za where access to all current and recent legislation, bills, speeches, government documents etc. is provided. Provision is not, however, made for interactive services on these web pages.

According to 'About Government Online' (2000:online):
One of the objectives of the South African Government is to operate as an integrated entity with a single corporate identity. The aim is to eliminate duplication and confusion. By developing a comprehensive government Home page, government has created a mechanism by which the information from government departments, provinces and other government bodies is accessible through a one-stop gateway[which will] enable users to:

- get a comprehensive overview of information available on government web-sites;
- quickly navigate the vast information resources available in government [and has the main objective to]:
- facilitate easy access to government information on the Internet;
- avoid duplication regarding the availability of government information on the Internet;
- ensure a co-ordinated approach to government Internet publishing meet transparency goals
- keep the electorate informed
- place information on the global network, [as well as providing]
- links to web pages of government departments, provinces and other government bodies
- information content as it is delivered (where it is not the direct line-functional responsibility of any government department; when it will enhance accessibility or when government bodies do not have their own web-sites yet);
- value-added features such as a search engine, maximum access points to government information feedback opportunity and access to additional government information.

Initiatives are however underway in South Africa to bring certain services such as the SA Revenue Service into a position where citizens may submit their tax forms electronically, these initiatives are however some distance away from fruition. Also, members of the public may access the web site of the Independent Electoral Commission (IEC) to verify their voting status and find out where they must vote etc. These are but a few of the web based services provided by the SA government yet are reliant on access to the Internet via traditional methods such as the desktop computer.

At a parliamentary media briefing held on 13 September 2000 in SA, the Minister of Public Service and Administration, Geraldine Fraser Moleketi announced that with the highest number of Internet connections in Africa the SA government recognises the role of IT in providing opportunities to assist in service delivery. Various electronic policy and service initiatives are to be announced later in 2000 but will include, *inter alia*, aspects relating to online applications for government services as well as projects designed to enhance integration of government department IT functions and services (Fraser-Moleketi 2000:online).

Although the need for a client centred approach is recognised and espoused in South Africa, present trends regarding e-government initiatives are focused on the integration of structures and processes between public institutions and not necessarily between public institutions and their primary clients - the public. Although, as mentioned previously, initiatives such as the provision of multimedia (computer based) kiosks are taking place within the country.

This is in many respects understandable as it could be argued that priorities for improving general government efficiency via informatisation and e-government initiatives take precedence over interactivity with the client at this particular developmental stage. Nevertheless, such an argument is flawed as developments in ICTs are proceeding at such a rate that the 'goalposts' for ICT systems in government and elsewhere are continuously subject to change and are always likely to be in a relative state of flux. Client driven initiatives should therefore be attempted and lessons and experience learned even if contemporary ICT systems in the SA public sector are not 'ideal' as they are unlikely to ever be so, here or elsewhere, in the foreseeable future.

No adequate provision has as yet, however, been made to provide any of these services via the mobile (cellular) phone.

7   Enabling E-government in South Africa via Cellular (mobile) Telephone Technologies

From the side of the public sector in South Africa no integrated mobile phone - electronic initiatives are presently on offer. Traditional methods of placing information on the web, such as the example mentioned in the preceding section, abound however. Although there is an extensive, yet not complete, presence of government departments on the web these are presently information driven with little scope for interactivity.

As previously mentioned access to 'traditional' ICT technologies such as desktop computer technology is severely limited in countries such as South Africa where even access to 'landline' telephones is problematic insofar there are only approximately five to six million installed telephones servicing a population in excess of 45 million persons. The lack of access to technologies such as desktop computers need not however be a limiting factor with respect to potential initiatives for electronic government. The alternative is readily available in the form of cellular (mobile) telephone technologies.

7.1   Cellular (mobile) telephone *status quo* in South Africa

The growth of the cellular telephone network and subscriber/user base in South Africa has been nothing short of phenomenal since mobile technology became (extensively) available in 1994. According to the SA Yearbook (1999:495) the South African market is growing at a rate of 50% per annum and is the fourth-fastest GSM (Global Systems for Mobile Communications) market in the world. The demand for mobile telephones has far exceeded market expectations as is illustrated by the forecasts of Vodacom (one of the two main service providers in SA with a market share of 55-60% versus the 40-45% share of the other service provider, MTN) who projected 250 000 subscribers in the first 10 years of operation yet after only six years has approximately 3.6 million customers (approx. 90% of whom use the prepaid system).

Present growth is approximately 300 000 to 400 000 new mobile customers per month with current projections indication market saturation at approximately 40% of the SA population according to the Chief Executive of Vodacom, Mr Alan Knott-Craig (Bennet 2000:6). According to Licken (2000:online) the EMC World Cellular Database is forecasting that there will be approximately 32 million mobile phone users in Africa by 2003 with 14 million of these being located in SA (presently there are approximately 6 million+ cell phone users in SA). One of the reasons for this growth being the very fact that there was\is limited access to landline telephones. At this stage South Africa has more mobile phones than landlines in operation which is unlikely to change due to the accelerated growth and demand for cellular phone technologies and services. Also, the technologies being used in SA are the same as that being rolled out in many of the 'developed' countries and offer the same services. Mobile telephone services [ie.Vodacom & MTN] in SA also offer potential coverage to approximately 80%+ of the population and 52%+ of the total land mass. Moreover, Vodacom alone facilitates approximately 1 billion calls per month (Latest statistics 2000:online)

Although access to mobile phone technology in South Africa is still less than that of the 'post-industrial' or so-called 'developed' world due to socio-economic circumstances, this is not comparable to the discrepancies that can be associated with computers and the like. The reason for this is that the distribution of cell phone technology in South Africa is not restricted to those on the higher socio-economic levels but is distributed throughout all socio-economic levels. Also the physical 'mobility' of cellular phones provides access to all in many communities where extensive sharing takes place, specifically with the use of prepaid recharge vouchers. Cellular telephone technology therefore provides in many respects an equalising role between the 'haves' and the 'have nots' very dissimilar to the disparities that exist with respect to other technologies.

7.2   Cellular (mobile) Telephone Technology and E-government in South Africa

The potential extent to which mobile telephone technologies may be utilised in electronic government initiatives has not yet received much attention in SA. Commercial initiatives are however gaining rapid pace with cell phone banking initiatives using Wireless Internet Gateway [WIG] technology at the forefront of developments. Such banking services on offer are not necessarily even WAP reliant and rely primarily on systems based on the Short Message Service [SMS] based services. Electronic banking via Automatic Teller Machine [ATM] terminals has been a feature of banking in SA for many years and has gained wide acceptance throughout the country partly due to the ease of use and ubiquitous presence of ATM terminals countrywide. This historical trend is likely to continue in the realm of cell phone banking as services become more available together with an increase in trust and acceptance of using this type of service.

Other commercial applications of cell phone technologies being used also have an indirect impact on the provision of public services and *ipso facto* e-government such as those linked to upmarket motor vehicles like some new Volvo models. These have facilities which automatically inform a call centre and despatch emergency services if necessary in the event of a motor vehicle accident and utilise both cellular and Global Positioning Satellite (GPS) technologies to fulfill this task. Although such systems are presently only available to those who can afford them it is likely that they will become standard features in motor vehicles within the next two decades. It is actually within the realm of the emergency public services such as those involving law enforcement, medical and firefighting services where cellular phones have become crucial in South Africa. Access to these services is available to all cellular phone users whether they are monthly subscribers or using prepaid systems [even if no funds are available on the prepaid system]. Initiatives are presently underway to have the system encompass all emergency services in the country via a general "911" style number [possibly 112] accessible from any telephone whether mobile or landline.

Mobile telephone technology is also being utilised to facilitate learning/educational initiatives in South Africa such as 'Dial-a-Teacher' which was implemented during the mid-year examination period [2000]. This highly successful initiative enabled and is enabling learners from grade one to twelve [matric] to speak to qualified teachers about their studies at discounted telephone rates (Vodacom's Dial-a-Teacher...2000:online).

Ad hoc initiatives from the part of government using mobile telephone technologies have been attempted in the recent past. An example being a new years message where all (enabled) mobile telephones received a voicemail message from the Deputy President of South Africa, Mr Jacob Zuma, regarding the threat of AIDs and the necessity for the population to adopt certain health precautions in this regard. This use of cellular technology to send voicemail was also echoed by private sector marketers in SA who attempted to market their products in this manner and through SMS messages. The resultant public outcry has prevented any recurrence of such cellular based marketing efforts. This indicates that although SA consumers are not averse to cellular technology they do not favour being 'spammed' with unsolicited information from their mobile handsets.

Client driven use of handsets to access information is however proving popular in many circumstances where for example students access their examination results from their cell phones and e-mail alerts are forwarded via the same medium to persons who have access to e-mail facilities.

The abovementioned examples are but some minor *ad hoc* examples of current trends and cell phone usage. However, can such trends be built upon to provide e-government services within the country? When examining official SA government publications as well as international literature regarding e-government initiatives very little is mentioned regarding the potential application of cellular technologies.

7.3   Future and Potential of Cellular (mobile) Telephone Technologies *vis a vis* E-government in South Africa

The reason why limited research has been conducted to date in the field of cellular telephone technology *vis a vis* electronic government and informatisation can largely be attributed to the historical limitations of these technologies when compared with those relating to computing. This, however, is no longer the case as a convergence is rapidly taking place with respect to all ICTs with mobile telephony playing an increasingly important role in the equation.

There are some justifiable concerns regarding the suitability of cellular telephone technologies for e-government and informatisation initiatives. Wireless Application Protocol (WAP) services are often touted as an example of the inadequacies of the technologies to address all but the most basic of potential e-government services. Primary concerns about WAP include the fact that it has been based on technology which is often expensive to implement and which has limited rewards so to speak. As Sykes (2000:8) notes many commentators are presently suggesting that WAP is merely a temporary [evolutionary] staging post from which other more efficient mobile interactive technologies will develop [possibly in conjunction with Bluetooth]. Nielsen (in Sykes 2000:8) is of the opinion that the focus "has shifted to future mobile services with bigger screens and faster, always-on connections" and that WAP is only likely to be temporarily successful until the next generation of mobile technologies come into being.

Presently, cellular telephone users in South Africa are being exposed to basic WAP commercial services such as those offered by iTouch Plc, a mobile information portal, in conjunction with Vodacom. Such services which are WAP reliant include live share prices, news, sport and entertainment. Similar initiatives on offer include those from MTN in the form of the ICE [Information-Commerce-Entertainment] network. Criticism of these systems however include the fact that they are somewhat incestuous in nature and may lock the user into a particular network loop thereby limiting freedom of choice on the part of the user - in effect the opposite approach to the ease of access and multi-platform approach utilised in the largely HTML supported Internet.

As cellular (mobile) new generation technologies develop such as General Packet Radio Service (GPRS) and Universal Mobile Telecommunications System (UMTS) they are likely to become more suitable for large scale e-government and informatisation initiatives. Notwithstanding this, standard cellular technologies such as those represented by GSM can be called upon to do service in a pioneering way with respect to such initiatives. It is imperative that people become familiar with using technology in order for trust in the technology to take hold. Simple e-government services such as paying utility bills via [secure] mobile telephone connections will go a long way to achieving this goal. With [relatively] secure mobile telephone banking on offer via the SMS based WIG it would not be an impossible task to arrange initiatives for electronic voting/referendums/plebiscites coupled with the necessary security considerations such as issuing e-voters with unique Personal Identification Numbers [PINS]. Challenges in this regard will also revolve around other issues such as guaranteeing voters anonymity in their voting etc. Such challenges, although difficult are not however insurmountable.

8   Conclusion

Cellular (mobile) telephone technologies should be accepted as being viable and crucial vehicles for initiatives in the realm of e-government and informatisation. Most contemporary literature, research and work in the field of e-government and informatisation has neglected the potential of cellular (mobile) telephone technologies in favour of more traditional approaches, which although often suitable for highly 'developed' countries, are not necessarily suitable for countries such as South Africa (and many others) where the information divide is an important contextual factor. In a sense, cellular (mobile) telephone technologies, have been the Cinderella of the e-government and informatisation debate, too often neglected yet with the potential to play a pivotal role in the future.

Cellular (mobile) telephone technologies may provide one of the solutions to the ongoing debate regarding strategies to overcome the 'information divide' in the contemporary world, specifically due to their rapid penetration in all markets throughout the globe including those of developing and partially developed states. As the functionality of mobile handsets improve with rapid advances in technology so too will their relevance as a 'great equaliser' become apparent in providing access to information and services via e-government and commercial initiatives. Cellular (mobile) telephone technologies have the potential, in conjunction with other converging technologies, to be one of the strongest catalysts in maintaining and facilitating democracy and democratic processes on a global scale.

Placing the role of cellular (mobile) telephone technologies on the e-government and informatisation agenda is, however, the first step on this path. The potential of these technologies is considerable if given the attention that has until now been sorely lacking. It is hoped that this chapter will in a small way contribute to the ongoing debate and provide a stimulus for more in-depth research in the field.

References

About Government Online. 2000. Available online at http://www.gov..za (2000/08/30).

AISI-Connect National ICT Profile South Africa (ZA). 2000. Available online at http://www2.sn.apc.org/africa/countdet.CFM?countries__ISO_Code=ZA (2000/09/14).

Batty, M. & Barr, B. 1994. The electronic frontier. Exploring and mapping cyberspace. *Futures.* 26(7):699-712.

Bell, D. 1973. *The coming of post-industrial society: a venture in social forecasting.* New York: Basic Books.

Bennet, J. 2000. Cellphone king who avoids the red carpet in his Midrand citadel. *Sunday Times Business Times.* 27 August.

Brown, N. 1992. *The strategic revolution: thoughts for the twenty-first century.* London: Brassey's.

Cleveland, H. 1990. The age of spreading knowledge. *The Futurist.* 24 (March-April):35-39.

Coutts, L. 1996. Pan-African thinkers wonder: does Africa's pain presage death or rebirth? *The Sunday Independent.* 12 May.

Dejoie, R. Fowler, G. & Paradice, D. 1991. *Ethical issues in information systems.* Boston: Boyd & Fraser Publishing Company.

De Mulder, R. 1998. The Digital Revolution: From Trias to Tetras Politica. In: Snellen, I.Th.M. & Van de Donk, W.B.H.J. (eds.). *Public Administration in an Information Age.* Amsterdam: IOS Press.

Farnham, A. 1997. How safe are your secrets? *Fortune.* 8 September, 136(5):114(5). Available at: http://web2.searchbank.com/infotrac/session/967/271/15552237w3/10!xrn_14&bkm (04/03/98).

Fraser-Moleketi, G. 2000. Fraser-Moleketi: Parliamentary Media Briefing, September 2000. *Ministry of Public Service and Administration.* Available online at http://www.gov.za (2000/09/15).

Giddens, A. 1993. *Sociology.* second edition. Oxford: Polity Press.

Halal, W.E. 1993. The Information Technology revolution. *Technological forecasting and social change.* 44(1):69-86.

Hepworth, M. & Robins, K. 1988. Whose information society: a view from the periphery. *Media, Culture & Society.* 10(3):323-344.

Ionescu, G. 1993. The impact of the information revolution on parliamentary sovereignties. *Government and Opposition.* 28(2):221-241.

Johnson, C. 1997. Cheap calls via the Internet will threaten telephone companies. *Sunday Independent Business.* 15 June.

Jones, B.O. 1986. Choices in an information age. *Information age.* 8(4):195-199.

Katz, J.E. 1988. Public policy origins of telecommunications privacy and the emerging issues. *Information Age.* 10(3), July:169-176.

Kotter, J.P. 1985. *Power and influence.* New York: The Free Press.

Kumar, K. 1995. *From post-industrial to post-modern society.* Oxford: Basil Blackwell.

Latest statistics. Vodacom Pty (Ltd). Available online at http://www.vodacom.co.za/press/presspack.asp (2000/09/13).

Licken, E. 2000. In Africa, Mobiles Blossoming. International *Herald Tribune.* Available online at http://www.iht.com./iht/tech/tek071599.html (2000/09/01).

Lilic, S. 1990. Information technology and public administration in Yugoslavia: the citizen's influence. *Information age.* 12(1):9-14.

Louw, P.E. 1994. Communication, technology and democracy in the development of South Africa. *Communicare.* 13(2):86-102.

Moran, A. 1994. The technology of television. In: Green, L. & Guinery, R. (eds.). *Framing technology: society, choice & change.* St Leonards, NSW: Allen & Unwin.

Mulgan, G.J. 1991. *Communication and control. Networks and the new economics of communication.* Cambridge: Polity Press.

NUA Internet Surveys. 2000. Available online at http://www.nua.ie/surveys/how_many_online/index.html (2000/09/13).

Patton, D.H. 1995. *Information warfare: towards a better understanding.* available at http://www.eagle.american.edu/users/david/papers/infowar.html (09/04/97).

Pauw, J.C., Boon, J., Louw, J.B.Z., Schlebusch, J.A. & Els, B.J. 1991. Unpublished report: *The structure of the South African system of libraries and information.* Pretoria: Department of National Education (National Education Policy).

Poor countries are fertile ground for a revolution in communications. 1996. *The Sunday Independent.* 26 May.

SA Yearbook. 1999. Pretoria: Government Communication Information Service (GCIS).

Sagasti, F.R. 1995. Knowledge and development in a fractured global order. *Futures* 27(6):591-610.

Sendall, N. 1997. Is all military information necessarily critical to national security? *African Security Review* 6(2):33-36.

Sunter, C. 1996. The high road: where are we now? Cape Town: Tafelberg, Human & Rousseau.

Sykes, P. 2000. Is this a wrap for WAP? *Itechnology.* Supplement to Pretoria News. 18 July.

Vorster, S. & Nel, P. 1995. Tracing power relations in the global knowledge structure: two case studies. *Politikon.* 22(1), pp.52-78.

Williams, R. 1993. Technical change: political options and imperatives. *Government and Opposition.* 28(2), pp.152-173.

Whiston, T.G. 1992. *Managerial and organisational integration.* Berlin: Springer-Verlag.

Authors

Roger van Boxtel
Roger van Boxtel is Minister for Urban Policy and Integration of Ethnic Minorities. He is also responsible for government information systems and related policy areas such as municipal personal records databases and travel documents (including passports). For further information see http://www.ministervanboxtel.nl

Frans De Bruïne
Frans de Bruïne is one of the Directors at the European Union. He is responsible for the design, implementation and follow-up of the program "Towards a User Friendly Information Society". He is also responsible for policy actions linked to the development of the Internet and the multimedia market in Europe. He can be reached through www.europa.eu.int

Eleanor Burt
Dr Eleanor Burt is a lecturer at the University of St Andrews, Scotland. Her research interests include technology, work and organisation, and governance and the new electronic media. She recently co-directed a project under the Economic and Social Research Council's Virtual Society? Programme, examining the uptake and application of networked technologies in the voluntary sector. She can be contacted at eb19@st-andrews.ac.uk.

Wim van de Donk
Wim van de Donk is professor of Public Adminstration, department for Law, Public Administration and Informatization, Tilburg University. He has published widely on the meaning of informatization processes for the political arena. More information as well as an overview of publications and (current) research projects can be found at his homepage: http://cwis.kub.nl/~frw/people/wimdonk

Bram Foederer is a researcher at the Centre for law, Public Administration and Informatization at Tilburg University in The Netherlands. He has research interests in the impact of information and communication technology on public administration in general and the maintenance of public order and safety in particular.

Martin Hagen
Dipl.-Pol. Martin Hagen has been a full-time researcher in the Telecommunications Research Group at the University of Bremen in Germany since 1997. He currently studies socio-technical drivers and barriers behind Electronic Government and its implementation. For more information about publications and related work, see http://www.fgtk.informatik.uni-bremen.de/hagen.

Herbert Kubicek,

Herbert Kubicek is Professor for Applied Computer Science, in particular Information Management and Telecommunications at the university of Bremen and head of the interdisciplinary Telecommunications Research Group. His work covers international comparative studies on e-government as well as practical systems development for online service delivery (see http://www.infosoc.informatik.uni-bremen.de/).

Klaus Lenk

Klaus Lenk is professor of Public Administration at the University of Oldenburg, Germany. For more than two decades he has published widely on informatization in the public sector. In his quality as chairperson of the committee on administrative informatics of the (German) Gesellschaft für Informatik, he has recently edited a Memorandum on Electronic Government. An overview of publications and (current) research projects can be found on his homepage:
http://www.uni-oldenburg.de/verwaltungwissenschaft/

Miriam Lips

Dr Miriam Lips is Assistant Professor of Public Administration at the Center for Law, Public Administration and Informatization at Tilburg University, the Netherlands. Her research activities and resulting publications covering the broader area of ICTs and public administration focus on both national and international comparative basis and concern topics such as electronic government, knowledge management and regulation of new media. Online information is available at:
http://cwis.kub.nl/~frw/people/lips/index.htm

Massimo Mecella

Massimo Mecella is a Ph.D. student in Computer Engineering at the University of Rome "La Sapienza", Department of Computer and System Science. His research interests include software engineering for cooperative information systems, middleware technologies, component-based and Web architectures, methodologies for e-Commerce and e-Government. More information can be found at his homepage:
http://www.dis.uniroma1.it/~mecella/

Kees Planqué

Kees Planqué studied at Leiden University and worked at the Ministry of Economic Affairs, Technology Policy. Currently he is Conselor for Science and Technology in Washington, USA. He can be reached at twawashington@mindspring.com.

Matt Poelmans

Drs Matt Poelmans (1944) is program manager OL2000 (Public Counter 2000), a special bureau instituted by the Dutch government in 1996 to improve public service delivery. He has a background in local government as a councillor and vice-mayor in the town of Oegstgeest near Leyden. Poelmans has been vice-president of the Dutch Liberal Democrat political party D66. At present he is member of the Provincial Council of South-Holland. He studied business administration at Nyenrode business school and graduated in political science at the University of Amsterdam. Poelmans published several articles on public administration and the use of ICT and regularly gives lectures on E-government.

Corien Prins

Corien Prins is a professor of Law and Informatization at Tilburg University, where she joined the Centre for Law, Public Administration and Informatization in 1994. She obtained a PhD in Law at the University of Leiden (The Netherlands) where she also studied Slavic Languages. Professor Prins' research topics include at present (international) regulatory questions surrounding ICT, e-government issues, anonimity and privacy in relation to electronic commerce. e-mail: J.E.J.Prins@kub.nl; website: http://rechten.kub.nl/prins.

Charles D. Raab

Charles D. Raab is Professor of Government in the Department of Politics, University of Edinburgh. He has published extensively in the fields of education policy and information policy. In the latter, his main interests have been in privacy protection and public access to information, information and communications technologies in government modernisation, electronic service delivery and electronic democracy. His current research includes a study of geographic information systems in relation to privacy, identity, and place.

Silvio Salza

Silvio Salza is professor of Computer Architecture at the University of Rome "La Sapienza", Department of Computer and System Science. His research interests include the design and evaluation of large database systems, workflow management systems, data warehouses and cooperative information systems. More information, as well as an overview of publications and (current) research projects, can be found at his homepage: http://www.dis.uniroma1.it/~salza/

Dr Perri 6

Dr Perri 6 is a Senior Research Fellow in the Department of Government at the University of Strathclyde. Perri 6 is Senior Research Fellow in the Department of Government at the University of Strathclyde In Glasgow, and formerly Director of Policy and Research at the think tank, Demos. He is author of more than twenty books, and he has published widely on many issues of public policy, public management, electronic government, privacy and data protection, health and social policy and social theory. His latest book "Toward holistic governance" (with Leat, Seltzer and Stoker) will be published by MacMillan Palgrave in 2001.

John Taylor

John Taylor is Professor of Management and Dean of Caledonian Business School at Glasgow Caledonian University in Scotland. He has written exctensively on the Information Polity and on organisations and ICT. His most recent work has looked at ICT and the changing shape of democracy, with reference in particular to the changing democratic role of the 'not-for-profit' sector.

Christopher Theunissen

Christopher Theunissen is Senior Lecturer in Public Administration at the University of South Africa. His research concentrates on Knowledge Management as well as the applications and implications of technological innovations on governance and public administration. He holds a Ph.D in Politica Studies obtained at the Rand Afrikaans University (RAU) with a thesis entitled "State Power and Intelligence in an Age of Knowledge". He can be reached through his homepage: theunca@unisa.ac.za.

Roland Traunmüller

Prof. Dr. Roland Traunmüller, Institute of Applied Computer Science, Johannes Kepler University Linz, A-4040 Linz, Austria; email: traunm@ifs.uni-linz.ac.at. Prof. Traunmüller works in the field of Information Systems, Telecooperation and applications of information technology in Government. He is member of the steering committee "Administrative Management" at the Office of the Prime Minister and is also the founder of the working group "Information Systems in Public Administration" (IFIP 8.5). Currently he serves as deputy chairman of TC 8 "Information Systems" within IFIP and as vice-president of the Austrian Computer Society.

Koen Zweers

Koen Zweers Master of Science student in Business Information Technology at the University of Twente in Enschede, the Netherlands. This article was written for an assignment of the Office for Science & Technology of the Royal Netherlands Embassy in Washington, DC, USA. It was published (in Dutch) in the scientific magazine Technieuws (http://www.technieuws.org/cgi-twa/twa.pl/Washington/1331.html). A summary of the article was published in 'De Ingenieur', a Dutch magazine for technology and management.

Index

Law and Electronic Commerce

1. V. Bekkers, B.-J. Koops and S. Nouwt (eds.): *Emerging Electronic Highways*. New Challenges for Politics and Law. 1996   ISBN 90-411-0183-7
2. G.P. Jenkins (ed.): *Information Technology and Innovation in Tax Administration*. 1996   ISBN 90-411-0966-8
3. A. Mitrakas: *Open EDI and Law in Europe*. A Regulatory Framework. 1997   ISBN 90-411-0489-5
4. G.N. Yannopoulos: *Modelling the Legal Decision Process for Information Technology Applications in Law*. 1998   ISBN 90-411-0540-9
5. K. Boele-Woelki and C. Kessedjian (eds.): *Internet*: Which Court Decides? Which Law Applies? Quel tribunal décide? Quel droit s'applique? 1998   ISBN 90-411-1036-4
6. B.-J. Koops: *The Crypto Controversy*. A Key Conflict in the Information Society. 1999   ISBN 90-411-1143-3
7. E. Schweighofer: *Legal Knowledge Representation*. Automatic Text Analysis in Public International and European Law. 1999   ISBN 90-411-1148-4
8. L. Matthijssen: *Interfacing between Lawyers and Computers*. An Architecture for Knowledge-based Interfaces to Legal Databases. 1999   ISBN 90-411-1181-6
9. K.W. Grewlich: *Governance in "Cyberspace"*. Access and Public Interest in Global Communications. 1999   ISBN 90-411-1225-1
10. B.-J. Koops, C. Prins en H. Hijmans (eds.): *ICT Law and Internationalisation*. A Survey of Government Views. 2000   ISBN Hb 90-411-1505-6; Pb 90-411-1506-4
11. C. Girot: *User Protection in IT Contracts*. A Comperative Study of the Protection of the User Against Defective Performance in Information Technology. 2001   ISBN 90-411-1548-X
12. J.E.J. Prins (ed.): *Designing E-Government*. On the Crossroads of Technological Innovation and Institutional Change. 2001   ISBN 90-411-1621-4

KLUWER LAW INTERNATIONAL – THE HAGUE / LONDON / BOSTON